SHATTERED
VOWS

SHATTERED VOWS

VOWS

DAVID RICE

✠ Triumph™ Books
Tarrytown, New York

TRIUMPH® BOOKS EDITION 1992

Published by special arrangement with
William Morrow and Company, Inc.
and Michael Joseph Ltd.

This book is based on original interviews; however, some names have
been changed to protect the privacy of certain individuals.

First published in the U.K. by Michael Joseph.
First United States edition published by William Morrow.

Library of Congress Cataloging-in-Publication Data

Rice, David, 1934–
    Shattered vows : priests who leave / David Rice.
        p.   cm.
    Originally published: London : M. Joseph © 1990.
    Includes bibliographical references and index.
    ISBN 0-8007-3037-2
    1. Ex-priests, Catholic.   2. Catholic Church—Clergy.   3. Catholic
Church—Discipline—Controversial literature.   4. Celibacy—Catholic
Church—Controversial literature.   I. Title.
[BX4668.2.R52   1992]
262'.142—dc20   91-29569
                                                                          CIP

Published by Triumph® Books
Tarrytown, New York
An Imprint of Gleneida Publishing Group
Printed in the United States of America

To
Luci

CONTENTS

ABOUT THE AUTHOR

DAVID RICE, born in Northern Ireland and educated by the Jesuits of Clongowes, the school made famous by James Joyce, was ordained a Dominican in 1958. He left the priesthood in 1977 to marry. He has worked as a journalist all his life and was an editor and award-winning syndicated columnist in the United States during the 1970s. He returned to Ireland in 1980 to head the School of Journalism at Rathmines. He lives in Dublin.

PROLOGUE

'REMEMBER ME'

I will judge no man until I have walked in his moccasins for six months.

Native American proverb

FOR NINE YEARS Don Franco Trombotto, aged forty-five, had been parish priest of Vilaretto, one of those Italian Alpine villages that come alive in summer for the tourists and drowse all winter under their blanket of snow.

On 26 January 1985, Don Trombotto hanged himself in the corridor of his parish house, just outside his bedroom door.

'We arrived and cut him down and put him on his bed,' the brigadier of the regional *carabinieri* said. 'Then Dr Francesco Visconti established that death had been instantaneous.'

The local newspaper continues the story:[1] 'He killed himself five minutes before the 6 p.m. Saturday Mass. They were waiting for him in the church. Not seeing him arrive, an altar boy went into the priest's house and called. Don Trombotto was hanging in shirt and pants, and his glasses had fallen on the ground.'

On the kitchen table were three letters. The first contained telephone numbers to be contacted immediately. The second contained the priest's will. The third contained his farewells and some thoughts on his life.

'In my last hour,' Franco Trombotto had written, 'here in the silence of my room, while snow is falling outside, I ask Jesus Christ to be my saviour. I say to him the prayer of the Good Thief—remember me. I have carried my cross a long way: now I fall under the cross.'

The letter made no reference to Don Trombotto's twenty-year-long love for a local woman. However, a priest-friend, Don Franco Barbero, wrote to the Press about it, angered at Church attempts to cover up the suicide as a sudden illness.

Barbero wrote bluntly that his friend had been in love for twenty years, but in the end, not being able to make it official, had killed himself. 'He had asked me', Barbero wrote, 'if people were talking about him, if I had heard anything. He feared above all that his mother might know he had left orthodoxy.'

The local paper stressed the utter loneliness of the dead man. For nine years he had tried to break through to his parishioners, learning their Piedmontese dialect, but to no avail. The long winter evenings were for him an obsession. 'They only look to me for baptisms and funerals,' Don Trombotto had once said.

The paper said that solitude is the condition of many priests in the Alps. 'Long ago people used to confide in their priests; they were invited from house to house. But today, even in the country, priests play a marginal role. The television is the *padrone* [master] in every home: Pippo Baudo [a television character] rules the Sunday.'

In his loneliness Don Trombotto had looked for love. 'He felt', said the local paper, 'that if he followed that love, canon law would have deprived him of his priesthood.' This he could not bear.

'He wanted to live in fullness **and** in the priesthood,' Barbero wrote. He could not, and he died.

The dead priest's letter asked pardon for the trouble caused to his bishop and his parents, mentioning that the church roof was now fixed, but that the kitchen stove was broken with age. His last thought was for the boys with whom he went climbing in the summer. 'Be more friendly and generous with your priest', he wrote, 'and do not leave him alone at the altar.'

Suicides of priests are not confined to the lonely Alpine valleys of Italy. I have come across a considerable number of such suicides – four in one city – in places as far apart as the United States and Ireland. One such priest who killed himself was personally well known to me. Within the last three days as I write this I have heard of two further suicides by priests.

It is the most final way of all to leave the priesthood of the Roman Catholic Church (or rather, the formal ministry, for one is a priest for ever). Yet it is but a symptom of one of the most grievous crises to have hit that Church since at least the Reformation. Hardly more than two decades after the Vatican Council*, Pope John's dream of a Church renewed, has shattered into 100,000 pieces, each of those a priest who has left his ministry. That is almost a quarter of all the active priests in the world.

Those 100,000 shepherds did not shuffle into the mist with downcast heads. Most of them marched resolutely out, vowing to take no more; others stormed out in fury and disgust; many simply got up from their knees, made the sign of the cross, and walked quietly away.

More than one every two hours, for twenty and more years, they have left and left and left. And still they leave: right now, according to sociologist Richard Schoenherr, 42 per cent of all American priests leave within twenty-five years of ordination.[2] That means that today half of all American priests under sixty have left.

Already, over two-fifths of the parishes in the world have no resident priests.[3] By the turn of the century it will be half. The hungry sheep look up and are not fed, as Milton said.

NOT SO SIMPLE

A picture of St Patrick banishing the snakes, which hangs in many Irish Catholic homes throughout the world, aptly captures the popular mythology of priests leaving the ministry. A fine upstanding bishop, noble of brow and resplendent in shining green vestments, points with outraged finger. 'Begone!' he is clearly saying. And the wretched creatures slither off over the cliff into richly-deserved oblivion. Except for one that has the temerity to raise its head and glare back at Authority. It is obviously uttering something unprintable.

The conventional wisdom about priests leaving is that the good priests stayed and the bad ones left. Or, if not the bad ones, at least the weaklings, the cowards, the selfish ones. It is not quite that simple. Sometimes it is even hard to decide who stayed and who left. What of a priest who marries with the Church's blessing, and continues working in a Rio de Janeiro slum at his bishop's request? Has he left? What of the priest who really

*The Second Vatican Council (1963–5) was summoned by Pope John XXIII to look at the position of the Church in the modern world.

wants to leave, but elects to stay inside the structure because 'to dig I am not able', and settles for a life centred on himself? Has he not left, even if it is only 'inner emigration'? What of a priest who is still 'celibate', but insists that celibacy excludes only marriage, not sex? Has he left anything?

What of priests who are given Church permission to marry, then continue to work as hospital chaplains, and bring up their children in the love of God? Have they left?

Left what, anyway? The Church? Very few leave the Church. The Priesthood? 'Thou art a priest for ever.' The ministry? I know hundreds who 'left', and have never stopped ministering in many different ways, and in many new ones.

What of this item, from the *Houston Catholic Worker*, August 1988?

> A young El Salvador priest, threatened by the army with death, decided to leave his parish against the order of his archbishop, who chided him for deserting his people. He says he is not an Oscar Romero and doesn't want to die. He is now in Canada.[4]

My heart goes out to that young man, and I dare not cast the first stone. But riddle me this: if he finds a bishop to accept him into a diocese in Canada, and resumes priestly work, has he 'left' anything? And what of priests in El Salvador or Colombia, who 'left' to marry, and are still threatened by death squads because of their work for justice? Who left what, when?

And what about why? Few in the Church dare to ask why this immense mutiny. It is The Unmentionable Topic. Is it the system? Is it anger at authority? Is it Church structures that are unacceptable? Is it celibacy? Celibacy was excluded from discussion at the Vatican Council, at the express wish of Pope Paul VI, in a papal letter read to the Council on 11 October 1965.[5] Again in 1971 the Synod of Bishops turned down a proposal that called for a married priesthood.[6]

WHY THIS BOOK?

Sociologists have given us clear statistics. We need now to look at the human lives they represent: we need to hang flesh on those statistical bones. We need to hear these men speak from the heart, and to hear their wives and children. And that is what this book is about.

Cardinal Aloisio Lorscheider, in an interview I had with him in Brazil in 1988, stated clearly what was needed: 'I would like more concrete information on the priests who left,' he told me. 'The reasons why they left. Their situation now. Are they living in anguish or in anger? If we could just see these priests and hear them more profoundly, and perhaps arrive at another solution to the one that exists today.

'There should be more exchange and dialogue. Because many of these priests were very faithful servants in the ministry, very dedicated. They suffered in coming to their decision to marry, and all of this should be examined more. I think it is a human and a Christian problem that is not being treated as profoundly as it should be.'

This book has tried to do what Cardinal Lorscheider now suggests. In the last several years I have travelled 38,000 miles to meet and interview priests who left, and their wives and children. In many parts of the world, throughout the United States, Britain, Ireland, Sicily, Italy, Holland, Germany, France, Spain, Peru, Brazil, Chile, Colombia*, I have lived with these families, dandled the little ones on my knee, gone for ice-cream with the teenagers, sat for hours with the wives and heard women's views on this crazy but still-loved Church that is ourselves. I have stayed up into the small hours with men who were once monsignors and even bishops, and watched their eyes, once opaque and cautious, now sparkle with candour and the sheer joy of life, or sometimes flash with unhealed anger, and watched a wife reach across to hold a hand, as her man wept over a grief he had not allowed to surface in fourteen years.

In the course of my travels I met a total of 442 priests who had resigned the ministry or married, and did interviews with 247 of them. Many of these were in-depth ones of up to four hours long. A number of them ran to twenty and thirty hours: this was when I was staying with some of these men and their families, and certain interviews simply became almost non-stop conversations spread over several days, sometimes up to a week. Others were

---

*During the course of my research, I also interviewed married and resigned priests from the following countries: Argentina, Australia, Austria, Belgium, Bolivia, Canada, Czechoslovakia, Guatemala, Mexico, Honduras, India, Japan, New Guinea, Nicaragua, Philippines, Poland, Portugal, South Africa and Zaïre.

group interviews with six or eight people, men and women, in which everyone talked, and I tossed questions into the ring from time to time. I took written verbatim notes and also carried a voice-activated micro-cassette recorder, which, when set at half-speed, could record up to three hours on a single cassette. I did similar interviews with 177 of the wives and women friends of such men, and likewise talked to 41 of their children.

I also stayed with many priests still in active ministry, living in anything from parish houses in Southern Italy to mission stations in Peru, Brazil and Chile, and from a priory in Germany to a rectory in Chicago. I estimate I met a total of 104 such priests, and did in-depth interviews or held serious dialogue with 65 of them. Some of these were also prolonged over several days, when I was staying with a pastor or in a religious house. A few of these active priests are among the most dedicated and downright good people I have met in my life. And some are in pain. But many said, like Cardinal Lorscheider, go, find out what is happening, and tell us. For all is not well in the Roman Catholic Church.

My notes from the interviews total nearly 10 miles in length (2,380 pages, 35 lines to a page, 7½ inches per line). It took many months simply to distil those notes enough to gain a mastery of them and make them serve this book.

ANGUISH AND HOPE

This book, based on those 530 interviews, as well as on participant observation and direct research from a considerable number of written sources, has turned out to be partly a story of anguish – the anguish that today runs from top to bottom in the Church. The anguish of a frail Pope Paul VI, crying out in 1967 against priests who are 'crucifying the Church', the old man choking on words like 'Judas'. The anguish of Pope John Paul II, arms outstretched, pleading that 'we do not return the gift once given',[7] as he ties a tourniquet on the haemorrhage of priests by cutting off all dispensations.

There is the anguish of indecision before a man leaves, and sometimes afterwards that of guilt, laced with hunger and poverty and rejection by churchmen. There is the anguish of the spouse, branded as Eve the Temptress; there is the shame of families and the heartbreak of mothers; there is the hurt and loneliness of fellow priests who choose to stay.

But the untold story is of the agony of the priests who do leave. Every one of those 100,000 statistics represents a breathing human being, anguishing, not about life and death, but about eternity.

'It got so bad,' one told me, 'that for sheer frustration of not knowing what to do, I can remember physically hitting my head off the wall, over and over again.'

There was a priest who lingered for five years, mesmerised by two absolutes: 'a love of the priesthood and a love of this woman.' Finally, he made a retreat, in a last agonising attempt to discover God's will. On the last evening of the retreat, he found himself kneeling in the darkness of that chapel near Portland, Oregon, begging with all his heart for a sign – any sign – to break through those absolutes.

He found a sign the next day. And when he did marry four days later (before a crusty old Illinois judge, as there was to be no permission from Rome for many moons), one of his former superiors wrote to him to say, 'You made the right decision. And whatever anyone may say, you are married in the eyes of Almighty God.'

When his dispensation came and he married again in church, four priests concelebrated and blessed that marriage.

How could I, as the writer, possibly know all this?

Because I am that man.

Anguish is, however, far from the whole story. Rather it is akin to the pain before birth. For I found on my voyages that something splendid is gestating inside the Catholic Church, as though the Spirit is using all this turmoil to bring about a marvellously renewed People of God.

Anguish there was and is, but what I found most was Hope. I was thinking the other day that I may have been inside more married priests' homes than perhaps anyone else in the world. I thought it, not with conceit but with gratitude – gratitude for the hope and joy I found there. I thought of St Paul saying how all creation is in travail, waiting. That is how I found the Church round the world.

This book will try to explore this hope in the hearts and hearths of the priests who leave the active formal ministry. It is not a book of statistics but of human probing. Both kinds are

needed. To learn of hope, you ask individuals to open their
hearts, often in the quiet of the night.

But before we touch on hope, we must deal with the shattering
and the sorrowing that comes first. And that is what the early
chapters must face. They are painful.

This, by the way, is a book about priests who leave, not about
nuns who do the same. Nuns are mentioned occasionally, but
only in passing. I know full well their experiences are equally
valuable, and their sufferings just as acute. It is simply that there
is not the space here for both topics. Nuns, anyway, merit a book
to themselves. Perhaps they shall have one.

I shall explore no new theology in this book. It is not what the
book is about. So the ordinary human joys and griefs recounted
here take place in a setting of conventional theology, where it is
taken as given that one is a priest for ever. Thus you will not find
the term 'ex-priest', except where it appears in quotation. I speak
always of leaving the formal ministry, not of leaving the
priesthood.

There has to be significance in the fact that no European
language has found a satisfactory word for a man who leaves the
formal ministry of the Catholic priesthood. The Americans often
use the term 'married priest', but what of those who leave but do
not marry? 'Resigned priest' is not really accurate either, for
some men simply married and never resigned. Others were put
out. I thought of suggesting 'sometime priest', on the analogy of
'sometime professor of . . .', with its overtones of once and
future. But it sounded too pompous.

The Austrians speak of *ein Priester ohne Amt*, a priest without
a role. The French have a nice term, *ancien prêtre* on the analogy
of *ancien combattant*, meaning an old soldier, or a veteran.
Perhaps we could take a leaf from their book, and call them
'veteran priests'? Actually in the book I mostly sidestep the issue
and talk about 'a priest who leaves . . .'.

The reader should be aware of the distinction between secular
and religious order priests. Roughly speaking, secular priests
belong to a local diocese, and are under the direct authority of
the bishop of that diocese. They usually live alone, or with one or
two others in rectories. They do not make vows, but Church law
requires that they be celibate – that is, that they do not marry.
Priests, however, who belong to religious orders take vows of
poverty, chastity and obedience, and normally live in a commun-

ity based on the tradition of the monasteries. Such priests are often called 'religious'. These orders are often multi-national bodies, and are in many ways independent of local bishops. But in a number of dioceses, and especially on the missions, their members frequently work under the local bishop. If celibacy eventually becomes optional for priests, it could come about that the secular priests would be free to marry, and that religious orders, with their community traditions, would be the natural and supportive environment for those who choose celibacy.

There are a few words on the following pages that might puzzle some readers – words like 'canon law', 'nuncio', 'retreat'. These are briefly explained in a glossary at the end of the book.

One final point. If I use the title 'Father', I am indicating a priest who has not left. I do not use it every time, however, as often the context will indicate whether a man has stayed or left, though as I have explained, it is not always clear what staying or leaving means.

1

THE SHATTERING

> The Devil's mirror fell and shattered into hundreds of millions of pieces . . . Two splinters from the mirror hit little Kai — one entered his heart and the other his eyes. Poor Kai, soon his heart would turn to ice, and his eyes would see nothing but faults in everything.
>
> Hans Christian Andersen (*The Snow Queen*)

IN OCTOBER 1968 the Archdiocese of San Antonio, Texas, mutinied. It was an eruption of fury, frustration and recrimination the like of which had not been seen before in the US Catholic Church. It began when local priests demanded that the Pope fire their archbishop, and got fired themselves instead.

The effects of that eruption are still being felt in San Antonio. I have watched men fall silent as they tried to recount for me those events two decades ago, and have seen tears run down their cheeks. I have heard others, bleak with anger, utter words of hatred I never thought to hear. I have also met men whose lives are dedicated to healing the wounds of that awful year.

The story of San Antonio is relevant, not just because wounds still bleed, but because events in the Texas of 1968 are a microcosm of the worldwide Roman Catholic Church today, where good men even now do bad things, and the consequent hurt and hatred are a virus poisoning the Body of Christ. The effects of that virus are alarmingly visible throughout the Church, in parishes without priests, people starved for the Eucharist, fear in the Vatican, and a resentful and over-stressed clergy sullenly switching off, and priests continuing to leave their ministries.

In the United States alone, where the number of active diocesan priests is 30,000, there are already 18,000 priests who have resigned.[8] But few realise that priests are continuing to walk out of their ministries at alarmingly high rates. In the prologue we saw how almost half of all American priests (42 per cent, and rising) are still leaving within 25 years of their ordination. Further on in this chapter and others, similarly daunting and documented figures from around the world will be presented.

Whatever it was that created such havoc in San Antonio (a failure in Christian values? A breakdown in communication? Or simply sheer evil?), it is working similar mischief throughout Christ's Church today.

The San Antonio mutiny was so concentrated, so visible and so cruel, that perhaps it holds some lessons for the rest of the Catholic Church. As Monsignor Balty Janacek, fired from his job in the uproar, yet today a priest in San Antonio, says, 'We still need debriefing on what happened then. Otherwise, we can never learn from it.'

So this book begins with what happened in San Antonio.

Church's Alamo

It was the best of times; it was the worst of times. The best, because those days after the Vatican Council shimmered with energy and hope for spring in the Roman Catholic Church. The worst, too, as the powerful leader of San Antonio Archdiocese grew progressively more autocratic. Archbishop Robert Emmet Lucey of San Antonio had this in common with King Louis XIV: he did not just rule his diocese – he was the diocese, and don't you forget it.

For most of his life, as priest, as Bishop of Amarillo, Texas, and later as Archbishop of San Antonio, he spoke out fearlessly for the underdog, and was a tireless champion of trade unions.

Except, that is, for the clergy of his own diocese. A champion of liberty, he was a ferocious authoritarian towards his own. His priests accepted it for years, went out and fought his battles and gladly preached his doctrine of civil and personal rights, because they believed in it.

But they learned it too well. 'Lucey created a monster out of us,' says Ray Henke, at that time spiritual director of the local seminary. 'He took us Texan farmboys and radicalised us in social justice. But then when these priests wanted to act out social justice, or to apply workplace democracy in the Church, Lucey could not handle it.'

Lucey came back from the Second Vatican Council a changed man. They say all the talk of collegiality had frightened him. When his own priests began to organise an association, just as the Council had told them to, he could not deal with it. He was growing old and, like an ageing lion seeing the pride drift away, he grew dangerous. And cruel. 'When they come after me,' he was heard to say, 'they'll come to kill me.'

In those years after the Council, things in San Antonio Archdiocese got worse and worse until, as Father Joe Till says, 'you could smell the fear.' Men seen as ringleaders were sent to rehabilitation homes for alcoholic priests. Priests were assigned and reassigned, over and over again, in a way that was clearly intended to punish them.

As a local priest pointed out to me, 'Even the military knows you just don't keep moving people round any more.' But to transfer people without any reference to where their social contacts are, especially when they are celibate and have no families or loved ones to go with them, was, he believes, 'tantamount to a breach of their civil rights.'

'A young man would be moved four times in the space of nine months, just like a pawn,' Joe Till recalls. 'After a while he wakes up one day, looks at himself in a mirror and says, maybe there's something wrong with me. As a result, guys had nervous breakdowns.' One priest recalls the diocese refusing to pay psychiatrist's fees for a man who had had a breakdown. 'There was a palpable sense of doom and gloom. There was fear, uncertainty. Guys would go into a tizzy if the phone rang. If they heard the chancery office [where the diocese is administered] wanted to see them, they'd go bananas, almost. It was intimidation.'

There was one old alcoholic priest called in to the chancery office. 'He was an alky, no doubt about it,' another priest remembers. 'They call him in, they tell him he's a no-good alky. "You are suspended, removed, get out of the diocese in twenty-four hours. We don't care where you go." Maybe they just want to scare him. Well, he goes home, puts a shotgun to his mouth, and blows his head off.'

A young Franciscan, teaching in San Antonio, put together a series of extracts from magazines and used them for class discussion. Archbishop Lucey got hold of a copy, thought the man had written it all himself, and wrote to his superior in Missouri:

> Dear Father Schwab
>
> . . . Father Nick Baxter seems to have lost his mind . . . Most of the language in the four-page memorandum is the raving of a maniac, and in order to save your time I have marked the parts which are particularly offensive to our Latin high school boys. I am wondering if you could find it possible to remove Father Nick from this archdiocese in the very near future [and] . . . not permit a recurrence of such insanities.

In the attached copy of the extracts, Lucey had circled a total of five words: bowels, bastards, balls, damned and shit.[9]

Two religious orders simply pulled out of San Antonio, including the Vincentians who ran the seminary. The Archbishop had to use his own priests to run it. They were young men and soon were running a lively outfit to which, for example, Peter, Paul and Mary came after a concert, to play a song or two and sit round the fire with the students. Within a year Lucey regarded the seminary as a hotbed of sedition.

'You and I are on a collision course,' he told Roy Rihn, seminary rector, who in fact had been his friend and admirer.

Justice without love

'It was an era in the diocese when justice without love was the order of the day,' Monsignor Balty Janacek says. At one point, a book by Jesuit John L. McKenzie, saying that authority should be exercised in a spirit of love,[10] was discussed at the priests' senate. The Archbishop was furious, saw it as an attack on himself, and denounced the book as heretical.

At a secret meeting in the basement of St Anne's Church, thirty priests got together to form a priests' association. Lucey's spies were there and told him. Then came the recriminations – picking off the leaders, firing them out of their parishes, sending them to the back of beyond in the Texas boondocks.

Jim Brandes, head of Catholic Charities in the archdiocese, called it witch-hunting, and was reported. He was summarily fired, and told to report as assistant pastor in Victoria, Texas.

'He was the first who refused to go,' recalls Roy Rihn, now a pastor in the diocese. 'He was the first one to say, fuck it, I ain't gonna go.[11] Jim was a strong guy. But he just crumbled. It got to me: people were being destroyed.

'Well, I was president of the priests' association. And what happened to Brandes really got to me. I got depressed, seeing this fine man destroyed. Emotions were running very high.'

Shortly afterwards, the men on the seminary faculty took a working weekend at a house on nearby LBJ Lake. There was tension in the air, as the Archbishop was in the throes of his disciplinary reassignments.

Roy Rihn: 'We were worried that Myron Swize was going to get it. The phone rang. I said, I'm sure they've got Myron. I went to the next room to take it. Strange to say, they hadn't touched Myron. But Joe Till and Clarence Leopold got moved. It was Myron himself on the phone. "Clarence says he'll go where he's sent, but Joe Till says he'll quit," Myron said.[12]

'I remember spending a sleepless night. We had to do something, I thought. This can't go on. So the next morning I announced, "Fellas, I can't go through with the planned business. I couldn't sleep last night: I can't live with myself and see people destroyed. We have to do something." What we didn't know, of course, was that one of the people there was reporting to the 'Bishop.'

The upshot was that the priests' association prepared a letter to Pope Paul VI asking for Lucey's resignation. It was signed by fifty-one priests on 16 September, and later by a further seventeen. Four signatories were from the seminary faculty.

'There is an atmosphere of fear, alienation and dissatisfaction on the part of many priests in this archdiocese,' the letter told the Pope. 'We are like camels crossing an increasingly arid desert, upon whose back there has just been placed the proverbial last straw.' The atmosphere was being made more tense by 'a long line of vindictive and repressive transfers' of priests, and by Lucey's 'aloofness, repression and paternalism'. The priests asked for a fact-finding commission to be sent by Rome, and requested a say in the naming of the next archbishop.

The letter was to stay secret, with copies to Archbishop Lucey, to the Vatican's representative in Washington, and to a couple of other key people only. But it ended in a warning: 'We want you to know that we are so determined that if we shall not have received within thirty days some positive sign of action on our requests, we will make this letter public to the news media, and we will involve the Catholic laity in our appeal.'[13]

Roy Rihn now thinks the ultimatum was a mistake. Lucey's comment was: 'You don't give ultimatums to the Holy Father.'

Under the cool crust of the archdiocese the magma was seething. Lucey himself passed copies of the letter to his loyal priests and laymen, telling them to get ready for a fight 'if the rebels publish their garbage'. He asked the Vatican for 'a canonical trial for the conspirators'. His principal targets were Rihn and the seminary men.

At the seminary they still talk of 'Black Friday'. That was the morning when two black Cadillacs slid up to the main door and the Archbishop climbed out in full regalia, flanked by eight officials. He ordered the seminarians to appear before him one by one, formally dressed in cassocks, for an inquisition on seminary discipline and on the behaviour of the faculty.

The first thing the rector knew was when someone called his office to say, 'Roy, you better get over here. There's going to be a riot.' He rushed across to find all the seminarians stamping their feet in unison outside the inquisition room. A faculty member feared the Archbishop might end up hurt.

Roy Rihn describes the scene: 'The students had formed a body-barrier in front of the door. "Father, don't try to do anything," they told me. "No more students are going in there." "Let me in," I said. I went in. I can still see those eight men, and this little guy in cassock and sash, being quizzed.

'The Archbishop looked up. "Now Roy, you're not welcome here," he said.

' "I know that," I said; "but what's going on here is obscene. If you want to get me, please don't involve these young people. They're innocent."

'I told him what was going on outside, and that I couldn't control it. Some of those are pretty burly boys out there, I impressed upon him.'

The students were surprised to see the doors suddenly open, and Lucey and his entourage swirl out, briefcases in hand. The Cadillacs hissed away down the avenue.

That month was like the time of the phoney war with all its feints and manoeuvrings. One day Lucey sent a message to the rebels through one of his priests: 'Tell them I have asked the Holy Father to send a neutral observer into the diocese,' Lucey said.

This was the long-awaited sign from the Vatican, but tragically no one realised it. Roy Rihn still grieves over their mistake: 'We just didn't recognise the niceties of Vatican protocol,' he says. 'We thought the Archbishop was trying to delay things. I've learned since that the Pope, through the Apostolic Delegate in Washington, ordered Lucey to do this. But at the time, not a single one of us spotted this as the sign.'

So they rejected the overture, and called the fateful news conference at the Menger Hotel. Father Charlie Hersig read out the letter, while a prepared statement filled in the background for Press and television, stressing that the action: 'does not destroy, nor does it intend to deny, the authority of the Church.'

All of a sudden the San Antonio Affair became part of the nation's headlines. And the diocese split from end to bitter end, with laity and priests marching on the Archbishop's house, and others rallying to support the beleaguered Church officials.

THE HOUSE ON PINTO STREET

Nine days later, the four key members of the seminary staff – rector, vice-rector, dean of men, and spiritual director – were ordered to report to the Archbishop, at five-minute intervals, starting 10.30 a.m. It was like the timetable for a hanging. They entered the Archbishop's sanctum one by one, to be told they were removed from office and that they were not even to return to the seminary. They were not being given alternative assignments, but were to report to Padua Place, a nursing home for elderly priests as well as those with difficulties.

The four, Roy Rihn, Ray Henke, Louis Michalski and Bob Walden, decided they would not go. Without a penny of income, they rented a house in a poor *barrio* on the city's west side. Soon Henke and Walden got jobs, and helped to support the others, and Rihn, one-time seminary rector, became sort of house mother to everyone. Gifts poured in from lay people. Gradually, it became known as 'the House on Pinto Street' and for a long time it was a kind of halfway house for any priest in trouble in San Antonio.

'The attacks and vilification really mounted,' Roy Rihn recalls. 'I'll never forget this scene: Bob Walden, a decent guy, came in from work. I helped get him a bite to eat, and I told him what I had learnt that day.' This was that a recent seminary graduate had married only six months after his ordination, 'and the Archbishop's office had got hold of our seminary evaluation of him, and circulated it among priests and laity to discredit us. When Walden heard that, he just broke down and cried. "I had thought I'd go back into the ministry," he said. "I'll never go back now, not with this kind of dirty pool."'

In the midst of all the stress, Father Joe Novak collapsed and died from a heart attack, the day after a confrontation with Lucey from which he came away angry. At the funeral Mass, Lucey preached, not altogether sensitively, on the Five Foolish Virgins.

The firings and the reassignments continued. After months of waiting, the rector of the other (preparatory) seminary was suddenly summoned, called a traitor, and fired. Lucey himself had planned to resign a couple of days later, which in fact he did.

Within a year over thirty priests of San Antonio diocese had left the ministry, and the exodus continued long after Lucey's retirement.

Roy Rihn continued the housekeeping in Pinto Street, 'until it became clear to me that my brothers had each found kind women to share their pain. It was obvious our arrangement was not going to last much longer. I became very depressed.

'Then I got an offer to be campus chaplain up in Oklahoma. I asked the Archbishop, and he refused. I hit the skids, and had to be hospitalised for depression. The doctor wrote to Lucey: either you let him go, or it'll be on your head. So he let me go. It saved my life.'

Today Monsignor Roy Rihn is a well-loved pastor in San

Antonio. Ray Henke is married and living in the city, a respected
psychotherapist. Joe Till and Balty Janacek have stayed priests.
Of those who signed the letter, at least twenty-four later married,
some waiting several years before leaving. Many live round San
Antonio today. Some have died; a couple have disappeared,
marital status unknown. Charlie Hersig is Bishop of Tyler,
Texas; Edmondo Rodriques is a Jesuit provincial. Larry Steuben
is personal assistant to the present archbishop.

In the years that followed, other priests who had never signed,
left the ministry to marry. The diocese, which in 1967 had 441
priests, today has 386.[14]

Archbishop Lucey died in retirement in 1977. To his dying day
he referred to the events of 1968 as 'the Massacre'. Others called
it 'the Alamo'. His chancellor, Leroy Manning, is pastor of
Boerne, Texas, where he keeps a loaded revolver on a table
beside the front door.

MO RANCH

Nearly twenty bitter years passed. Some of the priests who left
and married had formed 'Connections', a small association for
their wives and themselves. Gentle Roy Rihn, ever the brother
and bridge-builder, kept in touch and even conducted prayer
weekends for the married priests and families. A new kind of
archbishop reigned in San Antonio – Mexican-American Patrick
Flores. They call him the Mariachi Bishop.

Then came the little miracle of MO Ranch.

One day Roy Rihn was having coffee with his old married
friend, Ray Henke. He happened to mention that the San
Antonio priests were getting together for a weekend of prayer
and discussion at a retreat centre called MO Ranch.

'Some of us should come,' said Henke. 'We're priests too!'

Rihn laughed. Then: 'Seriously, Ray, would you like to come?
How about I put it to Flores that some of our married brothers
would like to join us?'

Finally, married priests Ray Henke and John Orr were invited
to come for the Friday evening and stay overnight. When they
arrived, thoroughly nervous, they were told, 'You guys are on at
7 p.m.' They were brought in to the assembled priests, and got a
standing ovation. 'It was electrifying,' a priest told me. 'It
brought tears to many eyes.'

Ray Henke spoke first. 'When I left, I was hurt by many of you,' he told the priests. 'But I also know my leaving hurt very many of you. For this I am sorry.'

One youngish priest got up and said, 'Ray, you really did hurt me when you left. I looked up to you. I admired you so very much – I looked forward to spending my priesthood side by side with you. When you left, my world collapsed.'

Ray just said, 'I'm sorry.' And the two of them came together and embraced.

That was the turning point. Others began to ask pardon. It was a reconciliation process that went on way past midnight.

The next morning, Archbishop Flores spoke at the Mass. I am ashamed, he said, that we had to wait for our married brothers to come to us for reconciliation. We should have gone to them. He said he had just returned from Cuba where he had met Castro. If we can do that with a Communist leader, Flores said, why not with our brothers who are no longer in the ministry?

He pledged that it would be a priority of his administration to bring these men and their wives and families back to use their talents in whatever way possible in the Church.

The group then established a Resigned and Active Priests' Committee, which the following March held 'Bridging the Years', a reconciliation retreat where over eighty resigned and active priests shared hurts and memories. It was a beautiful day, a priest told me, with much healing. There have followed gatherings of whole families with the active priests, and Christmas parties at the Archbishop's house.

But it was only a start and, now the euphoria has faded, there is a sense of anticlimax. For some priests, whether active or resigned, maybe it is enough to have buried the hatchet. Others, however, would like to see moves towards reintegrating married priests in the ministry. But, with Rome's present stance, they can go no further. One pastor, after MO Ranch, invited married priest Louis Fritz and his wife Rosemary to do a weekly communion service in a chapel that had no priest. It was very successful, until some other Texas bishops got to hear of it and came after Archbishop Flores. Fritz had to quit.

As Ray Henke puts it, it is a bit like ecumenism. Once the handshaking is over, where can you really go?

And tragically, there are some, both resigned and active, who have never been reconciled. 'They went their way, we went ours,' one active priest says. 'We have nothing to say to each other.'

'I couldn't care if I never saw one of them,' a married priest said to me about former colleagues. 'It's an evil organisation.'

When married priest Dan Heffernan died, his friends were bothered that so few of his active colleagues were at the funeral. 'The chancellor was there, in a black suit in the back row,' a married priest told me. 'The Archbishop wasn't. What bothered me was that everyone was denying the past: there was no mention of his priesthood, what he had done with most of his life. They just excluded that. I was horrified. No one accepted that these people put years into trying and trying.'

MANNING

Hatred and anger still claim their place in San Antonio. Rightly or wrongly, much is directed at Leroy Manning, who was on Lucey's staff during the cruel years.

I went to see Monsignor Manning, in his little parish house in Boerne. His hair is iron-grey now, and he looks his 73 years. 'Talk louder,' he told me. 'I've been round guns and airplane engines so much of my life that I don't hear so good.' There are guns on the walls, beside photos of light planes that look like Cessna 172s or 175s. And the loaded revolver at the door, against intruders.

In all the years he worked for Lucey, he never liked him, Manning told me. 'But boy, did I respect him. And I was loyal to him. People saw me as his hatchet man, which didn't make me too popular. But it didn't matter as long as they respected me too.'

Manning told me he grew up during the Depression in the only Catholic family in a 100 per cent Ku Klux Klan county in Texas. 'I never had a friend in school. I was born and raised fighting, and I was determined to be the finest Catholic priest I could be, and expected others to do the same. Those Klansmen were going to respect us.' But now after twenty years as a pastor, he says he has learnt to be more sympathetic to priests out in parishes.

Manning still maintains a grim view of the priests who wrote the letter to the Pope: 'Were you ever round a mob?' he asked me. 'It's not a group of persons, but a mob personality. That's how it was. I could get these priests one by one and talk to them, and make sense. I had known these boys since seminary. But when they got together, personally I could not cope. The Archbishop encountered the same thing. A sort of diabolical personality.

'There were four or five of them who wanted out of the priesthood. Remember in those days it was disreputable, shameful. So they kept needling the others, to create a furore. That would give them an excuse to get out of the priesthood. Of course, some of them stayed – they were the ones that just got drug [dragged] into the rebellion.'

Manning paused, and gazed out of the window. 'This, this is like an old wound,' he said at length. 'It hurts deeply. God, it hurts! The hurt done to the reputation of the Church – after the Klan pounding on me, I wanted to see the Catholic Church standing so high above all else.'

What about reconciliation?

'Those who left, I've seen very little of them. It would hurt them to see me. It would hurt me to see them. I've been invited to many meetings, but no, it would hurt too much. It would open those wounds again. There was a meeting recently: had I known about it, I would have purposefully avoided it.'

Manning is sad there are so few priests today, but he thinks God is teaching people to be less dependent on the Church. 'Maybe God said, I'll let y'all see how it feels to be without schools, nuns and priests. The Church has been in worse positions before – you can't kill it. But please God I won't live to see it. I'm seventy-three and I'm bone tired. But I can't quit.'

As we parted he embraced me and said, '*Vaya con Dios* [Go with God].' And then he called after me from the door, '*Oremus pro invicem* [Let us pray for each other].' As I drove away I recalled the question I had wanted to ask – something like how do you feel about Jesus saying, if you are in the temple and you remember that your brother has something against you, leave your gift at the altar and go first and be reconciled?

A few days later a married couple, people from out of state, were telling me about their holiday home in that same town of Boerne: 'One of the things we like is the old priest there. He is totally dedicated to the poor. They say he made a promise that no one would every be without food or a place to lay their head in that parish. Even the down-and-outs passing through. And he has kept his word. The priest's name is Manning.'

THE MEANING OF SAN ANTONIO

With hindsight the San Antonio story can be seen as part of one of the most turbulent years of the century: the year of the assassinations of Martin Luther King and of Robert Kennedy; the year of the start of Northern Ireland's troubles; the year of the Tet offensive that turned the Vietnam War round in the USA; the year of student riots in Paris, Mexico City and Tokyo; the year of the invasion of Czechoslovakia; and the year Cardinal Patrick O'Boyle suspended fourty-four priests in Washington DC for refusing to go along with the encyclical condemning birth control, in an uproar rivalling that of San Antonio in its intensity and anger.

It is not just history. The San Antonio story will not be ended until reconciliation is complete, until those priests hungering for ministry can find it, and those parishes hungering for priests can have them.

But, far more significant, are the thousands of mini San Antonios that are still happening throughout the Catholic Church every day. They can be as tiny as one man confronting his bishop, or as hidden as one man confronting his own loneliness. But together they represent a crisis that is without parallel, an enormity that no official secrecy or fear of scandal can bury. It is a crisis that will lead to a Church without priests and thus without the Eucharist.

Professor Richard Schoenherr, sociologist at the University of Wisconsin at Madison, presents some daunting figures for the United States:

> Look at the resignation rates and we find that by the tenth anniversary after ordination, on average, 20 per cent of the priests have resigned from the active ministry. By their fifteenth anniversary, an additional 15 per cent resign. So that by the time they reach their twenty-fifth anniversary, 42 per cent of each ordination class has resigned from the active ministry. Here is a startling figure that shocked even me. In three or four years there are going to be more resigned priests alive in the United States than active priests.[15]

By the turn of the century, the number of priests in the United States will be halved. What it means is this: in 1925 there were 15,000 priests for 16 million Catholics; although there are

30,000 priests today, by the end of the century the number of priests will have dropped to 15,000, but there will be 65 million Catholics for them to serve.[16] There will, in fact, be more resigned than active priests. And religious order priests cannot make up the deficit: studies show their rate of resignation is even worse.[17]

The consequences for the Church are appalling. The average age of a diocesan priest in the United States today is fifty-seven. By the year 2000 it will be sixty-five. That is retirement age. Already 1,950 US parishes have no priest, and the figure keeps growing.[18]

Stress is taking a terrible toll on active priests: the number who die before retirement (at sixty-five) has doubled in recent years. In 1985, according to a study commissioned by the US bishops, 40 per cent of US priests reported having 'severe personal behavioural or mental problems in the previous twelve months'.[19] With fewer priests trying to do more and more, 'you're seeing a kind of national burn-out,' Father Myles Riley of San Francisco told US News & World Report.[20]

Vocations, the other side of the coin, are also down – from 48,000 seminarians in 1965 to 10,300 today.[21]

Other countries fare no better. One diocese in Spain had 1,200 priests in 1965: it now has 200. That is one single diocese losing 1,000 priests in two decades. In another, 70 per cent of the active parish priests are over fifty-five.[22] Spain has 7,000 priests who have left the ministry, of a total of 28,000 priests in the country.

Le Figaro says the French clergy are facing the greatest crisis of their history. From 40,000 diocesan priests in 1969, there will be less than 25,000 in the year 2000.[23]

France has over 5,000 resigned priests.[24] Italy has 8,000.[25] Holland has 2,114.[26] Ireland's bishops admit to 488 who left the ministry through 'a definitive act' such as marriage, and the real total is thought to be considerably higher.[27] In Brazil the organisation Rumos lists 2,200 resigned priests, and estimates there are 1,000 more.[28]

Figures for Britain are almost impossible to get, as no statistics are published on priests resigning. From the Catholic Directory one can glean that, between 1968 and 1987, the number of priests in Britain dropped by 1,526 (from 4,962 secular priests and 2,788 order priests in 1968 to 4,276 secular priests and 1,948 order priests in 1987). During this period the estimated

Catholic population rose from 4,143,854 to 4,164,040. However, these gloomy statistics are not even accurate: the 1989 directory merely repeats the 1987 figures, which had already appeared in the 1988 edition.[29]

The total number of resigned priests throughout the world could be as high as 100,000, which is the figure generally accepted by the media, and is certainly above 80,000. The Vatican's own *Annuarium Statisticum Ecclesiae* lists the granting of 46,302 dispensations to priests to marry, between 1963 and 1983.[30] That was six years ago. And for every priest who gets a dispensation, there is another who was refused or never bothered to ask. So a figure of 100,000 is likely.[31]

Jesuit Professor Jan Kerkhofs has compared the number of ordinations each year with the combined totals of deaths and resignations for that year. He has done it for twenty-four countries. For every 100 priests resigned or died, Holland had eight replacements; Belgium fifteen; Germany thirty-four; France seventeen; Italy fifty; Ireland forty-five; Spain thirty-five and Portugal ten.[32]

Official Church bulletins sometimes suggest that things are better in the Third World. They are not. According to Kerkhofs, the extra bodies in Third World seminaries are far outweighed by the decline in foreign missionaries and the vast increase in Catholic populations. As another Jesuit, John A. Coleman, writes:

> Nor should we be fooled by statistics that show that the number of seminarians and ordinations increased in the last decade in places such as Zaïre, Nigeria, India, Indonesia and Mexico. In almost every case, these gains are offset by the decline in foreign missionaries or by a dramatic increase in the Catholic population that far outstrips any increase in the number of priests.[33]

In one Ugandan diocese, there used to be 6,000 Catholics to every priest a few years ago. Ten years later there were 13,000. In Indonesia in 1954, there were eleven priests for every 10,000 people. Two decades later there were only five priests serving that same number.[34]

In the whole world there were 368,000 Catholic parishes and mission stations in 1985. Of these, 157,000 did not have a priest.[35] That's nearly half. For millions upon millions of people that means no Mass and no Eucharist, which is the centre of their religion.

The priesthood of the Catholic Church is in deep trouble. As Father Coleman puts it: 'Any profession for which the following facts are true: declining absolute numbers in the face of growth of the larger population, significant resignations, a declining pool of new recruits and an ageing population – can be referred to as having a deep-seated identity crisis, whatever the internal morale of the group.'[36]

The Catholic Church has, in fact, become one huge San Antonio. In the next chapter I make a start in asking why.

2

THE SCATTERING

Do not be afraid of life's ending, but that you never lived.
John Powell SJ

'IN THE MIDDLE of life's journey I found myself in a dark forest, and could not find my way.' In the last two decades those opening words of the *Divine Comedy* came true for thousands of Roman Catholic priests, so that they scarcely knew if paradise or hell lay before them. With purgatory they became thoroughly familiar; a purgatory of greater anguish than Dante had ever conceived.

Some are still priests and still suffering. Others have emerged from their purgatory and are fulfilled and active priests. Close on 100,000 simply left, that is, they resigned from formal ministry. It is a figure that expresses one of the most extraordinary religious phenomena since the Reformation, a phenomenon as yet unexplained.

The men themselves who left — can they explain it? What were their reasons for leaving? I have put that question to hundreds of them around the world.

'Who is the woman?' Thus began a letter from Belgian Cardinal Godfried Danneels to a missionary friend who was leaving the ministry in Brazil. Danneels could not have been more wrong, that friend, Eduardo Hoornaert, told me. Yet *cherchez la femme* is everyone's presumption when a priest leaves. A pious Irish mother put it succinctly when her missionary son left: 'There's some bloody Brazilian bitch at the back of this!'

In fact, leaving the formal ministry is far more complex than that, and I found as many reasons as there were men to ask. I shall try here to organise those reasons under some general heads.

VOWS WITHOUT MEANING

The first reason was best expressed by Penny Lernoux, celebrated writer on Latin America, when she spoke to an international meeting of priests and nuns at Bogota: 'Religious are beginning to discover that vows lose their meaning unless the community in which they live tries to challenge society's dehumanising elements.'[37]

People don't leave Mother Teresa. They leave, like missionary John Carney in Honduras, after seeing kids crowding round to eat the rubbish thrown out by his community. They leave in circumstances like these encountered by missionary Mike Breslin in Paraguay:

'There were a quarter of a million in the diocese,' Mike told me. 'There were thousands of square miles with unpaved roads. We had one US bishop and half-a-dozen Franciscans with no Spanish or Guarani. Up to 130°F heat, in terrible conditions, with no water and no electricity. Infant mortality was so great that there was no time for funerals. We threw a rope from the steeple: when people rang it, we would just come out and say a prayer over the little body.

'That thing rang like the doorbell. I still hear it in my dreams.'

The hundreds of hamlets saw a priest once every three years. Mike and the others felt they had to train local lay leaders – it was the start of the base community idea. 'From all the villages we gathered the leaders together for training: they came to us; we shared their lives. I learned Guarani and, instead of staying at a big American rectory, I moved in with an Indian family.'

However, the priests received a visit from the Apostolic Nuncio, the Vatican representative in the region. 'The Nuncio got hold of the Bishop – "You can't do this," he told him.

'The Bishop called everybody in: "We'll have to reverse all

these things, because the Nuncio's against it." We told the Bishop the scheme had gone too far, that the leaders would lose face if we dropped the training now.

'But the Bishop called another meeting the next week, and put us all on the spot: "You do what I say, or I'll suspend you," he told us [Suspension means that a priest is forbidden to function as one]. One by one he asked us, "Will you do it? Will you obey?" Right down the line.

'There were unanimous NOs. Right on the spot he suspended the entire diocese. The entire diocese.'

Shortly afterwards came a cable from Breslin's parent diocese of Brooklyn. It read, 'Send Breslin home.'

Breslin is married now and runs a ceramics shop in Brooklyn. He is also one of the founders of the Nehemiah Project for building houses for America's poor, a project being taken up by Congress, and he has helped found a phenomenally successful bilingual state school for 850 mostly black and Hispanic Brooklyn youngsters.

The Vatican Council had brought enormous hope, a Brazilian priest told me. But new, conservative Church authorities are backing away from it even in pioneering regions like Brazil, away even from the option for the poor, and priests have been losing that hope.

In Nantes, France, Jean-Pierre Leroy brooded over what he called, 'a contradiction between pastoral work and social reality.' It was everywhere in France, but was more starkly evident in the Third World where he had spent much of his ministry. 'I saw the people dying at forty. Were we just to run to them with the sacraments when they were dying, or were we to care about the process or cause that made them die? I just could not make a bridge between this merely functional doling out of the sacraments and really participating in the social issues.'

Brazilian Ignacio Campo wanted a more virile church, break-ing out of the sacristy, a church where love and dedication to others would be fundamental, 'not just looking after yourself and your own soul. I give full value to the sacraments, but only where there is faith and commitment to others. Instead, for most people we are turning the sacraments into mere sentimental helps.'

For years before he left the ministry, Campo kept a giant map of the world on the wall behind the altar in his church, to remind people that God so loved the world . . . He had ten chapels, trained lay ministers to preach and do Eucharistic services and was organising groups to tackle problems in factory and community – this was the time of the military dictatorship.

He moved out of the parish house to a single room, and began hiding fugitives from the police. There were rows with Cardinal Rossi and with the local bishop: 'because I wanted to give importance to the groups demanding social reform, not to the Legion of Mary.'

Campo is married now and is a psychotherapist in São Paulo, where he works mostly with the poor. Some of his patients are sent by the local priests.

Men like Campo normally stay in the ministry as long as they see hope in changing church structures that need changing. When they feel there's no hope, or sense that they themselves could burn out, they resign from ministry, but not from the Church. Usually they marry later, remain dedicated Catholics and, free of all official constraints, carry on with whatever ministry is possible to them.

Sometimes these men don't leave, but are put out by Church authorities. Such a man is Giovanni Battista Franzoni. He has, quite literally, come down in the world. He just moved a few hundred yards down Rome's Via Ostiense, from the abbey-basilica of St Paul's Without the Walls, to a little community of local people, but it was all the way from an abbot's cross and mitre to a layman's sweatshirt and jeans.

The people still call him Don Franzoni, though for thirteen years he has had no legitimate claim to priestly honours. From his position as Abbot of St Paul's, the basilica second only to St Peter's in all of Christendom, he was, to use the official term, 'reduced to the lay state'.

From the moment he was elected Abbot at the young age of thirty-five, Franzoni was a thorn in the side of both Church and state in Italy. The real trouble began when in 1970 he wrote a public letter to the Italian President asking him to cancel the annual military parade, saying he was aware of 'a growing repugnance to glorifying of armaments, bearers of death, as though they were the nation's glory.'

Then he was taking the workers' side in industrial disputes; attacking the Vatican's concordat with Italy, 'which makes the

Church a power, in contrast with what the gospel says the
Church should be.' In 1971 he joined with other Rome pastors to
demand that unused Church property be handed over for the
poor, and asking the Pope to denounce the city's property
speculation.

Abbot Franzoni was forced to resign as Abbot in 1973; he was
suspended from celebrating Mass in 1974, after he declared
himself in favour of divorce in that year's referendum. In the
1976 elections he was to be found attacking the Christian
Democrats.

Then, interpreting Christ's words 'Blessed are the Poor', he
stated that poverty was not wished by God, 'but by rulers and
oppressors, and that God's disciples are called to confront this
anomalous situation.'[38]

Shortly after that outburst, Franzoni was 'reduced to the lay
state'. The priest for ever was now a layman. The sentence was
announced at the same time as the suspension of ultra right-wing
Archbishop Lefevre, for defiance of the Vatican.

By then Don Franzoni had moved to his new address just
down the street. He and a couple of monks had the abbey's
permission to start an experimental community on the Via
Ostiense. More than a decade later he is still there, and a vibrant
neighbourhood base community has grown up, with its own
services for the poor, its own centre for celebrating the Eucharist,
and even its own bookshop. They call it the *Spazio Commune*, or
'Common Ground'.

THE WRONG PLACE

And now for the second reason priests leave. There are priests
who quite simply feel in the wrong place. Either they cannot
stand the clerical environment in which they feel trapped, and
have to get out. Or they feel excluded from normal life and want
to get back in. These seem to be two sides of the one coin.

'I felt a sense of incredible domination, of being controlled,
waking and sleeping,' a now married priest told me in Ireland.
'They controlled me by tying me down to the breviary, by the
way they moved me round like a pawn, by censoring everything I
wrote for publication, even letters to the paper, by locking me
inside a black suit (and in Rome even putting me in skirts and

shaving the back of my head), by tying a collar round my neck, so that I could not relate to people and they could not relate to me. A railway carriage would fall silent when I entered. I finally felt I couldn't breathe, and to this day I feel physical nausea whenever I see a cassock or a black suit. It's like the Nazis making Jews wear the yellow star. And it's for the same purpose – control.'

A number of priests' wives have told me their husbands have almost a physical revulsion to black, and cannot be made to wear it.

I listened to a group of Italian married priests and their wives discussing the wearing of cassocks in the street, compulsory until the mid-1960s. *Un uzanza pessima* – a dreadful custom – one of them called it. 'I felt it was a violation of my identity and my personality,' one said. 'I could simply not be totally me while wearing it.'

'You know what the people called us?' another priest said. 'The third sex. They mocked us for wearing skirts. And that's why the Church made us wear them.'

'The role of the cassock,' a priest's wife told me, 'was to make the priest feel no longer like a man. A young man who came out of the seminary dressed like that was a stranger among people. He could not fit into daily life. And that's what the Church wanted. These men weren't to have a human personality, but a piloted one, directed by the canon law. The purpose is to put the priest in a caste apart, so that he is apart from everything, especially women.' The black suit and Roman collar has the same effect, and it is still required dress in most regions.[39]

While such men felt oppressed by symbols, others went straight for the oppression they perceived behind them. 'I wanted out of a system where there is no term of office, no control, no appeal,' a priest said in New Jersey. 'And where everything is cloaked under silence. And that's how it is: bishops are in for life; if they're unjust, there's nowhere to appeal, no higher court, no due process. And half the human race is excluded from all power – I mean the women. It's against the UN Declaration of Human Rights. I believe in the Church, but these are human abuses. It's just Ecclesiastical City Hall, and I couldn't fight it.'

Priests like that felt locked in. Others felt locked out – from the real world. 'I felt I had my nose pressed against the window of other people's lives,' one married priest said. 'I envied anybody, even gipsies, dustmen, the youngsters in the youth club enjoying first love. My heart would tighten up watching them.'

Another told me his hands would start shaking as he was giving out communion, 'and I just wished I was down at the back of the church, saying my prayers.' That man left, and his hands are steady now.

It is interesting that many priests resented their very privileges: the deference, people picking up the tab in restaurants for them, the 'clerical discount', the gifts of what they call 'celibacy vaccine' (liquor). 'In New York or Boston you just have to throw your breviary on the front seat of the car, and you never get a parking ticket,' a priest told me. A former missionary in Australia said he only wanted to be like St Paul the tentmaker. 'Just to earn my bread by the sweat of my brow. And after I left, it was such a relief to get that first payslip.

'You know,' this man said, 'I've never been an ordinary person in my life. I came out of school, went into the seminary. I never had the freedom to go out and make a fool of myself. And lay people don't help when they keep saying, "You chaps have a great time. You'd never survive outside." It was something I had to do – prove I could survive.

'Anyway,' he added, 'you're a better role model for everyone when you earn your bread.'

Some priests leave because they are no longer sure what a priest is, or is supposed to do. Father Clete Kiley, personnel director of the Chicago Archdiocese, told me the key question is the identity crisis of priests. With so few priests, many have to be 'circuit riders', going from place to place. 'Our fear for our priests', Kiley said, 'is, do they become sacramental machines? Technically, a parish must have a pastor, but the duty-person could be a nun or lay-person. Which leads to the ID question – what is the priest's role?' Add to this the growing indifference on the part of lay-people, their lack of support for their clergy, and the fact that 'our priests are very viciously attacked in the media, mostly by conservative and right-wing elements, and the Vatican seems attentive to these.'

My interviews bear this out. Many priests, faced with all this uncertainty and indifference, opt for the warmth and tangible certainties of job, wife, family and children.

LONELINESS

Closely linked to this is the motive of loneliness. A Mexican bishop was visiting one of his elderly pastors, and enquired about loneliness.

'I have my Rosary,' said the old man.

'But what about the long winter nights, all alone?'

'I have my Rosary.'

The bishop asked if he could have a cup of coffee, and the old man called into the kitchen: 'Rosary, would you bring out the coffee for his Eminence?'

Priests smile at little stories like that. But there is less to smile at in the bleak loneliness of many a priest's life.

I have seen it. While researching this book I stayed with an Italian pastor in a small town in Calabria, Southern Italy. Don Antonio is a man of prayer. Each morning he asked me to join him in praying the breviary in the empty church before Mass. I accompanied him on his rounds of parishioners and saw the respect with which they received him. The young men all had a smile and a nod for him.

But I could almost taste his loneliness. It was in his eyes during morning Mass; it was in his face the day he bade me farewell at the bus station. Don Antonio lives alone, and never cooks for himself, saying fruit and cheese are all he needs. He eats standing at the kitchen table.

Off the kitchen is a dining room, pleasantly furnished with a big table and six chairs, suggesting hopes and expectations of years ago. It is never used. Yet one day I cooked spaghetti alla carbonara for us both, and Don Antonio ate it with relish. We had some wine that evening, and during the meal I asked him point blank if he would live his life again the same way.

He shook his head. 'No. Not unless they changed the priesthood totally. Only then. Only maybe.'

Why had he never married? I asked.

He shrugged. 'Maybe just I never found my *grand' amore*, the love of my life,' he said.

What keeps Don Antonio going?

'*Dio solo* [God alone]. But I never ask him for anything. I just say, thank you, God. At first, years ago, I begged; I despaired. Now I don't know how to ask any more.'

One evening we sat together in the silence of the presbytery. I

was reading a book; he was sorting some papers. A Vespa scooter puttered past in the little street below our window, and it seemed that all joy and life was in that sound. It suddenly struck me that nobody had rung the doorbell that day, and the phone had rung only once. The terrible words of Swinburne went through my mind: 'Thou hast conquered O pale Galilean, and the world has grown grey with thy breath.' Only it's not really the Galilean's fault.

When Don Antonio saw me off at the bus station, I thanked him. 'I was happy here with you,' I said. I had been.

He embraced me, and whispered a line from the Psalms: 'How good and sweet it is, for brethren to dwell together in unity.'

Pamela Shoup, who married California Jesuit Terry Sweeney, winner of five Emmy television awards, told me this:

'I thought when I first met Terry, this man has more friends than the universe. At lunch one day Terry started to cry. I asked myself, who takes care of this person, who holds him when he cries? Where does he take his fear?

'When we were first married, Terry took a box out of the back of the closet. It was one of his Emmy awards, just sitting in there. He was so alone, he hadn't bothered to open it.'

Loneliest of all are missionaries and priests who have left their homeland. Few layfolk can grasp how lonely. Sean Connolly described it in Texas: 'Sundays were the worst. You did all the masses. All the baptisms. After Mass I'd sit on the wall by the church, and chat to the few people going by. I used to envy the local priests – they could go home to Ma on Sunday. I used to sit on that wall outside St Cecilia's: the intensity and the pain of it – feeling, I don't belong to anyone here.'

And returning home can be worse. Missionaries in Brazil call it the *amargo ritorno*, the bitter homecoming. The space you once had is overgrown, and no one knows what to do with you.

Father Tony Conry, still a priest in São Paulo, remembered visiting his Irish hometown, and sitting in a pub there.

'Where are you now, Father?' said a young man sitting at the bar, drinking a pint and watching Gaelic football on the television.

'I'm in Brazil.'

'Oh. Well, uh, that must be an interesting place, surely. Hey Mick, what's the score for Galway now?'

CELIBACY

Which brings me to celibacy as the next reason why men leave the ministry. I distinguish celibacy from falling in love, as they are quite different motives for leaving.

Celibacy is defined simply as the state of being unmarried. It is not the same as chastity, which means abstaining from genital sexual activity (or confining such activity to the marriage bed if one is married). So a celibate person could be either chaste or unchaste (and it is that possibility that leads to so many disasters, as Chapter Eight makes clear).

Professor Adrian Hastings of Leeds University, England, explained in 1978 why he left the ministry of the Catholic priesthood. He said that for over fifteen years he had not believed in celibacy, yet had lived by it and remained in the ministry, as it gave him a stronger base from which to argue against celibacy. He was not lonely, and loved his priesthood.

However, he changed his mind, and decided to marry, partly because he found that the Church heeds deeds more than arguments. Besides, he said, 'I do not believe it to be a just law or a good law, or a law which the Church had the right to make, and I am convinced that it does not express God's will for the Church today, if it ever did . . . Wherever one turns, the clericalism which puts celibacy above ministry is strangling the Church.'[40]

Scores of priests have told me how they were taken into seminaries and set aside for celibacy even before their teens, without a notion of the awesome undertaking it was. And they have spoken of their incredible ignorance and lack of preparation.

Bob Guidry remembers a conversation he had with another ninth-grade kid in Houston's junior seminary. Both boys would have been thirteen or fourteen years old, and were discussing problems with masturbation.

Bob: 'This celibacy thing – dunno how I'm gonna make it. But I guess God'll help me.'

Other kid: 'Do they cut your balls off?'

Bob: 'I dunno. But if they have to do it, I guess they have to do it.'

Kids like that sleepwalked into celibacy. Thousands of them awoke in their thirties and beheld with horror the cage they had wandered into. And they simply forced aside the bars and clambered out. Once outside, what they started looking for was that intimacy they had never had, and which they desired even more than sexual fulfilment.

At the Easter vigil in 1952, German youngster Heinz-Jürgen Vogels felt a powerful call from God to be a priest: 'So absolutely sure was I that this was my vocation, that I could not even pray "Thy Will be Done", without being a priest. But that very night, I went round home weeping for hours, not knowing why. In the end I realised it was because from now on I could no longer marry. I had a most tender relationship with a girl in high school. But I knew I would have to renounce everything.

'All during my seminary studies I had this strong and ineffable vocation to priesthood, and the inevitable sensation of incapacity for celibacy. An invincible sadness endured all through those years. But no one said you don't have a vocation.

'Three months after my ordination I entered a depression, without being able to move physically. It took me an hour just to get up out of bed. I thought continually of suicide. I was like an animal playing dead; the soul was aware that the door to marriage was finally closed by ordination. With that door closed, I cannot live any more.'

In both the Netherlands and Brazil I have heard priests describe an atmosphere of impending change in the 1970s. In the Netherlands it followed the famous Dutch Pastoral Council, that assembly of the Dutch Church that raised so many hopes before it was suppressed by Rome in 1971. The assembly sent Cardinal Alfrink to Rome to ask for optional celibacy. He got nowhere, of course, but, because of the Dutch bishops' openness, much seemed possible. In this time of almost renaissance euphoria, it seemed as if compulsory celibacy would soon go the way of Friday abstinence or fasting from midnight.

So some priests decided not to bother waiting. 'It was a kind of springtime,' Father Lambert van Gelder recalled, 'and many priests thought, now is the time to marry. I'll go and find me a woman. There were others who already knew a girl. They took the chance, and went ahead and married.'

A married priest in Brazil described the sense of expectation there: 'At the time, a married priesthood was in the air. Everyone was talking about married men being accepted as community leaders, and being prepared for ordination. All thought it would be the first step. It was tied up with the base community idea – we thought that each community would have a married man looking after it, who would later be ordained.'

Cardinal Arns evidently thought so, for he set up a four-year night course to train hundreds of parish leaders whom, one hoped, would later be ordained.

A missionary remembers the sense of expectation in São Paulo: 'In the early 1970s, the feeling was we were coming to the crunch. There would be a decision on celibacy, and a married priesthood was inevitable in Brazil. Well, we were mostly in our thirties: we felt that if we didn't make a move and set things up, you'd be high and dry when the Pope said, "it's all right, boys."

'They all thought worker-priests were coming too. So the boys went and did training courses at the *Cultura Inglese*, to become teachers. The idea was you were going to work, to marry and have a family, and be a priest in a small base community. Of course, it was never expressly put in those terms. You could just sense it.'

But nothing happened.

'I saw one of the lads when he turned forty. It was a sort of a crisis: he called his friends for a meal. He said, "I'm not going to reach fifty without knowing what it's all about."

'Later we saw him round with a woman.

'Then I guess this Pope came in 1978, and it was clear there wasn't going to be any change by anybody. We'd just continue working in a parish. I saw the boys who were still around – perhaps they had waited too long. I felt that one or two of them had their girls – you'd see them with them – but who am I to say? But after that, most of them withdrew from the teaching. They'd given up hope.'

Here I should mention what I call 'the Whittington factor'. Young Dick Whittington leaves with his cat for London, after an old villager tells him, 'Go now, my boy, while you still can. I wanted to go when I was young, but I left it until it was too late.'

Many a young priest has heard those words. A young Benedictine had almost a father-son relationship with his pastor in northern Minnesota. 'We had fun together. He had a hard time getting round to it, but eventually he did tell me, "You really ought to get out before it's too late."'

An Irish priest from Sligo remembers working in a parish in Liverpool: 'The parish priest was this old guy with egg down his cassock. His main interest was bingo – the principal object in his life. He'd look out of the rain-swept window. "What a wasted life," he'd say. "When I think of my brothers and sisters back home in Ireland, with their families. I wish I had my life all over again."

'Well, my hair stood on end when I heard him. And I swore then and there, if I ever think I'm in the wrong thing, even when I'm seventy-five, I'll quit.'

That man did leave, and is now a teacher. He is married with three children. His going was hastened when a young priest he knew became an alcoholic, fell down the stairs and died from a broken neck.

Vietnam was also a factor in leaving the ministry, for priests who served there as chaplains. I talked to a number who later married. Tough old Jim Butler of Vista, California, volunteered for two tours as chaplain in Vietnam. He was involved with the Marines in a Combined Action Platoon and was often under fire. These CAPs had among the highest casualty ratings: in one group photo Jim showed me, most of the men had been killed.

'Something happened to me when I was in 'Nam,' Jim told me. 'I talked to a couple of doctor friends about it. I guess it was this – I had seen so much death, I wanted to share my life more. I just did not want to go back to rectory life any more: I could not have taken it.'

Jim met his wife in Arlington Cemetery when he was visiting the graves of his men, and she was visiting her husband's.

Charlie Liteky, the only chaplain to win the Congressional Medal of Honour, said almost the same thing on a visit to Dublin. He just needed a spouse. He chose life, after all that death.

Mike McPartland spent his years in Vietnam being dropped out of helicopters with twenty minutes to say Mass, and unzipping green bags and anointing whatever he could find inside.

'But the massacre of the innocents on both sides, the death, the destroying and the maiming, I think it sobered a lot of us. All the guys who served there whom I knew left the priesthood. I think 'Nam had tremendous impact on our relationships with God and the diocese – positive with God; negative with the diocese. Every priest walked out of there needing to be loved. As a man, and sexually. Something happened to me: it will never be the same again. I left, because I wanted to be loved, and 'Nam was the catalyst of that. 'Nam destroyed so many, it's ironic that it made a lot of people whole.'

FALLING IN LOVE

A priest may leave the ministry for any number of reasons, and later meet a woman and marry her. Another may be struggling with authority or doctrine, suddenly encounter a woman and leave to marry her. Such a woman could be seen as the occasion on which he leaves, rather than the cause.

But there are thousands of priests, completely happy with their ministry and with the Church, who quite simply fall in love, and marry. Maryknoll missionary Father Dan McLaughlin, himself a lifelong celibate, described it to me with compassion: 'It could well be that a man makes a vow and lives it. And then meets a woman. There is an attraction, but deeper than that, there's a goodness in the person who draws out a goodness in the man. The man says, God wants me to spend my life with her.

'Do I have a right to deny God's action? I could once have said in all sincerity, I want to make this vow for life. But none of us has power to see down the line. Grace happens not just the day I was born: God acts on us every day of our life. And God could choose to give me the grace to continue in celibacy, or the grace to react to love.'

The love often leads a man to a deeper ministry, rather than to a desire to abandon it (even though authority may force him to do so). Married priest Everardo Ramirez is a writer in Cartagena, Colombia. He is also a political activist under constant threat of death. He explained to me, from his own experience, how the love of priest and woman can take place in a social context:

'In the same *barrio* where I worked as priest, lived her family. They were great supporters. She and I worked together in the *barrio*. There began a sympathy, which gradually reached a more profound relationship than I have ever had with another woman. The love came in the context of our real work together.'

Ramirez recently stood for mayor, representing the left. He lost, and threats against his life have now grown critical. 'But,' he told me, 'my life today is more complete, richer, even though a lot more dangerous, The best of my life, the best of all my books, the best of my effort with gospel and people, has been since my marriage. I have lived with more courage.'

Over and over I keep meeting this phenomenon, of love arising in a context of ministry, and the couple just wanting to continue their ministry. Brian Eyre, of the Irish Holy Ghost Fathers, and Martha Almeida, of Recife, Brazil, were working together in one of Recife's *favelas* (slums). They organised St Ignatius-style thirty-day retreats for the local people.

Eyre: 'The Ignatian retreat is one of the riches of the Catholic Church. But it's not offered to the majority of the poor – it's too long, and it costs money to stay over for thirty days. Well, we broke it up over thirteen weeks, and began offering it to the poor. We combined our personalities to give the retreat, and there was a communion of ideas. One day we discovered it was better to continue this journey joined together (*caminhada juntos*).'

They married, and continue their work for the poor. Brian teaches also now to make ends meet.

Joe and Jacqui McCarthy are another instance of love in context. Jacqui is quite literally a golden girl from one of Brazil's wealthy industrial families, and threw it all up to work in a São Paulo *favela* with retarded and abandoned children. Joe was a Kiltegan missionary priest working in the same slum community. They married with that community's blessing, and the people asked them to stay on there and work with them.

When they later moved north to Recife, the community leaders said, 'We're sending you as missionaries up there, where there's more need than here.'

Joe and Jacqui have a little house on the edge of a Recife slum where they are bringing self-reliance and confidence to the people there. There is, of course, no money from the Church any more, so the couple depend on a small stipend sent by an Irish lay relief organisation. It is due to end shortly.

Doctrine

Priests also leave over doctrinal difficulties, but among the hundreds of resigned priests I have interviewed, the only doctrinal difficulty ever mentioned had to do with *Humanae Vitae*, the papal encyclical forbidding artificial birth control. It must have been some kind of historic watershed: the astonishing thing is that many priests, resigned and active, can remember exactly what they were doing at the moment they heard the news of the encyclical. It is almost like when Kennedy died: as though, somehow, something died when that encyclical came out.

'I just don't belong to this,' one priest told himself on a London street one afternoon in 1968. He was looking at an *Evening Standard* hoarding: 'Pope Bans Birth Control.' It was the day *Humanae Vitae* came out. That same day another priest was reading Ireland's *Evening Press* aboard a Liverpool–Dublin ferry, and decided he wanted to get out. He left some years later. 'My leaving was tipped by *Humanae Vitae*,' he says now. 'That encyclical seemed to say, "Never mind what this does to individuals – we must mind the system."'

Jim Brandes was having breakfast in his Texas rectory when one of the lay ministers brought in the newspaper announcing the birth control encyclical. As he remembers it, 'The first words out of my mouth were, "Oh shit!" It was extraordinarily devastating. All my abdominal muscles knotted up and stayed that way for weeks. I actually went for help, professional counselling. And then one day I was sitting in the rectory, again at the breakfast table, and the words went through my mind: "Boy, you have to leave." Almost immediately my gut relaxed.'

Dan Dierschke ministered on the Mexican border where, he says, most of the families had nine or ten children. 'When that encyclical came out, I was on a deserted ranch-road, 40 miles from the nearest town. I heard it on the car radio. When I heard it I just said, "I quit!"

'I felt even worse when I heard that the majority of the Pope's commission had favoured birth control. I mean, if the voice of the people and clergy could be so disregarded on such a fundamental issue, how can you say the People are the Church?'

Jim Dillon of Tulsa, Oklahoma, was down at his diocesan mission in Guatemala in that fateful year of 1968: 'I found there Indian families with a dozen kids, where it was better that the weakest would die as an infant than go through life with such malnutrition. The mission had set up a little health care centre, and was introducing the people to the notion of birth control. Then came the encyclical.' And that was that. Everything had to stop.

For Bishop James Shannon, auxiliary of St Paul and Minneapolis, and the only Catholic bishop to march with Martin Luther

King at Selma, the encyclical was the last straw, which brought him to leave. He declared he would not keep 'two sets of books', privately believing one thing and teaching something else. When he left, he wrote a letter to the Pope: 'I cannot in conscience give internal assent, much less external assent, to the papal teaching in question.'

Eighteen years later, when I interviewed him in his office as a vice-president of General Mills in Minneapolis, Shannon had no doubts on the correctness of his decision.

I myself had a moment of truth some weeks after the encyclical came out. A young woman came to see me in the Black Abbey, Kilkenny, Ireland, where I was a Dominican priest. She wanted to be told it was all right to use the Pill: in those days people expected the priest to decide for them, and I was silly enough to accept that.

Her husband, she said, was not bright. 'He's awfully good to me when he gets It – y'know what I mean, Father. But if I refuse him, he beats me up, and then he does it with the dog. And I do get sick, Father.'

Those were her actual words, which I cannot forget.

Since the encyclical she had been saying no to her man, and life had become unbearable. Yet deep down, she loved him, and wanted to stay with him. So could I let her use the Pill? she asked.

I was scrupulous in those days, and had felt I must always counsel obedience, although the struggle between obedience and compassion had been tearing me apart. But something snapped in me: for the first time, I did what my gut told me. Go and use the Pill, I told her. And never mention it to a priest again.

To myself I said, I'll have to face God for my disobedience, but she'll be off the hook. Maybe that's my ministry, to carry God's anger for her and for others like her. I remember thinking of Yeats's very first play, *Countess Cathleen*. There is a famine in the land, and all the people have sold their souls to Satan for food. Countess Cathleen offers her own soul in exchange. In the play, of course, Satan accepts the offer because Cathleen's soul is totally good and pure. Unfortunately, I couldn't exactly match that!

Such was my thinking in those days. But I was never quite the same from the moment I followed my heart. I think maybe I began to grow up.

Humanae Vitae is one thing. The Faith is another. A François

Mauriac novel describes priests continuing to minister long after they have lost the Faith. I can only say that I have never met a man who left the ministry because he lost the Faith. I have met several whose faith withered after they left, but that seems to have been tied up with shock and bitterness at the way they were dealt with. I will touch on this later in the book.

Burn-out

There are priests who quietly grind to a standstill after many years of dedicated work. Some are just bone tired; others find themselves yearning for a little bit of warmth and humanity. It often happens when there is deep commitment to ministry in very difficult circumstances, combined with the growing realisation that Church authorities are either indifferent or hostile.

When I was one of the editors on a paper in Washington State in the 1970s, I sometimes handled stories about a sixty-year-old chaplain in the strife-torn state penitentiary at Walla Walla. His fight on behalf of the prisoners, his charges of brutality against the guards, and the harassment he suffered from the prison staff, made this priest a sort of hero to me, even though I had never met him.

During the terrible prison-lockdown of 1979 that lasted 146 days, he became the link with the outside world for inmates confined in often sweltering conditions. Once, when he entered a cell block at the height of the turmoil, the inmates rose to their feet to applaud him. One enormous, burly lifer grabbed his hand: 'I never had no use for priests, Father,' he said. 'But you're an all-right mother!'

Eight years later, when I returned to the Pacific north-west to research this book, it was arranged that I would stay a couple of days in Portland with a married priest called Bob Beh. It was a while before it dawned on me that this big, white-haired, gentle soul, a full colonel in the Army Reserve, with a wife who adored him and whom he deeply loved, was the same man as that Walla Walla chaplain.

In November 1981, Beh had resigned as chaplain. After five and a half years in the prison, he had 'reached burn-out stage'. But the burn-out ran deeper than his role as chaplain. Because Bob Beh then resigned as priest, and married.

Wrong reasons

Dominican theologian Father Liam Walsh said to me lately, 'Be sure to point out that just as some men remain priests for the wrong reasons, there are some who leave for the wrong reasons.'

Indeed there are, and I have met a few tragedies. Only God can judge, of course, and those who leave for wrong reasons do not easily confide their motivations. But one gets the impression of a few men who were self-serving in the priesthood, and left for what seemed an even more comfortable life outside. Usually it isn't. If such men make it big on the outside, they can be distressingly materialistic. If they do not make it financially, they can grow very bitter, and sometimes pathetic. The only generality I dare make is that selfish priests seem to become more selfish after they leave, and one or two men who were Don Juans in the priesthood did not easily settle for one wife later (although many did, and changed for the better beyond recognition, as is reported elsewhere in this book).

Then there are some who were neurotic as priests, and are neurotic as laymen. Sadly, they sometimes become more neurotic after leaving. Whether such people left for wrong or right reasons, which of us dare say? It is difficult even to write about many of them, because such people often disappear off the radar screen.

But I grieve for them, and I wonder how many there are, and where they are. And I wonder why they are not sought out and cared for by the Church they once served. They should be first among our concerns. I know of one who sits alone in a tiny room all day, without even a book to read except the Code of Canon Law, too proud to come out for a drink if he can't buy his round. I know of another, dismissed from his diocese for paedophilia, who died a down-and-out on the streets of London. And there, but for the grace of God, go all of us priests, be we active or resigned.

The 100,000 reasons

This chapter has tried to touch on the main causes of men leaving the ministry. These are not mutually exclusive: often a man leaves for several different reasons.

He may have problems with his bishop and with preaching *Humanae Vitae* at the same time; he may feel the institution is messing with medals instead of real ministry; he could also be dying of loneliness; he may be grossly overworked, and suffer serious burn-out; a good woman may reach in and touch his heart and he may feel that with her he can better minister to others.

Or his mother may have just died – plenty of men have stayed priests as long as their mothers were alive. There are as many combinations as there are men out there, and that's nearly 100,000.

A final point. Neglect of prayer does not figure largely among the reasons I encountered. It would seem to be a fallacy that priests leave because they have long neglected prayer. The majority of these priests say they prayed as in Gethsemane for months or years before they left. Sometimes the very words they prayed were Jesus's own: 'let this chalice pass'.

A Jesuit, now married, describes it thus: 'It was a struggle – how does God stay in your life? On my Provincial's advice we set up a discernment process, praying through things with the help of another priest. There was colossal anxiety in the early stages, until I realised God was going to love me whether I stayed in the priesthood or married.

'One thing God asked me was that He would stay in my life, and that I would continue to serve Him. Once I said yes to that, I had a growing sense of peace.'

3

THE SORROWING

Love in action is a harsh and dreadful thing, as compared with love in dreams.

Dostoevsky

FATHER JOHN X came from an Irish country village, and was a curate in Dublin. He decided to leave the ministry, and sent word to his family. However, he stayed on in the parish for a few weeks until a replacement came. A colleague tells the rest:

'A few nights later the priest was set upon outside his presbytery and beaten up most viciously by members of his own family, who had travelled to Dublin for the purpose. They were cousins and relatives from the country — presumably they were doing it for God's sake. I remember thinking, such violence comes out of a great fear.'

There in a nutshell is gathered all the sorrowing of the priest who leaves: the anguish of the man himself, and the grief, humiliation and often anger that could drive others to such a pass.

A priest who leaves goes through a particularly fearsome ordeal. It is an ordeal of both fear and loss. There can be fear on the level of intensity of Death Row or of front-line warfare. But whereas the condemned man or the soldier fears for his life, the priest fears for his soul, with a fear carefully nurtured in him since childhood. And where the soldier's fear lasts for those hours or days in jungle or trenches, the priest's can last for years.

There is fear of a world the priest has never lived in, and for which he has been deliberately and expressly unfitted.

There is a paralysing fear of failure and even destitution, that fear which scripture describes so well: 'To dig I am not able, to beg I am ashamed.'

There is loss of father, mother, brothers and sisters, who so often totally reject their loved one when he most needs them and with a ferocity that leaves him numb with dismay.

There is loss of home, of income, friends, colleagues, security.

There is a quite devastating loss of status: 'One day I was idolised in the parish,' a priest says. 'The next I was washing dishes.'

There is the horror of seeing a beloved Mother Church, which had been his life and breath and his salvation, turn into a cruel stepmother that first spurns him like a cur and then denies his existence.

This is not to say that priests are the only ones who suffer so. Suffering is a part of life, a part of growing. The transition to adulthood frequently brings acute suffering, and much of what these priests endure is a delayed form of such suffering. And there are many other transitions in life that bring similar sorrow. Divorce is an obvious instance.

In fact, leaving the ministry is rather like a divorce – where the parish is the spouse, the people are the offspring, and the Church is the parent. There is, however, one way in which it can be harder than a divorce. If a doctor divorces, he remains a doctor. If he marries, he still keeps his role. A priest does not. But he loses something far more than a role – he loses his very identity. For a priest is so trained that his person and his ministry are one and the same. So he almost ceases to exist as a person, and must try to build a totally new personality. It takes years and it takes tears.

'When you marry you want to rejoice, to scream it from the rooftops,' said a priest's wife in Phoenix, Arizona. 'Instead it is a march through hell.' And many priests when they leave do not even have such a partner to march beside them.

Of all the terrors of this path, probably the most awful is that, until recently, relatively few had trodden it. And fewer still had told of their experiences. There were no models, no examples for the priest to follow when he left. John Dubay, married priest of Binghampton, New York State, describes it: 'It is a journey that has no historical precedent . . . It is indeed a dark night, since our journey has so few handholds or footholds to guide and direct our way. This sense of having no reference in reality by way of history, legacy, legend, experience or knowledge, adds to the dark night.'

In a sense, a Catholic priest who leaves takes with him neither a future nor a past. He has nothing except his own strength of character, his personal qualities, and the grace of God. Yet these turn out to be enough.

A KIND OF DYING

When a priest leaves, the whole process is redolent of death. And a sense of bereavement swathes it like a shroud.

'I thought I'd be burying you in your thirties,' one father told his priest son after he left. Today that son, now married and a father himself, pulls out a photo from those days, in which he looks as if he is terminally ill.

'Indeed it is a dying,' says a married priest who had spent much of his ministry in terminal wards. 'But it was my ministry that was terminally ill. There comes a stage where you grieve for the man that was, because you can never have that quality of life in the future. Kubler-Ross calls it detachment – pulling into oneself to weigh one's life.'[41]

For the man who leaves, the acutest anguish usually comes before he decides, or before he acts on his decision. It is endured in silence and loneliness. And it can go on for years. The anguish is as Hamlet's: to be, or not to be? What does God really want of me? What of scandal? What of hurt to parents and family and fellow priests and bishop? Sometimes, quite often, there are thoughts of suicide. And sometimes, the act of suicide.

'Even to think these thoughts is treason.' So said Rommel, pondering a move against Hitler. The priest is like Rommel: thinking about leaving is itself unthinkable. He must not scandalise his people. He will not distress his family. He fears to trust his colleagues. And he feels he dare not trust his bishop. 'Put not your trust in princes,' the Psalm says, and sometimes the priest later finds how wise he was to have kept his own counsel.

So the idea of leaving the ministry is conceived in loneliness and born in isolation. The maturing can take years of silence. Sometimes the priest does finally seek help from someone he trusts: maybe an older priest, a colleague he looks up to, or a priest in confession. Instead of help he may just get a stern lecture. Or worse, he may sense that the other man is having similar problems.

What happens then is crucial. According to sociologist Eugene Schallert, if no help is found, that is when he decides to leave, without perhaps fully realising it. 'Once that decision is made, he may develop a close relationship with a woman,' Schallert says. And it could still take 'an average of four to five years' agonising . . . before walking out of the door.'[42]

Many priests experience a moment of truth.

'Don't drag Jesus in the dirt,' a Scottish Presbyterian minister in Glasgow told a priest friend who was having an affair. The priest went home and prayed, and that same evening asked the woman to marry him.

A Minnesota priest wanted to marry, and earnestly believed celibacy would soon go. When the parish got its first married deacon, the priest overheard a parishioner say, 'There goes your married priesthood, shot to hell!'

That priest has been married now for years. 'That was my moment of truth,' he remembers. 'I realised then the Church would not take the celibacy problem seriously. That's when I just started walking in the other direction.'

To try and decide whether to marry or remain a celibate priest, Frank Bonnike of Chicago went on a retreat, based on St Ignatius's Spiritual Exercises. 'The very first Exercise had the words from Scripture: "This is everlasting life, to know God and His Son Jesus Christ." Nothing about celibate priesthood. I couldn't get those words out of my mind. By the time of the fourth Exercise, I went to the retreat master and said, I'm free.'

Nature can bring a sense of proportion. Missionary Mick Caheny, returning to Europe from South America, stopped off at Easter Island. 'I was brooding so much on Christ's words, "He who hears you, hears me." Are all these tiny Church rules covered by that mighty premise? Or is it being abused?

'But, looking at those waves rolling in for 3,000 miles, I felt the insignificance of so much. Here am I worried, thinking I'm

the centre of the universe, and I'm not. Here am I halfway
between two continents. I felt I had a unique chance to size up
everything. There were longings in me. I'd walk round and look
at the stone statues. I went with the fishermen, and they'd cook
the fish on stones on the shore. It was very Paschal. I had a
massive inundation of Paschal and gospel occurrences. It was
like a great retreat: I relaxed in nature and stopped fighting
against it.'

After that Caheny returned to work in Ireland, where he had
to wear black and where his Monsignor in Athlone would not
allow the priests to preach at their own Masses. Caheny did not
last long there.

Before he left, Allen Moore took a post with Christian
Ministries in the Grand Canyon National Park. 'You don't have
to go far along the canyon rim to get away from tourists. I'd just
sit there, and look out into this marvel of God's creation. It was
very easy to pray. Things just seemed clearer. Nature does it for
you.'

LIFE

A woman, if she enters a priest's existence amidst all this grieving
and dying, is perceived and experienced as almost the quintes-
sence of Life. Often the transformation in the priest is dramatic.
As a light bulb burns brighter in the last moments before it fuses,
so a priest's ministry, in those last weeks or months before he
leaves, is often noticed to be richer, more alive, more com-
passionate.

'Who is she?' Jim Peterman asked a fellow chaplain in
Vietnam. The priest blustered that he didn't know what Jim was
talking about.

'Come on, Frank,' Jim said. 'There has to be a woman. You've
been just too effective as a chaplain lately.'

Frank finally admitted that there was indeed a woman. Later
he left to marry her.

Texan Louis Fritz, before he resigned as campus chaplain to
marry, was trying to help so many divorced people get Church
annulments that his colleagues called him Loophole Louis.

At this point, of course, there comes a quite new kind of
anguish – the struggle between this new Life and celibacy. The

relationship may be chaste, but it is driving inexorably towards marriage. A marriage that is unthinkable.

Etienne was chaplain to a Paris student group, of which Marie-Christine was a member. Everybody else had noticed, before the two even realised they were head over heels in love.

Marie-Christine: 'We resisted. We made it a rule never to be alone together. During the summer holidays, we decided not to write to each other.

'But that first Mass after college reopened, I just knew. I tried to say adieu. We separated. But afterwards we were both desperately unhappy.

'In the end Etienne said, I have no right to abandon you. He asked his bishop to get him laicisation. We're married now, and Etienne continues to serve God. And I have never had such strong faith as I do now.'

This is the point where a woman can get hurt, if a priest becomes paralysed by indecision. And the image of the callously scheming female, manipulating a simple cleric into matrimony, seems to be mostly myth. Too often she is the one manipulated. But more on that in Chapter Eight.

It is also a point where a priest frequently takes what is called 'leave of absence'. Technically, Church authorities allow him to opt out of the active ministry for a year or more, take a job, and think things over. Sometimes a priest returns at the end of the leave, ready to resume ministry. More often he leaves for good.

I have found that the manner in which a priest leaves is important to later peace of mind. 'I'm glad I didn't just run,' an Irish resigned priest told me. 'I'm glad I asked for a dispensation. And I'm glad I said goodbye to the lads, and tried to explain it to them. That way we're still friends.'

I met another man who didn't leave like that. 'The way I left was terribly wrong,' he told me. 'I just went over the wall, no note, nothing. Nobody knew where I was. It was bloody awful for me to have done it like that – I'm pained every time I think of the unnecessary distress to my family and to my fellow priests. I was just not man enough to face the option and say to the bishop, "I want out". If I could put the clock back, my mode of exit would be different. I believe in the infinite mercy of God – his arms extended on the cross – but I find it harder, almost impossible, to forgive myself.'

TRANSITION

There is often a sense of euphoria when the priest does leave.
One priest, now in counselling, thinks it is because most of the
grieving has been already done: 'There has been anticipatory
grief. Like when watching a long-term illness of someone close to
you (although in this case it is yourself): the muscle of the spirit
has strengthened through the constant exercise of grieving. By
the time the rock drops, a person is better able to catch it and
hold it. At least it doesn't crush you.'

But that 'first, fine, careless rapture' doesn't last long. There
are new pains to bear. The first of these, and it comes fast, is the
loss of status and the second is loss of identity, both of which
have already been mentioned. The third is poverty.

'I encountered poverty such as I had never known,' a resigned
priest told me in Britain. 'That first winter in London, I didn't
have an overcoat. I was so poor I couldn't afford alcohol,
although I had been drinking a lot before leaving. It was a hell of
a shock, going from inside to outside. I had been a Franciscan – I
knew next to nothing about money: I didn't even know what a
building society was for.'

Charlie Barfield was an Australian priest working in the
United States when he left. 'At thirty-five I go into some
government office: "What's your social security number?" the
woman asks me. I had never heard of it. She was a big woman,
and she sat back: "I can't believe you don't know what a social
security number is. The first thing we'll have to do is get one for
you."'

For two decades after his 1948 ordination, Augustinian friar
Antonio Corsello had been one of Sicily's best known priests,
champion of workers and of young people. He had a high profile
in sporting circles, and his Sant' Agostino Sporting Club had
carried all before it. He left simply and solely for love of a young
Sicilian woman.

'After we married,' Corsello told me, 'we had a year and a half
of near destitution in Rome. Ina was pregnant. I wrote personally to the Pope, telling of my hunger. The Vatican replied,
sending me prayer and blessings. I wrote again that I couldn't
live on that. Then they sent me 15,000 lire [about £10, or $14].
Imagine, 15,000 lire after twenty years of service.'

In a book he has written about those days, Corsello says: 'I looked for work in a thousand ways. Nothing. My clerical education had so "incretined" me that even easy work was difficult for me. My way of presenting myself, my seminarist face, did not inspire confidence . . . I came back home with empty hands, with great bitterness. And with so much anger, that even now, after so many years, I am still unable to soften it.'[43]

Corsello also sought work and help in Church institutions and parishes. 'I went in need,' he writes, 'but principally for a spiritual need: I needed personally to find out the level of charity that reigned in the centre of Catholicism. It was an interminable series of disillusionments, insensitivity and hardness of heart that bewildered me.'[44]

The Corsellos had married in January. By the following Christmas they were living, Bethlehem-like, in the Torre Maura district of Rome – close to starvation. 'But news gets round,' Corsello remembers. 'Word got round the houses that here was a married priest with a pregnant wife, and hungry at Christmas. Well, the neighbours came in with everything: olives, cheese, sugar, the lot.'

It was like the gifts of the Magi. 'A neighbour saw us through the window, saw that we had nothing. She even brought us a Christmas tree. Do you know, we still use that tree every year. And when Giulio was born, that woman became the god-mother.' Elvira Mastrosanti was the neighbour's name. I met her recently, nearly two decades later, spending her vacation down in Sicily at the Corsello home. The Corsellos remember kindness, too.

Corsello tells of one poorly-dressed old woman who brought him gifts that Christmas, 'with such discretion and sensitivity that it moved me deeply.' He later went to her little flat to thank her, and found her living in extreme poverty – 'far worse than our own,' Corsello says.[45]

A few priests were kind, and Corsello insists that they be remembered. 'Without their comfort,' he says, 'perhaps I would have definitively left the Catholic Church.' Cardinal Pellegrino gave him help and comfort. There was a priest who telephoned a number of bishop friends begging a teaching post for Corsello, but without success. There was Don Balducci, who also tried to help. 'I remember,' Corsello writes, 'the first time I told him my sad story, he was so moved that, trembling visibly and getting up from his chair, he came and embraced me tightly, so tightly that it seemed I could feel the beating of his great, noble heart. He said, 'Corraggio, Antonio. Non sei solo [Courage, Antonio. You're not alone].'

'Today I say, thank you, Don Balducci.'[46]

Antonio Corsello is today national secretary of a powerful Italian trade union. The grim days are over. But for many resigned priests, especially in certain countries, that kind of poverty is their lot for the rest of their lives. The following, for example, is part of a letter from Sri Lanka:

> About ninety priests have left during the last fifteen years, a big number considering there are only 500 priests on the island. It is very difficult for a resigned priest to find a job here. His seminary studies are not recognised. Those who leave are mostly in the age group thirty-five to forty-five. As such they are too old and inexperienced in a trade or even in administration.
>
> Most of my colleagues who have left are living in small sheds constructed by themselves. My own house has only one room. There is no electricity. There is a pit lavatory, and water has to be drawn from a very deep well. It is far away from a bus route, and I have to walk over one mile to a main road. However, one gets used to living in such situations, and as such we have nothing to complain of. Although we are no longer bound by the vow of poverty, we practice it to an extent which surpasses the most strict monastic order.[47]

Poverty and unemployment are not, however, confined to the Third World. I have encountered many priests in Germany, Spain, Ireland, Italy, France, Britain and throughout the United States, who have had bleak and bitter experiences of unemployment. 'I had always dealt with people down on their luck, but I have a greater appreciation of poverty now than when I was a priest,' a young priest told me, who is unemployed in Phoenix, Arizona. 'Until now I had never realised the permanence of poverty: I can see now how people face the downward spiral they call the poverty trap.'

The man who told me this has a wife and two-year-old child.

Another American married priest, now a prominent government administrator, described to me his years of unemployment, with a wife and two children to support. 'I hit bottom one Christmas,' he told me. 'I got so mad at God that night – at least it shows I still believed – that I came home and threw away every religious object I had. How I've regretted that. How I wish to God I had my mission cross back. At least I have my rosary; I couldn't find it to throw it out.

'The day after Christmas I was sitting there talking of suicide. Luckily, we had this wonderful old Grandma: she came and slapped me across the face. She told me things about my own worth, and how much I had done for her. She said I had been more a priest to her in the few months she had been with us than any priest in her life.'

Job interviews hold particular terrors for a man who has served as a priest. In France, for example, when you go for interview, you have to be a man without a history, French priest-sociologist Julien Potel says. The years of priesthood have to remain hidden because French employers are scared stiff of 'marginal, confrontational types'.

Mark Zwick of Houston tells how his priesthood used to pop up to haunt every interview: 'In my job search, priesthood was written all over my face. Inevitably, we came to the word "Father". Once you hit the magic word, you knew you were going down the tube.'

The real miracle is that in spite of everything being loaded against them, the vast majority of resigned priests throughout the world do ultimately find themselves in worthwhile jobs, often in positions of high responsibility. On my contact list of resigned priests I find psychologists, doctors, social workers, personnel managers, journalists, editors, writers, a mystery novelist, film-makers, radio producers, a police chief, a member of the West German parliament and an executive of Germany's Christian Democrat Party, a provincial governor in Brazil, a millionaire inventor (who uses his millions for the poor), Greenland's negotiator with the European Community, a US diplomat, a secret service agent, a vice-president of General Mills, an Episcopalian bishop in Ecuador, university professors in at least three continents, college lecturers, teachers, psychotherapists, government administrators and civil servants.

The preferred professions? Whichever deal with people rather than things, and especially professions that help. 'Nature breaks out through the eyes of the cat,' as the Irish proverb says.

The very success of thousands of priests has itself led to changing attitudes, particularly in the United States. According to the *Wall Street Journal*, in a special news report on people and their jobs, 'Ex-priests and nuns make excellent employees, many companies discover.' The paper quoted a bank executive as saying, 'They're super performers, and are good at dealing with bureaucracy and office politics.'[48]

The completeness of this turnaround in attitude, at least in the United States, can be partly attributed to one man. Marty Hegarty is nothing short of an apostle of resigned priests and nuns: he has made it his life's work to help them get jobs after they leave. A Chicago priest until he left in 1969, Marty quickly built a name as an industrial psychologist, starting his own consultancy. With the independence it gave him, he set about helping his ex-clerical brothers and sisters in need of work.

He founded an organisation called WOERC, which had the single objective of finding jobs, and it has found them for many hundreds of resigned priests and nuns. Its principal tool is a regularly-updated directory of the nation's resigned priests who already have jobs and are willing to provide job leads for others. The directory is backed up by a regular newsletter.

I went to see Marty Hegarty in his East Point apartment, eleven floors above Lake Michigan. I found a blunt, leathery man touching sixty, brimming with humour and quite devoid of sentimentality. WOERC, he explained, is just the Old English spelling of work, and pronounced the same. Simple. How come he has been so successful? By just going after jobs, and staying out of all the campaigning for letting priests marry. Simple, again. A narrow field of fire.

Yet this same pragmatic, unsentimental Marty was the only one to write to an Illinois priest, who was starting a long prison term for molesting children. 'When you get out of jail, you'll be looking for work,' the letter said. 'Come and see us when you get out.'

Marty only seems blunt. In fact, he is infinitely diplomatic, and gets much done for his priests and nuns by delicate and carefully-nurtured links with the Church establishment in Chicago. When Marty speaks, many listen. Including Cardinal Bernardin.

Above all, the media heed and report Marty, and down the years he has hammered home the fact that priests make marvellous employees. So nowadays American priests face only the same level of prejudice as that met by military men or academics who look for jobs. As Marty says: 'The expectation will be that the academic is too smart, the military man is too rigid, and the priest is too "good".'[49]

Priests who leave need counselling and advice, not just on work, but on all aspects of their transition. A Minneapolis group called Transition, founded by married priest Gary Meitz, provides career assessment, job-seeking training, follow-up services, and women's support. Several resigned priests have told me their lives were practically saved by the Career Program Institute, run by John Mulholland in Washington DC.

Britain has a group called New Bearings, founded to help priests and religious in transition. Even though it is a small organisation, the advice and contacts that New Bearings provides have been a lifeline for many priests and nuns who leave. It is described in more detail in Chapter Ten. The other more general associations of resigned priests, such as Advent, Leaven and Corpus, are also described there.

In talking to many of these groups, I found they stressed two basic pieces of advice for priests who are leaving. Firstly, a priest should try and get a secular qualification, if at all possible before leaving. Secondly, he should not just look for any old job to keep body and soul together. Aim for a career, they said. And aim as high as you can: your potential will astonish you.

RELATIVE PAIN

Sooner or later, then, with the passing of years, many of the priests who leave manage to get on their feet. They find careers, take wives and father children. Much of the grief dwindles.

Much, but not all. There is one grief that can stay and stay for years, perhaps until a man dies. It is twofold: the grief and hurt of the family, and the grief of the priest when his family rejects him.

'I have never seen my nephews and nieces in twelve years,' Eoin, an Irish married priest, told me, 'and I suppose I never will.' This, although they all live within 40 miles of one another. Eoin's two sisters just don't want him round their families, and they certainly do not want his wife. 'I was told, if you want to marry her, for God's sake go to Australia. They see my wife as the scarlet lady that led me out of the Church.'

Sisters, next to mothers, seem to find it hardest to get over a priest who leaves. Several men have sisters who do not speak to them. 'I have one sister,' says a Liverpool priest, 'who has never forgiven me, refuses to speak to me or to acknowledge my children. That's very sad.'

A man from the North of England speaks of what he calls the appearance of forgiveness: 'Their attitude is, we forgive you, but do you realise you did something awful?' The effort is made, but it's only the glimmer of twilight, never glad confident morning again.

Joe Gerharz of Seattle told me shortly before his recent death how his family reacted to his leaving:

'I was a priest in LA at the time, and my sister came down on a business trip. I told her I was going to grad. school. She got up from the restaurant and walked out – she interpreted it as leaving the priesthood. She said, no matter what you do, don't ever tell Mother.

'I did call my Mom, and told her I was going to graduate school. She said to me, "He who puts his hand to the plough and looks back . . . If your father was alive he'd horsewhip you!"

'I'd never said this to Mom before, but I said it: "You goddam sonovabitch," I said to her, "I'm going to do my thing and I never want to hear that from you again!" I slammed down the phone.

'She called right back. She said, "Jody, I'm eighty years old and I'm dying, and I never want you to come home again, 'cause you'd be an embarrassment to your brother and sisters."

'My brother called up a short time later: "Mom tells me you're going to graduate school and that you might leave. I want to tell you I'm a businessman and I don't think you're tough enough to make it on the outside."

'My younger sister called, and said, "The bishop who gets you your dispensation, and the Pope who grants it, and the girl you're going to marry, and you yourself, you're all going to burn in hell." '

In 1983 Joe Gerharz's mother was dying, in Billings, Montana. Let Joe tell it: 'I walked into the hospital room and she said, go and get your hair cut. I spent three days listening to her at a deep level, during which she told me things I never knew. That she was the only one of eight children married in church, one of the few who was not an alcoholic, the only one who was educated. All this time I listened and listened, and we became good friends. One of the things I said to her in those days was, "Y'know Mom, it's because you taught me never to be satisfied, and always to search, that I now have courage to re-examine my life and make the changes I need to make."

'The most beautiful thing [Joe was crying when he told me this] – she called me over to the bed, and took my hand, and said, "Jody, forgive me. I hope I haven't ruined your life."

'She was a great little lady.'

Joe's younger sister died of cancer, without their being reconciled. Joe: 'She was five months in hospital. I flew from Seattle every month to see her. She knew she was dying. The first time I came, the nun went in to see her first. "Peggy, your brother's here. Don't you think it's time to reconcile?" I have time, my sister said. She wouldn't talk.

'Every time I visited her, she would not talk. I'd sit there, holding her hand. One time I was sitting there looking at her. She turned: "Quit staring at me," she said. I was racking my brains – what could I do?

'I was back here in Seattle when she died. If I have any regret, it's for what happened to my sister. She made her choice. But I grieve that she lived with all that anger for so many years.'

And I grieve now for Joe. During my days in Seattle to research this book, that gentle, sensitive man became my friend. And then he died suddenly, before I could ever get back to see him again.

When Sicilian priest Antonio Corsello decided to leave and marry, first he went quietly to his superiors in Rome to ask for a dispensation. 'But as soon as they found out,' Corsello says, 'they told the girl's parents back in Sicily. The parents beat her up, and immediately engaged her to a cousin.'

When Corsello heard that, he took the next plane back to Sicily. As he remembers it: 'My first call was to the local magistrate, to ask his advice. His advice was: "Son, this is Sicily. Down here the only way is to meet violence with violence. But don't say I told you."

'So I went to the girl's parents and I told them, "Have her ready to leave by this afternoon, or I'll kill you with these hands." Well, it was finally arranged for her to go to a college in Rome until it was all sorted out.

'Then the diocesan office in Messina called me in, and offered me money to take care of her pregnancy, if I'd stay a priest.

Pregnant? They thought she was pregnant! "*Chè vergogna!* [Shame on you!]" I said to the Bishop.'

It is the priest's mother who usually suffers most when he leaves. Mothers have been heard to say, when a son leaves, 'I'd rather he had died.' In fact, the grief of such a mother is greater than bereavement, for there is added shame, public humiliation, fear of the neighbours, where-did-I-go-wrong remorse, and fears for the eternal salvation of a son gone astray.

Yet over and over again, so many times, it is the mother, more than anyone, who finally reaches out when the long grieving is over. Sometimes the outcome can be beautiful and happy. A year after Joe and Cathy Grenier married, they took Joe's mother to live with them in Pennsylvania, and she was with them for five years until she died in 1986.

In Minneapolis Terry Dosh's parents, and his wife's parents, all helped the Dosh family buy their home. At different times Terry's father, and Millie's mother, lived their final years in the Dosh home, where they were nursed until they died. The relatives, however, never had need for reconciliation, as they were supportive from the start.

The birth of a child can often be the catalyst of reconciliation. There is a certain undeniability about children, even priests' children, and their very existence can bring the grandparents running.

A priest colleague, still in the active ministry, can help a man's family towards acceptance and reconciliation, as the family will often take its cue from him. Would that more priests realised this. When Frank Prior of New Jersey wrote to his mother in Ireland to say he was leaving, she took the letter down to her parish priest. He, wise man that he was, took her carefully through the letter and explained that Frank's reasons were sound. It changed everything, Frank says.

One German missionary returned home with his bride to find his parents at Frankfurt airport to meet him, as were several of his priest colleagues, and their very presence was enough to reassure the parents, and help the new relationships off to a healthy start. Indeed, perhaps the greatest kindness fellow priests could render would be to provide a counselling service for parents and family of a priest who leaves. They sometimes need help more than the priest himself.

But why in the first place is there such grieving and anger from family? In fact, it is understandable. One resigned priest who knew much rejection explained it to me: 'They say those who mind don't matter, and those who matter don't mind. But that's not really true. There's a bereavement that has to go on in a family. The relationship was all bound up with your being a priest, and it has to be unravelled. It's a measure of their love for you that they mind so much.'

A great deal of the hurt has to do with status. In rural Ireland they used to say a family got respect from having 'a pump in the yard, a bull in the field, and a son in the priesthood.' To lose that son means acute humiliation, friends looking away, neighbours sniggering and wagging their heads.

It can be traumatic if the 'prodigal' comes home to visit. And yet that is the most effective healing of all.

'The resigned priest must try to be present to the family as much as possible,' one of them explained to me. 'They deserve a chance to grieve with you and over you, every time they confront you, or are confronted by you in your new capacity. It's like with dying: the widow must have reminders of her husband, to push against, so to speak. Otherwise there's no draw on her grief.

'When I quit, one of my uncles took it very badly. The local priest went to visit him and was rebuffed at the door – an unheard-of occurrence. But my sister made it her business to talk about me every time she could. "I had a letter from Luke," she would say to the uncle. "Wait till I tell you his news." She was making me real to him every time and giving him a chance to grieve.

'Then came a day when I knocked on his door. Uncle Jim threw his arms round me and burst into tears. "What was wrong with me was pride," he said.'

4

THE BRETHREN
AND THE INSTITUTION

It is easy to suffer for the Church. The difficult thing is to suffer
at the hands of the Church.

Georges Bernanos

ONE MORNING IN 1978, the priests and brothers of the Dominican Priory of Tallaght, in Dublin, Ireland, stood round the altar
to concelebrate Mass. Later that day, 6,000 miles away, one of
their number would stand before another altar, awaiting his
bride.

In that Dublin monastery a young priest stepped forward to
read the petitions: 'Let us pray for David Rice, once a member
of this community, who is getting married today in Portland,
Oregon, that God may bless him and his bride and give them
happiness. Lord hear us.'

Around that altar forty voices answered, 'Lord graciously
hear us.'

Some hours afterwards, as my church wedding began in St
Andrew's Church, Portland, I noticed a basket of flowers before
the altar. The label read, 'From your Brethren'.

If I should forget you Dominicans, let my right hand be forgotten.

I was fortunate to have belonged to a group of enlightened

men, members of a worldwide religious order ancient and great enough to act with magnanimity and even with love. That level of warmth and care for men who leave is not found in every religious order. Still less is it found in every local diocese.

It is understandable. Priests suffer almost like relatives when a colleague leaves, and go through a similar process of bereavement.

Steve and Bertie were priests, both teaching in a famous rugby-playing boarding school in Ireland. They were bosom friends, went dog-racing twice a week, were always in and out of each other's rooms, and worked together on training the rugby team.

One day Bertie said, 'Steve, there's something I have to tell you. I'm leaving.'

'Where are they sending you?' Steve asked.

'I'm not being sent. I'm leaving to get married,' was the reply.

A pause. Then Steve said, 'Do you think I should play young Murphy as scrum-half in Wednesday's match?'

For a whole week after Bertie left, Steve just sat gazing out at the Wicklow Mountains. He could not talk to anybody.

The grief and loneliness of those who remain priests when others leave, is one of the untold stories of the Church today. 'It's like someone dying,' one priest says. 'Especially if you are good friends. It leaves a hole, a gap. And those holes in your life are never really filled. I am conscious of those holes as I grow older.'

He thinks there is turmoil in the heart of a man who remains. 'Should I go too?' he finds himself asking. 'Or, what's wrong with us here, that he had to leave us?' You become acutely aware of the imperfections of your institution when someone leaves, he believes.

At times like these it can sometimes require immense reserves of strength and personal faith to remain a priest, and the marvel is that so many do. One Jesuit identified for me three stages in a priest's reaction when a colleague leaves: 'First, **shock** – "Not so-and-so. He wouldn't leave. Impossible." Then **denial** that it has happened – you just carry on as usual. Finally, it becomes a **forbidden topic** – people who have left are, by consensus, not discussed. Or they are only spoken about in a restricted way: "I saw so-and-so down at the traffic lights today." Reply: "Oh?" And the conversation lapses.'

'I believe', this priest says, 'that such communities need to go through a bereavement process. We need to sit down, talk it out, and work out our grief.'

Bereavement of this magnitude can take years, and it is understandable that some priests remain hurt and hostile. The hostility can range from pulpit denunciations to cold indifference that lasts for years.

Paradoxically, those who are understanding and warm to men who leave are usually the priests most fulfilled by their own priesthood and celibacy, or those who have been through a crisis, but have endured and grown. Often they seem to be men genuinely striving for spirituality: they are frequently members of priestly prayer groups like Jesu Caritas. And they seem more concerned for the happiness of the individual who leaves than for the effect of his leaving on the institution. The institution will get by, anyway, their actions say, but my friend Jim here needs support right now.

A curate (assistant pastor) in a lonely County Cork parish, Ireland, was "in the throes" of deciding to leave, and had no one to confide in. Finally, he got up courage to tell his parish priest.

'I sat him down and I told him. The old boy thought for a while, and then he said, "I've a bit of money put aside – you'll be welcome to it. And remember, you will always be welcomed in my house, you *and whoever comes with you.*" Those were his exact words. That for me was a sign of resurrection. It was one of the best experiences of my life.'

I have come across individual priests who are true samaritans, and are cherished by their married brothers. In Houston, Texas, they speak with love of the late Father Bill Steele who, for sixteen years until his death, regularly gathered his old comrades and their wives for dinner at his rectory.

In Rio de Janeiro, American Oblate priest Ed Leising is a legend. In FASE, the educational and social assistance organisation he founded in Brazil, he has given employment to 120 resigned priests since 1964. Some move on to other posts; some have remained as FASE administrators. 'We are committing mortal sin', he told me bluntly, 'by not using the talents of these men. Ninety-five per cent of them have the deepest Christian belief, without a blink of doubt. We are educators, and I need people who can relate to others in terms of belief.'

There are individual bishops, too, who are true brothers to their married priests. When Augustin and Anne Marie Joseph went from Haiti to an international meeting of married priests in Rome, their trip was paid by bishops in Haiti. Auxiliary Bishop Gerald Mahon of Westminster did the same for an English couple.

Archbishop Pat Flores of San Antonio has set out to be a peacemaker between the married and celibate priests of his still wounded diocese. 'I want to be a friend to those who were my friends prior to their leaving,' he told me in an interview. 'I will not close the door on them, or my love or my heart to them, even if, unfortunately, I cannot offer them participation in liturgical services.'

There are some other bishops who try to do what they can, but like Nicodemus they can come out only at night. For they operate in a Kafkaesque climate of fear that has to be encountered to be believed. Over and over in my travels I have been told please do not publish, or please do not identify – look what they did to Hunthausen [the Archbishop of Seattle who was publicly deprived of his functions by the Vatican for, among other things, his supportive attitude to resigned priests].

On 2 February 1988, I had an appointment for an interview with Cardinal Arns in São Paulo. I was presented to him in the hall of the big old house that serves as diocesan offices. This is a journalist from Europe, the priests introducing me explained. 'Ah, good. You're welcome,' said the Cardinal. A warm handshake for me. He's a married priest, they said to Arns. '*Muito bem* [That's fine],' replied Arns, and gave me a pat on the shoulder. He wants to interview you on married priests, they told him.

Arns stopped cold. 'Absolutely not,' he snapped. I do not give interviews on that subject.' And he scurried into the room off the hall, where he stood leaning over a work table and looking up to see if I had gone away yet. For no reason at all I found myself thinking of the hard-pressed White Rabbit in *Alice in Wonderland*.

Arns is far from being a rabbit, and has in the past been a courageous and consistent campaigner for a married ministry. However, it was explained to me that right now he is under intense Vatican scrutiny. If he puts a foot wrong he may be whisked off to Rome and put in charge of some meaningless office, thus ending for ever any further chance of accomplishing something for his beloved Brazil. He was not going to risk that for the likes of you, the Brazilians explained gently.

In the matter of priests leaving and priests marrying, this fear pervades the Roman Catholic Church from top to bottom. At the top it is fear of loss of office, or loss of promotion; in places like Africa, it is fear of losing Rome's financial support; at the bottom of the heap it is a fear of dismissal, homelessness and destitution, and sometimes of death, by suicide. And those fears have grounds, as what follows will bear out.

The African Church's anxiety about losing financial support was amply borne out by a talk given in London by Malawi's Bishop Patrice Kalilombe:

> As far as I am aware, there have been moments when African leaders did wish to examine the whole question of priestly celibacy, but were told in no uncertain terms not to do so. Since African leaders have no intention of presenting themselves as rebellious members in the Church, they have simply stopped speaking about this question. They have only too well understood the risk they would be taking if they disobeyed. The consequences would be too expensive even in terms of practical considerations. Such is the helplessness of our dependence on the higher authorities even for our budgets and very subsistence, that it would be suicide to offend the hands that feed us.[50]

PERFECT FEAR DRIVES OUT LOVE

When I began research for this book, I thought I would encounter a series of heartwarming stories of kindness from merciful Church authorities, reaching out to a brother who was hurting, as the Dominicans in so many ways reached out to me. What I found instead was that the deeper into the institutional Church I penetrated, the higher up the pyramid of Church authority I went, the more indifference and sometimes cruelty I encountered. I had to make a choice between a Polyanna-like recital of only the nice things, or telling it as I found it.

Institutions can do strange things when they sense a need to protect themselves, and the Catholic Church, composed of human beings, is no exception. But in the light of its mission of spreading God's love, some of the things it does are very strange indeed.

Take what happened in 1981 in the Dublin suburb of Templeogue. There is a word that lies deep in the memory of the Irish people, a word that still sends a shiver down the spine of anyone of Irish descent. That word is eviction. It evokes images of a ragged family huddled in the cold; of bailiffs with battering rams sent by a cruel landlord to demolish the thatched cottage; images of helmeted police holding back the sullen crowd; the arrogant sheriff astride his horse with the eviction order in his hand.

Those century-old scenes came to life once more on 11 December 1981 in Templeogue. There were a few differences this time: the crowd wore modern jeans and carried umbrellas against the pouring rain, and the police wore civilised caps instead of helmets. It wasn't a thatched cottage, but a suburban semi-detached. Television cameras focused on the front door. The sheriff, as he climbed out of his Mercedes, wore a natty business suit and tie.

But there were two other differences: the man waiting inside to be evicted wore a black suit and a Roman collar; and the landlord who had called in the sheriff to evict him was His Grace, Most Reverend Dermot Ryan, Archbishop of Dublin and Primate of Ireland.

The priest was Mayo-born Father Michael Keane, and he was being evicted from his rectory because the Archbishop had suspended him and ordered him out. A Dublin diocesan spokesman told me that the Archbishop 'had agonised an awful lot before taking the decision to evict', and had waited four years before doing so. However, what shocked the people of Ireland was that an archbishop would evict a priest under any circumstances, that Mother Church would do that to one of her children, one of her priests, for any reason whatsoever. As an active priest wrote in the *Western People* newspaper:

> What about all the theory we hear about community and love and brotherhood? What about all the sermons we hear on forgiveness and Christian reconciliation? What about the scripture quotation about turning the other cheek, going the extra mile, giving your cloak as well as your coat? Or is the preaching (people ask) not for the preachers, too? Is keeping the clergy in line such a priority in our Church that our leaders prefer to place their faith in a civil court before the Gospel of love that Christ preached?[51]

The answer would sometimes seem to be YES. In 1969 in Cleveland, Ohio, two priests were celebrating an unauthorised protest Mass at which they were going to read a statement on racism, poverty and war. Somebody at the diocesan office must have known what was going to take place and told the police. One of the two priests told me what ensued: 'By the time we got to the offertory, all the people but one couple had been removed, and there were about forty cops around the altar rails. It came to communion time. We had to give communion to the couple still there. We had to go through the ranks: it came to scuffles and the Host went flying. I was dragged out and carried away in the paddy wagon, still in my vestments.'

That priest now works as a layman in Seattle; the other was later reinstated in the diocese.

THE WHITE HOMICIDES

In Italy they speak of the 'White Homicides' of the Church. It was priest-journalist Gianni Gennari who coined the phrase, to describe Italian Church cruelty and indifference to priests and nuns who leave.

In an article in the daily *Paese Sera*, Gennari printed a letter from a nun who had left her cloister after twenty-five years. She had taught during those years in the convent's school, and had no pension. Her letter reads:

> Fourteen years wandering the streets of the city, seeking home and work; nine changes of residence; four years completely unemployed and in despair. A few days ago I fell at the feet of the superiors, begging for work in the institute's school, since I had no other possibility. I was told an ex-sister could no longer teach . . . I'm hungry . . . At another institute I asked for help, and was rejected. Am I to die in despair?[52]

In the same article Gennari tells of another nun who also left, and who finished as a prostitute on the streets of Florence. Gennari has her name, and the name of the priest who found and rescued her.

He writes of people leaving religious life after ten years, 'with

500,000 lire and *arrivederci*'. That figure is about £250, or $300. In the last twenty years, Gennari says, thousands of nuns and priests have found themselves thus, 'without guarantees and without social dignity, forgotten by all, regarded with suspicion by their brethren and by those who had shared their lives for years, treated as half-men and half-women, worms and not men, as the scripture had said.

'Only God remains to them, and the friendship of those who reject that terrible law that values the institute more than the person, good name more than gospel, and appearance more than substance. They are abandoned to themselves, annulled both in memory and in friendship, so that it can be said with ferocity, "Look what a fate you have, if you are not faithful." '[53]

It is the equivalent of murder, Gennari says. These are the White Homicides of the Church.

It goes back a long way. Guistino Zampini, now a very old man living in Genoa, was forced to live as a vagrant, sleeping in doorways and under bridges, with his young wife, after leaving the ministry over fifty years ago.

It was not always a matter of mere Church indifference to the fate of the 'lapsed' one: sometimes these men were vigorously pursued and deliberately deprived of work by Church authorities, even when they were in state employment. The 1929 Concordat between the Vatican and the Italian government contains the following article:

> Art. 5. No ecclesiastic may take up, or remain in, employment or office of the Italian State or public bodies depending on the State, without the *nihil obstat* [permission] of the Ordinary [bishop] of his diocese. The revocation of the *nihil obstat* deprives the ecclesiastic of the capacity of continuing to exercise such employment or office. In no case may apostate priests, or those subject to censures, take up or continue in a post as teacher, or in an office or employment in which they will come into a direct contact with the public.[54]

From the moment the concordat was signed, a bishop could actually call on the Italian state to dismiss a resigned priest from state employment. Could, and did.

THE BUONAIUTI CASE

A tragic instance is that of Ernesto Buonaiuti, who has been
called 'the most excommunicated man in the history of the
Church'. Accused of Modernism early in the century, he was
hounded from job to job.[55]

In 1906, at the age of twenty-five, he was dismissed from his
post as lecturer in Church history at the pontifical major
seminary in Rome, after the review, *Civiltà Cattolica*, had
attacked his teaching. Thence his life was one long ordeal of
being suspected, interrogated, threatened, condemned. He continued always to pray and to wear priest's clothes, in spite of
several excommunications which followed.

In 1915 Buonaiuti secured a post outside the reach of the
Vatican – that of professor of the history of religion at the
University of Rome. However, one year later, when it seemed he
might die after an operation, Cardinal Gasparri visited him in his
hospital bed and offered him holy communion, on condition
that he gave up his university post.

Buonaiuti refused, and was refused communion.

In 1926 he was declared *excommunicatus vitandus*. This was
both an excommunication and an official Church sentence of
boycott. Catholics were required to shun a person so excommunicated, to avoid such a person absolutely, even in professional
or social contacts.

This meant that no Catholic could attend Buonaiuti's university lectures, and it forced the university to move him out of
teaching altogether. He was given editing work by the university
authorities.

Then, in 1929, the Concordat was signed between Mussolini's
Italy and the Vatican. Incredibly, it contained an article that
seemed made to measure against Buonaiuti – the Article 5
already quoted in this chapter.

Article 29 was also made to measure, for a man who persisted
in wearing clerical clothes and collar:

> Art. 29 (i). The use of the ecclesiastical and religious habit
> by laymen or by ecclesiastics or religious who have been
> definitely forbidden to wear it by the competent ecclesiasti-
> cal authorities (who should officially communicate the fact
> to the Italian Government), is forbidden, and shall be
> punished with the same sanctions and penalties with which

is forbidden and punished the improper use of military uniform.[56]

Not long afterwards, the secretary of the Fascist Party had an audience with Pope Pius XI. A week later, Buonaiuti was called in by a government minister, who referred expressly to the secretary's meeting with the Pope, and ordered Buonaiuti to stop wearing clerical clothes: 'Professor,' he said, 'you are aware of Article 29 of the Concordat. It provides for the arrest of anyone wearing ecclesiastical garb while under excommunication. If you do not comply, the government will be obliged to proceed against you.'

The following year Buonaiuti was dismissed from his university post, ostensibly for refusing an oath of loyalty to Fascism.

Ernesto Buonaiuti died on Holy Saturday 1946, and was buried without any religious ceremony. He had written, years before, that the thought of leaving the Church filled him with 'an obscure terror', as it would have abandoned him to 'the dizziness of a lay world, empty of any spiritual consistency and of any Christian idealism.'

Even after all his excommunications and suspensions, he continued to say the rosary daily with his mother until she died and, for her sake, to leave the house every morning as though he were going to celebrate Mass.

The Concordat has recently been replaced, but old ways die hard. Last year Don la Bella, parish priest in Sciacca, Sicily, took me to a local café which is run by a married priest. 'After the priest left the diocese to marry,' la Bella said, 'he asked the Bishop if he could teach Christian doctrine in the local school. The Bishop consulted his priests. I was all for it. The others, no. So he didn't get the job. His wife's people had this café. So now he runs that.'

Rosario Mocciaro, married priest in Rome, told me: 'There are still many cases in Italy where married priests cannot get work teaching religion. And this, even under the new Concordat we have. The problem is, for many of these priests, it's the only way they know how to live.

'And especially if they don't manage to get a dispensation after they leave, they are immediately fired from teaching religion. But dispensations are nearly impossible to get.'

Mocciaro told me that teachers of religion, even in state

schools, are still regularly nominated by the local bishop, so even there the same old problems arise for resigned and married priests.

Father John McHugh was a pastor in Corpus Christi, Texas, during the 1960s and early 1970s. 'He was regarded as one of the best priests in the diocese – bishop material,' a colleague recalls. 'When he left, in 1973, it was a bombshell for all the priests, because he was so outstanding.'

The rest of the story is in a letter John McHugh wrote for me recently:

> I went to work for Oscar Soliz, the District Clerk of Nueces County, on 1 March 1973. This was two months after I had left Sacred Heart Church. I had spent a month in San Antonio looking for a job, but to no avail.
>
> At the beginning of April I got a call . . . requesting that I come to see Bishop Drury . . . He offered to make me the first pastor of his new mission in Arteaga, in Latin America. Obviously, I did not accept the offer.
>
> Some time after that, a prominent member [of a certain Catholic lay organisation] came to see my boss. He suggested that Oscar should not keep me on his payroll, since my presence in the courthouse was a great source of scandal to the Catholics of the Diocese of Corpus Christi. We do not know if he came as a representative of the Bishop, but Oscar felt that he was not acting on his own . . . Oscar explained that he did not have any problem with my working for him . . .
>
> I do want to stress here that I always found great support among the clergy of the diocese, and to this day I can count on just about all of them as my friends. That was especially helpful during the three years that I had to wait for the dispensation.
>
> There was one more incident that bothered me very much. After I had left the ministry, and I was already working at the courthouse, Del and I went to St Joseph's Church for evening Mass one weekday. The assistant pastor (I do not even remember his name) publicly refused to give communion to Del and me. He just stood there and told us to move on, because he could not give us communion.[57]

Sixteen years later, John McHugh is still working with Oscar Soliz, in the district courts of Nueces County, Texas. He is as respected in Corpus Christi as ever he was, and his work for the Mexican Americans is highly regarded and appreciated.

In the Netherlands, an eminent churchman asked the University of Utrecht to fire seven professors who were married priests. Three have now resigned, of their own accord.[58]

In Fortaleza, Brazil, the Papal Nuncio ordered Cardinal Lorscheider to fire three professors at his seminary for the same reason. (One of them told me what happened there: 'Cardinal Lorscheider replied that if the Nuncio would provide him with three other teachers, he would obey the Nuncio's wishes. Otherwise he would keep them, and take all the responsibility for it!' They're still there.)[59]

Married priest Francis McNutt, today a distinguished figure in the Christian healing ministry, was struck off the list of speakers at a US West Coast conference after a bishop objected. At a healing and prayer seminar, another bishop called officials and threatened to cut funding if McNutt remained on the programme.[60]

A Sri Lankan priest writes: 'I know cases where, when prospective employers refer to the superiors about an ex-priest, he has really been condemned. I am glad to say that now some bishops and superiors take a more sympathetic view.'[61]

John Dubay, married priest and family psychotherapist in Binghampton, New York State, has worked for years with priests leaving the ministry. In a letter he speaks of his concern 'for those men who were honest or attempted honesty in their resignation from the active priesthood and were treated in a monstrous, unchristian, and inhuman manner by fellow clerics':

> The range of stories approaches the absurd [Dubay writes] when we learn of the devices of evil that were brought against them by men of God. Men have spoken of phone calls from the diocesan office at 2 a.m. to their family residence. Others have spoken of pressure on prospective employers, possibly with the hope that if unsuccessful at work, he would return to the active priesthood.
>
> Transcripts have been witheld by some bishops' offices, presenting difficulties in pursuing education and getting employed, or licensed for employment. When asked of this by one married priest who needed work to support a wife and four children, the bishop's office responded that it was not their problem, and should have been considered at resignation time.

Married priests have spoken of calls to their families that put pressure on relationships that were vital during transitional times.

Some who attended local Catholic colleges after leaving active ministry often became aware of pressure by bishops or superiors on the college to affect their status and presence at the college. Some college professionals stood strong, and to them we say thank you. Others did not. Some of them have subsequently apologised for their moment of weakness and made gestures of reconciliation.

Five years ago a bishop stood up at a gathering of married priests. He asked for forgiveness for the Church and the way that it treated its men who had served it in active ministry but had chosen to resign. I was moved by his openness and humility and courage.[62]

John Dubay is writing of the treatment that resigned priests encountered in the recent past, the 1960s and 1970s, the decades following the Second Vatican Council. Bad though it may have been, it is nothing compared to the way such priests were treated before the Council. Father Paul Winninger, writing in 1963 for the bishops of the Council, describes it:

The situation of these unfortunates is horrible . . . we have succeeded in creating around them a . . . myth of the infected . . . They themselves seem to be dumb with stupor, and bury themselves in silence, refusing to defend themselves.

Will no Father of the Council have the heart to become their advocate? Their misdeed does not deserve such a punishment, and this sentence is not worthy of the Church. Such a sanction is not that given by a mother. It is interpreted today as a brutal reaction, similar to that of parents who reject their child, an unwed mother for instance, who has 'dishonoured' them.

Authoritative voices assure us that the Church carries sorrowfully the burden of these 'fallen priests'. That is not true, since she excommunicates them . . .

In countries (Italy, Spain) where civil law recognises only the religious marriage of baptised persons, the injustice reaches a rare extreme: these priests cannot get married even under civil law. Deprived of religious rights and excluded from the Church, deprived simultaneously of essential civil rights and banned from society, with wife and children, they answer perfectly the definition of the infamous untouchable: the pariah. Indeed, the only example of a pariah in Western civilisation is a Catholic product, and they are priests.

Is there an international tribunal to avenge the rights of man? If so, these priests can well bring their case to such a court.[63]

Active priests are kept in line, and those who leave are punished, by downright tight-fistedness on the part of Church authorities. It is hard to know sometimes if it is simply the result of indifference, or of a failure to grasp worldly matters, or a deliberate use of economic sanction.

My research notes contain many instances: there was the English priest-teacher, about to leave, who handed his final pay to his superior. The superior took it and gave him back £25 to start him off in his new life. I know of Irish priests who found themselves on the boat to England with the clothes on their back and £20 in their pocket – a parting gift from their order – and no qualifications whatsoever. By way of contrast, certain religious orders have been fair and generous to their men who leave. The Dominicans in Ireland customarily give several thousand pounds to a man after he leaves, and often make the down payment on a house when a man is taking out a mortgage.

In Portland, Oregon, Father Gerald Linahen retired at sixty-one because of poor health. Three years later he was laicised and got married. When he died in February 1988, a priest said in the funeral homily that 'Gerry went by the book. He waited until he had been laicised before he got married.' The rest of the story comes in a letter from Bob Beh of Portland:

> What was not mentioned in the homily was that after he was laicised . . . somebody then cut off his medical insurance. His wife got a lawyer and threatened to sue [the new] Archbishop Levada, so Levada started sending him $100 per month. He never did get reinstated in his insurance and died with a lot of medical bills and in relative poverty.[64]

Gerald Linahen's widow has verified these facts for me.[65]

Several priests have told me of the main thing that keeps men in line – the fear of losing their pension and insurance. One of them put it thus: 'Once you retire, you have your pension.

Marry, and they cut it off. If I serve faithfully for seventy-five years, I'll be ninety or a hundred years old. I marry – and they'll cut me off. They'll say, "Old man, how dare you quit on us!" '

THE COW SYNDROME

One of the saddest of all ecclesiastical cruelties I have encountered is what I call 'The cow syndrome'. It hurts women as well as men. When I was a very young priest trying to cope with celibacy, an older priest passed on to me a well-worn piece of wisdom, 'Always remember, young Rice, if you want a glass of milk, you don't have to buy the bloody cow.'

It is an attitude that can poison the personal life of a priest, but when it emerges as part of official policy – or rather, unofficial policy – it poisons the Church itself. In its policy form it amounts to a Church demand that a priest abandon his wife and children. I quote a letter from a certain US bishop to one of his priests who had 'strayed':[66]

> Dear . . . ,
> It was with great sadness that I learned of your decision to leave the priesthood and attempt marriage. As your bishop I am required to inform you that you have violated the canons of the Church which regulate your clerical life. You are in violation of canons 2388, 188, 132 no. 1, 1072, and therefore, having attempted marriage, you are now excommunicated *latae sententiae*.
>
> If after receiving this letter and having given its content thought and prayer you wish to return to the clerical state, *you must leave your wife and your children if any* [author's italics], and obtain a civil divorce and do penance. After a period of time we will apply to the Holy See for reinstatement to the clerical state on your behalf.
>
> With every best wish.
>
> + . . .
> Bishop of . . .

In the southern United States I was given the name of a fifty-two-year-old priest from a certain diocese. 'He met this lady,' another priest told me. 'They fell in love, and he decided to leave. She gave up her job, and moved from her house and town to marry him. She had been twice widowed, and was a very lovely person.

Anyway he couldn't get a job, and he wanted to go back into the priesthood. He went through a civil divorce, the whole bit. She was extremely upset. Then our bishop gave him a parish.'

On my desk is a photocopy of a letter, dated 12 April 1983, sent by the vicar-general of the Archbishop of Cologne, and addressed to Dr Heinz-Jürgen Vogels, married priest of Bonn, Germany. It informs him that the Vatican's Cardinal Ratzinger has stated he can never return to priestly duties. However, even if he wants merely to have his excommunication lifted, and return to the Church as a layman:

> . . . you must stop living with your wife, as you are only civilly married, without Church permission and against the norms of Church law.
>
> If you can come to an unequivocal decision, both to renounce any claim to priestly rights and powers, and also to seek a release from your marriage obligations, then the Congregation of the Faith will recommend to the Holy Father the granting of a dispensation [the reduction to the lay state].[67]

This means that Vogels was to lose both his priesthood and his wife, as the price of reconciliation with the Church. And tragically that is precisely what happened. Vogels pined so much for peace with his Church that he did what the Vatican demanded, and divorced Renata.

Now he still lives with her, but in a 'state of divorce'.

The Vatican has no reason to demand that Vogels leave his wife: her previous marriage had already been annulled by a Catholic Church court, so it had been no impediment to her marrying Vogels.

I stayed with Heinz and Renata for a few days recently, and found two intensely prayerful Christians. But both also suffer intensely from a church cruelty that is almost byzantine. And Heinz has never got back his church editing job – he had been part of a team preparing the definitive edition of the Complete Works of Albert the Great. As late as February 1989, Cardinal Ratzinger met Vogels in Rome and promised to speak in favour of his re-employment in that job. However in April 1989 Vogels got a letter from Cologne's new Cardinal Meisner, saying there was no possibility of his reinstatement, and asking him nevertheless to stick to his original promise of celibacy. So this gifted German theologian remains unemployed.

Frank was a priest in his early thirties in a diocese in the US south-west. Nearly three years ago he got a girl pregnant, and told his bishop. 'But the bishop's only concern was not to tell anyone,' Frank recalls. 'He said, give the child away. He figured that would be the best solution. I think he felt embarrassed by the whole thing.

'After Jimmy was born, he wanted me to stay away from Margaret. I was wanting to talk to him about my responsibility, but he didn't want to talk about it.'

When the child was eighteen months old, Frank felt he had to stick by the mother and child. He wrote a letter simply telling the parish he was leaving. They all wanted to know why. So he wrote another letter, admitting what had happened, and explaining that he felt he should marry and be a father to the child. Fifty couples from the parish organised a big shower [in the United States a 'shower' is a party to present gifts, usually before weddings or births] to provide gifts for the baby. Frank got the following letter from the bishop:

> I just received copies of your letter to the parishioners before you left. It is certainly too bad that you had to write a second letter. I feel sorry for the people of the parish . . . I can hardly believe that you divulged your personal situation to them and rubbed their noses in it . . . Your conscience and your common sense have left you. Faithfully yours in Christ. . . .[68]

As I read that letter sitting in Frank's kitchen, his little boy, now a flaxen two-year-old with the mischievous face of an elf, was climbing on my knee. His young father, on welfare, was washing dishes at the sink. The mother was asleep in the next room, as she does night work.

LET MY PEOPLE GO

A constant source of suffering for priests who leave is the curious process that used to go under the term 'laicisation', and is now more frequently called 'dispensation' (although Archbishop Pio Laghi, Apostolic Nuncio to the United States, was using the word 'laicisation' as late as 1985 in a letter to Archbishop Hunthausen). Put very briefly, it is official Vatican permission to leave the formal ministry. However, Church officials have often made it a lot more than that: it has been termed 'a reduction to the lay state.' But how can a man be thus reduced, if he had been made 'a priest for ever'? Besides, the document of laicisation states that if anyone is in danger of death, this 'layman' must give the Sacrament of Reconciliation, which is something only a priest can do.

However, that is far from being the end of the complications of this strange matter. Journalist Gianni Gennari in 1984 published in an Italian newspaper 'A Christmas Letter to the Pope', accusing him of a triple unfairness to priests who marry. Firstly, Gennari told the Pope, you won't allow priests to marry without getting a dispensation to leave the ministry. Then you refuse that dispensation. Thirdly, after refusing the dispensation, you insult them by saying they are in an unlawful condition.[69]

'*Vergogna*,' roared Sicilian married priest Antonio Corsello, as he tramped with me across the black volcanic slopes of Etna, high above Linguaglossa. 'I say *vergogna*, shame! Shame on the Pope for what he has done to us married priests. The Pope has a Christian duty to take people out of their sin. But by refusing dispensations to priests who have left and married, he is forcing these men into a state of sin. And then he keeps them there. Christ came to save, and this man is forcing them into sin. Where is the Christianity?

'When Stalin and Hitler killed millions, well, they were atheists; but when the Pope leaves priests in their sin, in a state of spiritual death, I am ashamed. Shame on him. Shame, shame, *vergogna*!'

Somehow the black cinders scrunching underfoot, and the smoke curling from the mountaintop above us, seemed appropriate to the utterance.

The president of the Brazilian bishops, Dom Luciano Mendes, told a meeting of Brazil's married priests, in May 1987, that it depends on who in Rome handles the application for dispensation. If it hits one particular desk, it moves faster; another desk, and it just crawls. So it's not surprising, he observed, that the results are often against all expectation.[70]

But is it in fact true that the present Pope has practically cut off any hopes of getting a dispensation? Has there been a cutback?

Jim Cantwell, press officer for the Dublin Archdiocese, says there has. 'Under Pope Paul VI, dispensations were given fairly routinely,' he says. 'But an analysis of the situation would reveal that in some cases a person had entered a marriage which he was unable to sustain, or after a while has wished to return to the ministry. So there have been cutbacks.'[71]

I hardly met a priest, resigned or active, around the world, who would accept this explanation. 'It just drives priests into the registry office to get married,' one man says. 'It doesn't keep them in the priesthood. And if it does, then it's even worse. If a man were to remain a priest only because he couldn't get a dispensation, then he'd be like a trapped animal. What use would he be as a priest then?'

Yet the Pope, asked recently by a group of US bishops to speed up the process of dispensation, replied, 'I'm in no hurry. They left us: we didn't leave them.'[72] I keep thinking of how the father of the Prodigal Son espied him from afar, and came hurrying to meet him.

The Pope is indeed in no hurry. One married priest penetrated the Vatican as far as to meet an official in Cardinal Ratzinger's office. That blond young German cleric told him there was no likelihood of dispensation, 'until you are on your deathbed.'[73]

The application process for laicisation is both demeaning and offensive. For the application to have the slightest chance, you have to admit to being either mad or bad, or that you should never have been a priest in the first place. In other words, that you are devoid of sexual control; or that you are a psychiatric case; or that you were pressured into becoming a priest. The whole thing is copied crudely from the marriage annulment process.

A missionary in Lima, Peru, told me how he had to give evidence before a tribunal on behalf of a colleague who wanted a dispensation. The findings of the tribunal would be forwarded to Rome. 'He needed the dispensation, because his wife had wanted a church wedding. Well, I had to witness that he should never have been a priest. They warned me, there's no point in going in there and saying he was a great guy. You'll help him only by saying negative things. It was as if we were imitating the Russian show trials.'

'What kind of negative things?' I asked.

'That there had been coercion from his family. That his father had been a school teacher, and that he had not been as bright as his father would have liked. That his father was fiercely negative towards him, and that if the guy had left the seminary, he would have said, "I knew you'd never make it". I was basically to say he became a priest only for his father: that's exactly what they wanted to hear.'

An Italian married priest says that Church authorities in Rome itself told him the dispensation would be speeded up if he went to a psychiatrist and got a certification to say he was mentally ill. A Monsignor advised him how to comport himself for the psychiatrist: 'Be sure to talk angrily, and to switch from smiling to weeping.' The Monsignor wrote out on a Church letterhead the addresses of two psychiatrists. The priest, now married, kept the paper and gave me a photocopy of it.[74]

What these men told me is amply borne out by a questionnaire, which has been administered to priests wanting to leave a certain religious order in the United States. The following are some of the questions it contains:

- How old were you when you entered the Order?

- Did you freely enter the Order or were you influenced by others to enter the Order? If you were influenced by others, who were they?

- What was your parents' attitude to your entrance to religious life and the priesthood?

- Prior to your solemn profession, did you know the obligations flowing from that solemn profession and from the law of celibacy?

- Prior to your entrance into the Order and during your years of religious and priestly formation, did you experience difficulties regarding chastity?

- Are these same difficulties leading you to petition for laicisation and a dispensation from your vows and the law of celibacy?

- Were you doubtful about your vocation during your years of formation? Do you feel that you took adequate means to overcome these doubts at that time? Around what did these vocational doubts centre?

- After you were ordained, were you or are you troubled

by moral problems relating to the vow and virtue of
chastity and the law of celibacy?

- Do you or did you experience any problems with
  drinking? Are you an alcoholic?

- Have you suffered from any emotional disturbance or
  mental illness? If so, please specify.

- Have you contacted any doctor or psychologist or
  professional counsellor about your decision to leave the
  priesthood and religious life? If so, do you have a
  document or statement from him regarding this decision
  or will you sign a document releasing him from the
  obligation of professional secrecy and authorising him
  to make such a statement in support of your petition?[75]

These questions clearly invite the petitioner to declare that he did
not become a priest freely, but was influenced by others; that he
could not keep sexual control of himself both before and after his
ordination; and that he had emotional, mental or alcoholic
problems. It is also clear that a psychiatrist's declaration to that
effect would help the matter of dispensation.

In all of this the Church is no different from any organisation.
Dahrendorf and other sociologists point out that any group will
defend itself against rebellious or threatening members by
declaring them either ill or amoral.[76] The point is, however, that
the Church came to teach a new and different way, that of gospel
love.

The dispensation, if it ever comes, can be as humiliating as the
application process. It claims to be a reduction to the lay state.
Even if one were to accept that it is really a return to the lay state,
and that such a return is a 'reduction', in fact the person 'laicised'
is reduced below the level of a lay person.

He is expressly excluded from many functions open to lay
people. He cannot be an Eucharistic minister; he cannot read the
lesson in church. An official instruction from the Vatican's
Congregation for the Faith (formerly the Holy Inquisition)
expressly forbids 'laicised' priests from 'taking any liturgical part
in celebrations with a congregation where his situation is
known; he may never preach the homily.' It also forbids him to
occupy any administrative office in seminaries or similar insti-
tutes, or to teach there. 'Likewise he shall not occupy the office of

director of Catholic schools, or religious studies teacher in any schools, Catholic or otherwise.'[77]

According to the same document, a priest who is laicised 'should not stay in a place where he was known as a priest'. If the wretch chooses to marry, the bishop 'should take care that pomp and display are avoided and that it takes place before an approved priest and without witnesses, or if need be, two witnesses. The marriage should be recorded in the secret archive of the diocesan curia.' It is left to the bishop 'to determine how the dispensation and the celebration of marriage are to be kept secret . . . An annotation should be made in the baptismal register of the parish of the petitioner and of his wife that the local ordinary [bishop] is to be consulted whenever information or documents are requested.'

This secrecy would seem to contradict the very nature of marriage, which is essentially a public act.

The Church's 1983 revised book of laws (called the new Code of Canon Law) makes things even more complicated. While now in cases of emergency it allows lay people to perform various ministries according to need, laicised priests are to be deprived 'of all offices, functions and any delegated power' (Canon 292).[78]

However, it is far from clear where the new Code really stands. Canon lawyers see it as riddled with loopholes, and some of them have been studying it at Catholic University of America, to see if it can be used to the advantage of laicised priests. Some are considering the possibility that the Code could be used to allow such priests to perform some ministries, rather than to exclude them.

But whatever interpretations may be put on the new Code, documents of dispensation, as late as 1988, are still substantially imposing the above listed restrictions and rules, in the few instances when they are actually issued.

I asked Dom Angelico Sandalo Bernardino, auxiliary bishop of São Paulo, Brazil, what he thought of the dispensation circus. While infinitely cautious, he seemed not to take it too seriously. 'This whole problem of laicisation is just a legal measure,' he told me. 'The priest continues as a priest: there's no doubt of that. At the present moment [Rome is] acting in this way. In Paul VI's time, things were one way; now they are another. In the near future it could be different again. There used to be no way out at all. Then came a way out. This is a big advance, and if we practise holiness, authentic Christian life and fraternal dialogue, there will be new steps forward. I don't know when, but the Holy Spirit always illuminates.'

So why does anyone now bother even asking for laicisation? One reason is that you can't have a church marriage without it, which means your children would be bastards in the eyes of the Church.

Another is that a priest is excluded from many jobs if he is not laicised. His wife can be too. In a certain Californian diocese, for example, a priest's wife applied for the principalship of a Catholic school, and got the post. But, her husband tells me, the diocese found out that her husband was a married priest without dispensation. 'The offer was pulled immediately,' he says.

The late Victor Power, playwright, author, and one-time speechwriter for Mayor Daley of Chicago, had once been a priest in Waterford, Ireland. He left in 1968 after studying journalism at the University of Iowa. Shortly before his death, he wrote me this description of returning to Ireland to look for a job:

> After I came back from Saudi Arabia, I applied to Dundalk Regional College for a post that was advertised. To my astonishment I found that the chairman of the board was a priest, Monsignor Peter McKevitt of Termonfeckin, County Louth, who had written a book called *The Just Society*.
>
> When I went for interview, about nine people were there [on the interview board], including a token elderly Protestant who nailed his eyes to the ceiling all the time.
>
> 'I've talked to your bishop in Waterford,' began McKevitt. 'Are ye laicised?'
>
> I said no.
>
> 'Don't you think,' he said, 'you are very naive to be looking for a job here when you're not laicised?'
>
> I told him I thought this was a secular college.
>
> He snorted. 'Don't you think a teacher should have some moral values?'
>
> I said I did, but mine no longer coincided with his. I said I was an Irish citizen, and entitled to a fair consideration. He said I had some gall applying for the job where there would be kids from several counties round coming to the college. I

left the interview with my tail between my legs, but furious. The college principal, a Dr somebody, followed me to the parking lot, apologising on behalf of everyone, and said the chairman was senile.

'Then what's he doing as chairman?' I asked.

Goodbye Ireland.

I then embarked on a happy decade in the Midwest, as one of the highest-paid executives in Chicago.[79]

A book, published by Gooi & Sticht in the Netherlands in 1986, under the title *Pastor*, lists eighteen points that are required in persons seeking to work in any Church-related field. They were put together from accumulated pastoral experience of the previous ten years in the Netherlands, and have been neither denied nor conceded by Dutch Church authorities.[80]

Some of the eighteen points discriminate against married priests. Those without a dispensation are totally excluded from all consideration. And, since the Dutch Synod in 1980, even priests with dispensation can no longer be nominated in any role whatsoever.

Yet, by giving a dispensation, the Church is releasing a man from his promise, and declaring that promise non-existent. Married priest Antony Padovano asks, 'Why then are we punished, and God's people with us? Would any of us release a child from a promise and then punish the child?'

Apart from the question of employment, laicisation is still a matter of conscience for many priests who leave. I met a man who left many years ago, and has now been waiting seven years to marry the woman he loves. 'But the law is important to me,' he says. 'I want laicisation before I marry Diane. If I went ahead without it, I feel I'd be cutting my lifeline to God.' So far there is not the sniff of a dispensation.

For some men who do marry, waiting for a dispensation that never comes is like Kafka's man waiting all his life, until he dies, for permission to enter the Castle. It can bring a lifetime of anguish and it has led, in cases that I personally know, to marriages breaking up. One married man whose heart is breaking from repeated refusals by Rome, showed me a photocopy of the latest letter from the Vatican to the head of his order:[81]

Most Reverend Father:

This Dicaster [Vatican Congregation] has examined the request for dispensation from priestly obligations, presented by the Rev.——, of your Institute.

Not having discovered, in the documentation presented, sufficiently valid motives, in the light of the criteria indicated in our letter of 14 October 1980, this Congregation has not been able to recommend to the Holy Father the request of the aforesaid Petitioner.

Your Paternity will not fail to support the Petitioner spiritually, offering him the encouragement and the help of which he will have need.

+ Joseph, Cardinal Ratzinger

As I read that letter, the man's young wife sat watching me silently. From across the table I could feel her grief, whose only crime was to have loved. I looked up, and her eyes seemed to be pleading. They filled up with tears as I looked at her.

It is not surprising, then, that more and more priests are simply not bothering to ask for laicisation. It's just no longer important to them.

But the refusal of dispensations hurts the Church even more than it hurts priests. A group of Austrian married priests made that point to the Pope, prior to his 1988 visit: 'Although we try to console our confrères', they wrote, 'and to strengthen their hope, they experience this treatment as inhuman and unchristian. There is a danger that not a few of them will become enemies of the Church, as you yourself predicted when you were auxiliary bishop of Cracow.'[82]

Even the people are going their own way. In Recife, Brazil, Holy Ghost missionary Brian Eyre was preparing to marry a local girl. Eyre: 'The day before the wedding, the people organised a concelebrated Mass in my church, and invited all the neighbouring priests – four came; so did Martha's parents, and brothers and sisters. The church was absolutely full of people, with Martha and me sitting down among them. At one point, the people called us to the front, and everybody put their hands over us and they said, "Even if the official church won't give you a blessing, we, the People of God, give you our blessing." The next day we had the civil wedding at her parents' house.'

HUMAN RIGHTS

One could make a case that in their treatment of priests, especially those who leave, Church authorities are in contempt of the United Nations Universal Declaration on Human Rights.

Missionary Cathal Cullen specifically lists the articles contravened: Article 2 is violated by *discrimination* against married priests and against their spouses, who are fired from jobs and deprived of work. Article 10 is violated, in that *due process* is denied to any priest in confrontation with Church authorities. Priests are punished, dismissed, evicted, deprived of pensions and insurance, without any recourse whatsoever. Even in the rare instances where voluntary arbitration is being introduced into Church disputes, there is still no independent, impartial tribunal to ensure fair treatment. Those accused are not told the charges, nor allowed to confront their accusers.

Article 16 stating the *right to marry*, is violated in the treatment of priests who attempt to marry, and in the arbitrary refusal to grant them laicisation. Article 21 is violated in that priests have no say whatsoever in Church *government*. Article 22 is violated by depriving priests and nuns who leave of all *social security*, whether it be stripping them of their pensions or perpetrating the White Homicides.

Article 23 is violated, in that priests have no *protection against unemployment* and are allowed no unions to protect them; neither priests' senates nor priests' associations are permitted to perform such functions.[83]

As Anthony Padovano puts it, 'Any policy which must be maintained with terror and dishonesty creates a heart of darkness in the Body of the Church, a spirit which Christ resists with all his love.'[84]

There are frightening parallels to what happens in dictatorships. In 1986, Rosemary Radford Reuther put it thus in the Jesuit magazine *America*: 'It is hard to believe a Church that defends religious liberty, freedom of dissent, the equality of persons before the law, just wages and fair political processes, and then fails to apply these principles within its own institutional walls . . . Theologians have been called for investigation before the renamed, but unchanged, Office of the Holy Inquisition. There they are denied the basic rights, guaranteed by modern judicial systems, to know the charges against them and

to confront their accusers. Some have been deprived of their jobs
or their official positions . . .'[85]

There was power-grabbing and injustice even among the first
twelve apostles whom Christ chose. And all that is happening
means only that Church authorities are still human beings.
However, to be human does not merely involve mild little
pecadillos – combine humanity with tremendous power, remove
all checks and balances, and the results can be monstrous.

John Dubay suggests that resigned priests sometimes feel the
same numbness towards the official Church as Jews can feel
towards their former Nazi persecutors, a numbness beyond even
hatred: 'In looking at married priests I wonder if their experience
with the Church officials when they left was so inaccessible to
any conception of how Christian religious men were going to
treat them, that they were left in a perpetual state of spiritual
shock. They are beyond anger and hatred. Never in their wildest
imaginings would they have thought that a bishop, chancery, or
pope would have so dealt with them as they were crucified. The
consequences is that to live with these painful realities, bishop,
chancery, and pope have become faceless and almost nonexis-
tent . . . The Church has become a faceless source of their
spiritual condition. They live in a world unaware of their
spiritual numbness, beyond despair, hatred, forgiveness and
reconciliation.

'Many roads back are open to them, but they do not remove
the responsibility from the faceless ones. One of the tasks that
lies before us is to speak the hard words that call those
responsible to face up to their part in the present crisis in the
priesthood in the Church. The present situation is a grace for the
priesthood, which will be lost if reconciliation is not sought.'[86]

Chapter Twelve looks at this question of reconciliation. I close
the present chapter by touching briefly the question that occurs
to everyone who encounters this phenomenon of the Church's
faceless cruelty: how can it be happening in the Church that
Jesus founded?

The Church is in crisis, and is facing the age-old dilemma that
French writer St Exupéry expressed: should the individual die
for the group, or the group for the individual?

In its human dimension, the Church is a group like any other.
When there is internal conflict, a group will defend itself by
neutralising or expelling the troublesome. A group's harshness

is, however, usually softened by structures like courts and juries to ensure fair play. But the Church has not yet developed such structures, so there is nothing to protect the individual from the full fury of its defence mechanisms.

But there is more to the Church than the merely human dimension. It happens to be a community that derives from Jesus Christ, he who taught that the Sabbath was made for people, not people for the Sabbath. The Church's real crisis lies in ignoring that very instruction. The great Trappist monk, Thomas Merton, speaks of 'the crisis of authority brought on by the fact that the Church, as institution and organisation, has in fact usurped the place of the Church as a community of persons united in love and in Christ. Love is equated with obedience and conformity within the framework of an impersonal corporation. The Church is preached as a communion, but is run, in fact, as a collectivity, and even as a totalitarian collectivity.'

We speak of *ecclesia semper reformanda* [the Church for ever in need of reform]. Jesus taught that 'by this shall all people know that you are my disciples, that you love one another'. That love is already alive among Church members as individuals, at whatever level they are found, and there are many moving instances of it. But that same love now needs to percolate upwards through the structures, transforming them to the words of Christ: 'Do not lord it over them as the Gentiles do.' So far it has signally failed to do so.

One married priest wonders if this could explain the puzzle of 'a church of beautiful persons, but who have a public or ecclesiastical persona – a sort of group personality, if you like – that is far from beautiful. It's almost like ecclesiastical schizophrenia,' he says.

The old Latin tag goes back a long way: *Canonici boni viri; capitulum autem mala bestia* ['the priests of the cathedral chapter are decent fellows; but the chapter itself is a wicked beast'].

'There's a scene in Brecht's *Galileo Galilei*', a married priest friend recalls, 'where Galileo is talking to the Pope. The Pope is enthused by Galileo's theories . . . A rapport begins to develop between the two men.

'Then the Pope dresses to leave. As each vestment goes on him, the rapport diminishes. The whole texture of the Pope's language alters . . . He begins to cite scripture, to cite Ecclesiastes.

'The Man begins to recede, and the Office Holder is standing there, condemning. The rapport ends in canon law and censure, and finally the Pontiff is standing there, denouncing, accusing, condemning.'

Eppur, se muove.

5

A PRIEST FOR EVER?

The Lord has sworn and shall not repent:
Thou art a priest for ever according to the order of
Melchisedech.

Psalm 110

ONCE UPON A time an Irish priest was travelling by train across the United States. Down by some shunting yards, somewhere in the Midwest, he came face to face with an old tramp who was climbing out of a railway wagon. Their eyes met and held.

'*Tu es sacerdos in aeternum* [Thou art a priest for ever],' the Irishman said. A statement, not a question. And the old man nodded.

The story has various endings, and used to be told regularly to students in Maynooth and sundry other seminaries. It could well be true.

For men who were once ordained really do seem to stay priests for ever. Apart from theological aspects, one could say there are subtle, and not so subtle, marks about such men, which they never seem to lose.

In this chapter I look at what kind of men they are, what kind of marriages they make, what their wives and their children think and are like. I got much of the material from simply living in their homes with them, endeavouring to become a participant rather than just an observer. As well as watching, I listened and listened: to the insights of the wives and the children, just as much as those of the men. It was a splendid experience.

The wives are the first to point out that priesthood leaves its mark. 'Financially they are hopeless,' one wife says. 'They haven't a bull's notion about money. Sometimes it would drive you out of your mind.'

'Priests aren't very practical husbands,' another wife says. 'All their training is intellectual, and idealism can be rather cloying. It could frustrate some wives, because they never get that material wealth that they would have had if their husbands had more drive. There's a lack of ruthlessness in most of them – I mean, idealism doesn't wash in business, where promotion is important.

'They say the Pope gets letters saying, "please take him back, and I'll rear the kids on my own." Some people say that's why he's not giving dispensations, but I don't believe it.'

The men themselves mostly admit to not being wildly ambitious. 'I just can't shake off St Augustine's words, which I lived by for so long – "It's better to need little than to have much,"' one of them explains.

'I just don't feel I need wealth for my own self-worth,' says another, who works in personnel for a German multinational company. 'I get more kicks out of simple things – good company, a good relationship. They're worth far more than going out for a big meal.'

Does that mean he'd let his wife and kids be poor?

'Certainly not. Poverty has its own anxieties. It's just a question of moderation.' He rejects what he calls the false god of careerism: 'going for promotion at all costs, and using your present position just as a leg-up for the next promotion. For me, success isn't measured in promotion or praise.' Success, rather, is being really useful, he says. It is getting results, or seeing someone's face light up when you're able to help them.

But it would be a mistake to think that these men don't care about success: for them it is probably the most important thing of all. 'As a priest, society had you on a pedestal,' one recalls. 'So you feel stripped of a sacred overlay, and you need some sort of success to restore your sense of worth.'

It's just that these men seem to have slightly unconventional notions of success. And they seem happiest in service-oriented jobs. Those in business often give leisure time to working for others like the aged or the poor, or do some counselling.

One man, who left the priesthood because he was gay, offered his services as a counsellor to a gay organisation. 'But it didn't work out,' he says. He found himself at odds with too many of their attitudes, and they found him too conservative.

Bringing up Father

The priests who leave to marry are frequently men of outstanding potential – potential winners, rather than losers. But they have a lot of developing to do.

To begin with, they come from a particular gifted group of men. A couple of decades ago you could not even have made it through seminary without being intellectually well endowed. Ray Henke recalls IQs of 130 as not unusual in the San Antonio seminary. 'I taught there and at a Catholic university simultaneously,' he recalls. 'The difference was unbelievable. There wasn't a single course at the university with the same abstractive level that we had at the seminary.'

The men entering in those days were also mostly what the Americans call 'jocks', popular, athletic, most-likely-to-succeed types. Several priests, including a vocation director, tell me such types flooded the seminaries from the end of the Second World War until the early 1970s. Some think these youngsters were attracted by the heroism of the wartime chaplains, but they certainly shattered the Victorian stereotype of the priest as a genteel wimp in skirts.

A clerical and seminary environment, however, could hold back the emotional development of even such a gifted group of men. In the early 1970s, psychologists Euguene Kennedy and Victor Heckler were asked by the US bishops to do a socio-psychological profile of the American Priest.[87] They found only 6 per cent of priests fully mature and developed, while 29 per cent were in the process of growing and developing, 57 per cent were underdeveloped, and 8 per cent were maldeveloped. These figures were thought to derive from certain unfortunate aspects of seminary training. As Kennedy and Heckler explained it, in their book published by the US bishops' Catholic Conference:

> Their difficulties are precisely those you would expect if you took a group of young men, sent them to special schools, virtually eliminated their contact with women, and then put them to work in circumstances that continued to reinforce all-male living in a socially restricted, public religious role.[88]

In a talk he gave in Los Angeles, Kennedy further pointed out that at least 80 per cent of those who leave come from that developing category. These are people who 'have had their personal growth suspended or delayed, and now, through circumstances or personal decisions, find themselves challenged anew by the problems of growth.'[89] In these priests one can see vitality, a sense of purpose, and a determination to move forward in personal development:

> Some event, or series of events . . . reactivate the dormant development processes. Common experiences that lead to development are a new job or work assignment, death of one's parents, especially the mother, new educational experiences, the effect of Vatican II, a serious failure, a profound religious or personal experience, particularly with a woman. This realm of personal experience is probably the most potent and frequent force in reinitiating growth in the life history of the individual developing priest. Such a confrontation leads the person more deeply into himself than he has ever been before. He begins to put aside the very controlling defences with which he has restricted his life experiences, and he moves into human realms that he can truly say he never knew existed before this kind of experience occurred.[90]

Some of these men remain in the ministry and mature into the outstanding priests I describe in Chapter Seven. Others find that their growing and maturing continues in the context of marriage, family and workplace, and it is these I discuss here.

When a priest leaves, the biggest mistake he can make is to

continue to hang around the sacristy. I found almost unanimity on this point. Get really out, get away from everything for a while, do some growing, is the advice one Brazilian bishop gives his men who leave. Maryknoll's Father Dan McLaughlin explained to me how his missionary order consciously backs off and gives space to its men who leave. But Maryknoll, 'like a good mother', is ready and waiting whenever they want to get back in touch, which many of them eventually do.

The maturing can take years and it can be very painful. There is anger and guilt to be faced and dealt with. But more than anything there is the building up of a new person, a new identity.

At a dangerously early age, the seminary had set out to bond together the young man and his priestly or clerical role so tightly that they were almost one. It succeeded so well that a man has almost to flay himself alive to discard that clerical skin.

'I was trying to integrate my mind and emotions,' Mick Caheny of São Paulo told me. 'I was trying to deinstitutionalise myself. It was like peeling an onion: the more you took off, the more you cried. In the end I felt like Adam coming from the hand of God,' lying there raw and new, waiting to be touched into life.

Some priests changed their names after leaving, in an effort to acquire a new identity. Others went through such anguish that they could not bring themselves to go out of the house. And the dreams some of them had: 'I used to have nightmares for years,' an English Dominican, now married, recalled. 'I'd find myself in my secular job with my Roman collar on, and trying to explain it. Or I'd find myself back in the religious community, celebrating Mass in my lay clothes, and people saying I shouldn't be here. Or fellows putting the habit back on me. I used to wake up in a sweat, especially in the earlier stages. . . .'

For such a man to find a new identity, there is nothing as effective as love from a woman. A person only realises his identity as someone else affirms it and builds it up for him. And it has to be someone who matters very much.

Psychologist William Graham of Houston, himself a married priest, knows it from his own experience: 'The person who valued me was my own wife,' he told me. 'To be cared for by another human being promotes a huge increase in self esteem. There is no deeper relationship than that between two loving, healthy people, and it can help both grow a lot.'

One needs to be quite a woman to put up with all the growing, however. 'I think that women who marry priests have to be very strong,' priest's wife Edna Berres says. 'Especially if the guy doesn't have a job, or is not financially secure. The women they marry have to be real supporters, not naggers. Allowing the guy to move from adolescence to adulthood in one easy year. You've got to be willing to listen: if it doesn't come out, it never gets healed. Look at our friend X——: how long has he been married? Fifteen years, and it's just coming out now.'

Irishwoman Maura Wall Murphy observes that priests do, in fact, tend to marry strong women: 'They always seem to choose independent, stronger women who have careers of their own or have a lot of interests. At first they are very dependent on the women, but, as the years go by, it changes. The men grow up, the women are more cared for, and they love it. The men have settled down and have founded their own careers and no longer need to be so dependent.'

Many psychologists have wondered whether a person can mature at all without some kind of relationship with another person.[91] And while such a relationship would not have to be sexual, there is no doubt that a healthy sexual relationship can be powerfully maturing. 'Sexuality matures you in other parts of your life,' says a married priest, now a psychotherapist. 'The maturing goes far beyond sexuality, to responsibility in thinking about someone else, to sharing your life. I twice carried my wife, unconscious and bleeding, into the hospital (it was during those weeks after a birth). I carried my own son into the hospital after a seizure. The family is a new reality, expressed in a sexual relationship of man and woman. It creates a new social group, where feelings are a basis.'

In particular, the naivety which some priests bring to their sexual relationships could daunt many a woman. 'I was educated in a narrow mentality,' Lauro Motta told me in Brazil. 'The first time I saw a naked woman, I was thirty.' In Reggio Emilia, Italy, Carla Camellini described to me how hard it was for her fifty-year-old husband to get used to family living, after having been a genuinely celibate and chaste priest all his life. 'Do you know,' she said, 'that Paolo didn't even know how a woman is made when he married me!' Across the table Paolo grinned sheepishly and blushed. I guess he found out, for the Camellinis now have a nine-year-old son. Usually, however, the physical side causes less trouble: the real problem is learning to relate intimately so long after late adolescence, at which stage such learning should have taken place.

The adjusting to married life can be traumatic. Peter Beaman of Los Angeles went from a pastor's spacious rectory to a three-bedroom apartment containing a wife and five stepsons, aged from first grade to teens. 'I expected people to be deferential to me,' he recalls. 'One of the boys who most resented me I had trained to be an altar boy in the parish. It was very difficult for him to accept the priest who had trained him, as a replacement for his father. We had a real falling out. Finally, in one confrontation, he said, "You were a wonderful priest – you're a rotten stepfather!" Of course, he's accepted me long since.'

When I was a Dominican seminarian they used to read us passages from a book by thirteenth-century Humbert of Romans, on 'How to be a Good Monk', or some such title. There was one chapter on 'The Bad Monk' and that was the only bit that stuck with me. The bad monk never refused a command: he always obeyed promptly, willingly, and badly. So they'd never bother asking him again: it was easier to ask someone else the next time.

It struck me as a brilliant idea, and I think I subconsciously practised it for most of my Dominican life. I even brought it into married life, and it worked like a dream – there were simply certain things 'David's no good at', like painting walls or balancing cheque books. It worked, that is, until one day I was dumb enough to mention the story of the Bad Monk. And that was that.

It was good while it lasted. But nowadays, all my wife Luci has to say is, 'I know Somebody who's being the Bad Monk!' and I hang my head, and do whatever it is I can't weasel out of.

Shirley Ara of Los Angeles tells me she had to teach her husband, Charlie, what to do in a supermarket. 'He'd push the trolley – he'd hesitate. I'd have to tell him where to find things, give him the brand name. To tell you the truth, he still really can't handle it. And he was used to having people wait on him: run and get me a glass of water sort of thing. At the first party we gave, Charlie sat on the couch and expected to be served drinks. In our house we get you the first drinks, and then you get your own. But Charlie still forgets.' In the early days Charlie was shocked when people no longer volunteered to help with things like typing – they now expected to be paid for it.

'Marriage has made me a better priest,' explains a Spaniard who lives in Barcelona. 'I feel myself more of a priest now, than before my marriage. Today I am more chaste than I was as an active priest: I am more loyal to my wife than I ever was to my celibacy. When I was a priest, I was inclined to be an adventurer – with women, I mean – now I am devoted to my wife and my family. I do not stray, as I used to.'

I met a French priest who told me that from his seminary days and all through his years as a missionary, he had been actively and indiscriminately homosexual: 'I lived a life that was totally selfish and irresponsible,' he told me. 'But when I married, I resumed a normal heterosexual life. I have a son and two beautiful daughters now, and I've never looked back.'

FAMILY AND HOME

Most priests seem in the end to achieve mature and stable marriages. In Brazil, the resigned-priest organisation Rumos gives a figure of 95 per cent successful marriages. At a 1985 meeting with representatives of married-priest associations, the Vatican's Monsignor Canciani spoke of 10 per cent of married priests divorcing. That indicates 90 per cent of priestly marriages succeeding, which is a far higher figure than the secular norm for most countries.

However, Terry Dosh, national co-ordinator of the Corpus organisation in America, questions this Vatican figure of 10 per cent. 'How does the Vatican know such a percentage', he wrote to me, 'when half the priests who marry don't even consult them? The two US studies that I have seen put the figure under 5 per cent – in fact, one of them has 2 per cent.'

Malcolm Muggeridge once said he would like to give Jesus Christ a tour of the Vatican and watch his reaction. I think I would like to take Jesus on a tour of the married priests' homes which I have visited around the world. Come to think of it, Jesus doesn't need such a tour – he's in most of those homes already. The person I would really like to take round would be John Paul II. I doubt if it would change his views, but he would certainly see home after home where Christianity is lived and breathed as nowhere else I have ever been or seen.

Across the world I was astonished at families who began the day with prayer around the breakfast table, families where the rosary survives and thrives, families who read the Bible daily, who pray together – parents and children – without the least embarrassment, families who manifest happiness, humour, social awareness, service, and what looks very like holiness.

'Your lives', Cardinal Bernardin told some married priests in Chicago in 1987, 'continue to be characterised by the same spirit of dedication and generosity which marked your priesthood. I will offer a special prayer for you, your wives and your children that God may bless you.'[92]

In a 1987 interview, Dom Angelico, auxiliary bishop of São Paulo, Brazil, spoke to me of his admiration for the families of married priests: 'These married priests, in the silence of their life, should feel much loved by God. I hope God will give them full peace. There is a lot of love in those families, and they are profoundly missionary.'

There are no homes quite like those of married priests, and going from one to another around the world became for me a kind of joyous pilgrimage. As a journalist I am no longer starry-eyed, and I am a competent enough observer. As I left one family I would find myself saying the next one could not measure up to this. Yet nearly every time I was surprised and delighted. Whether the crucible of the early years refines, or whether love blooms in adversity, I am in no doubt that a priest's family life can be very good indeed.

'A good priest makes a good husband' – it's almost an axiom with priests' wives. 'There's a lot of things going for us, especially if we come from a religious order,' one husband explains. 'The give and take of a religious community can rub off the corners and make for a good family man. Having counselled so many marriages, a man knows the pitfalls. And a man learns compassion through counselling and hearing confessions.'

Those wives who sound off about the impracticalities of their spouses are often the same ones who say that otherwise they make ideal partners. According to an Irish wife, 'they seem to have a strongly developed anima [as opposed to animus, the macho, dominant, controlling bit], so that there's a lot of feeling, creativity, sensitivity. It certainly was fostered in the order to which Eoin belonged. That's rare in normal male training here in Ireland.

'And our men are marvellous with children – sometimes I think they would even have them if they could. They're good with their kids, I think, because they tend to be childlike themselves. And they are a lot freer of social restrictions (which, of course, can be embarrassing to the children when they grow older).'

One wife thinks priests make excellent parents 'because they have a sense of fatherhood and the mystery of life. Maybe it's not that other men don't have it, but these guys can express it better, often in a very poetic way.'

She says they are sensitive to women: 'I watch them with their women. There's a respect there that you don't see with others – a caring. And I think their experience as confessors gives them a deep respect for confidences, a sensitivity. They become excellent listeners.'

This wife, a professional counsellor, guesses they make good sexual partners: 'There's no way to measure how good they are as lovers, but they seem to be able to recognise their feelings and deal with them.'

She concedes there may be initial awkwardness on the physical side, 'but dealing with feelings comes easier to them, so in the long term they have a better chance of a good relationship.' Wives say their men show a noticeable concern with sexual giving as well as getting, treating them as 'partners in joy, to be brought to arousal and fulfilled, rather than as objects of an exercise.'

Some women regard their priest-husbands as 'fantastic lovers'. Even if a man has led a totally celibate life, it seems that, after that initial adjustment, he is far from inhibited sexually. On the contrary, it is as though floodgates open and the wife finds herself carried along on torrents of physical passion and imaginative creativity that hardly seem to dwindle, even years into the marriage. There is one man, Tobias-like, who is heard to murmur, in the middle of the whole thing, 'Thank you God, thank you – I never thought it could be like this.' He's been doing it for years now. (By the way, I did not expressly ask for this information. But wives talk among themselves, and a few of them volunteered these general impressions to me.)

A wife in Birmingham, England, finds priests more open in relationships: 'They haven't been as hurt as many young people who went through all the agonies of dating, so these men are less protective, less cautious. They are so free, they can build up relationships without any double entendres.'

'I'm often amazed at how fortunate priests are when they leave,' says another wife. 'They just come out, and within a year they have a fine girl. I think it is that women are so delighted to meet someone so upfront. With some others in their thirties, there'd be questions: Is he two-timing? Has he a mother problem? Is he gay? Is he AC/DC? Is he divorced or separated? Or is he just a bachelor who's protecting himself?'

In sum it would seem that being a priest makes a man a better husband, and being a husband makes him a better priest. Terry Dosh speaks of the process as 'incarnational love'. It takes time, he says, to arrive at the full insight of such love:

> . . . the profound experience of being human and hence limited; God as real through family; my wife as a sacrament; the birth of children as a sacrament; the preacher as a participant in life, not a coach on the sidelines. There is the sense that incarnational love makes us better priests and more dedicated to Christ, that personal spiritual dimensions aid in strengthening commitment to family, that one's wife reinforces my image of self as priest, and that having been so loved engenders the responsibility to love.
>
> Family union enhances ministry itself. Each loving act deepens one's sense of consecration; in a truly committed marriage, these occur very often – such as in caring for a sick wife or child; the many reconciliations daily; an ecumenical group acknowledges my gifts and thanks me for exercising them. Many say family has enabled development, given many chances for service, opportunities for involvement in community that they could not have had as celibate priests. Day-to-day problems create a clear and stronger focus on more incisive prayer-life and a 'reality orientation'.

These families, of course, are faced with the very same challenges of any other family immersed in today's culture. Dosh again:

> Busyness is the obstacle to prayer and service in family life. Detachment is harder in married family life. The culture offers so much and the family cries out for possessions. Fighting cultural obsessions is easier for two people (who correct each other), but children make it harder when they want what the obsessed culture wants. The simple gospel life seems harder for a married priest, and can be a constant

battle for some. But detachment comes from inside, rather than being imposed.[93]

Faced with so many obstacles, it is not surprising that some married priests and their families appear to sell out to the prevailing culture. I have not found many, but those I found are sad. A priest who turns exclusively to big money and worldly success becomes a man haunted and driven. As Dr Michael Nichols of Albany, New York State, said: 'As long as we refuse to acknowledge our connection to others, we can never be fully reconciled to ourselves.' It is even truer in a man who is a priest for ever.

However, for some such priests the lurch towards Mammon is a temporary aberration. It is often due to feelings of insecurity at the time of leaving, and to hearing people predict they 'would never make it on the outside'.

'When I was a priest,' Mark Zwick of Houston told me, 'we heard stories of all the guys who left – stories of failure and dope. After those stories we had lots of anxiety about making it out there without the collar. Two years later, there I was on the pavement, just left the ministry, with a wife, no job – a basket-case.'

A very few years later found Zwick as head of the psychiatric emergency team for Stanislaus County, California. 'I had a good position, money in the bank, two kids, two cars, a new house. Even the Church had more to do with me, because I had money.' And Zwick loved it.

'But there was a Jewish lawyer in one of our groups, and he kept challenging us – what are you going to do next with your lives? It got to me. We're not by nature materialistic people, and I told my wife, this is silly – I don't see enough of the kids. I suggested we work half-time and share the kids, and she got immediately into graduate school. But giving up the job was very hard: I could have been director of mental health for the whole of Stanislaus County. Then we decided to join Maryknoll as lay missionaries, to be part of a team in Venezuela. But in the end we moved to El Salvador on our own steam, on the invitation of a priest there, who was then deported. . . .'

Mark and Louise Zwick now run the Casa Juan Diego in Houston, Texas, as shelter and support house mostly for

Hispanics and for illegal aliens. Mark has no salary at all. I have heard the couple compared to Mother Teresa of Calcutta.

SUFFER THE CHILDREN

'The moment they put our baby into his arms meant more to me than anything.' Louise Lynch of Phoenix, Arizona, is talking about her priest-husband Terry. 'I think all doubts leave you then. The joy in his face – just to see that joy in his face. The joy as he held his child for the first time had to be a gift from God.'

I myself have never had that experience, as I don't have children of my own. Maybe that's why, from all my travels, the most sparkling memories I have are of priests' children around the world. There are so many vignettes:

• The ten-year-old Brazilian boy in Recife, wheeling out the next-door-neighbour's infant, and shouting to the kids playing football in the street: 'Stand aside there. Make way for the Padre's daughter!'

• The little Irish girl rooting in a wardrobe, and finding a picture of Daddy in a black suit and Roman collar. She comes scrambling downstairs: 'Hey, Daddy, I never knew you were a priest!'

• A nail-biting father telling his teenage daughter the big Secret, that her Dad is a priest. 'I think it's just fabulous, Dad,' the girl replies, and gives him a terrific hug.

• The Camellinis' little nine-year-old Down's syndrome boy, in Reggio Emilia, Italy, taking his father and me both by the hand to lead us in to supper, looking up with that warm loving smile that makes all Down's syndrome kids seem like members of one family.

• Sixty-two-year-old priest Lucien Rupin, of Santiago, Chile, sitting talking with me while his seven-year-old son perches on one of Dad's knees and his eight-year-old daughter reads a book on the other knee.

• Three-year-old Londoner, Isabel, flourishing an old photo of her father celebrating Mass: 'Look at my Daddy with Jesus in his hands,' she says.

• The grade-school teacher in San Diego explaining solemnly that priests can't marry. 'They can, too!' pipes up a moppet. ''Coz my Dad did!'

I interviewed the youngsters wherever possible, and I ended with a strong impression that priests' children absorb a considerable amount of their parents' idealism. I came across many instances of this, and much of the idealism was quite down to earth and practical. For example, sixteen-year-old Sylvia Benedito of São Miguel, Brazil, gravely explained to me that the most important things in life were to serve God and help others, and that they were one and the same thing.

'But,' she said, 'to help others you have to open them up and get them aware. Like these landslides down in Rio that killed all those people – get them aware it's not just God's anger, but there's other causes. Like if somebody dies of sickness, it doesn't have to be God's will. You find the cause and you change things.'

So Sylvia would like to be a journalist: 'I want to open people's minds,' she told me.

Shortly before one Christmas I was staying with Terry Dosh's family in Minneapolis, and I gave a very few dollars to each of his two boys for Christmas. 'Gee, thanks,' said Paul, 'that'll help me pay for presents.' I then went to Martin's room upstairs, and found him recording tapes – to give as presents.

Sixteen-year-old Kelly Derden of Houston was so interested in her father's priesthood that she researched and wrote a paper on the effects of compulsory celibacy on the Catholic Church, which was published by the Texas State Historical Association in the January 1987 issue of *Texas Historian*. The paper draws on a range of sources, from nineteenth-century Henry Charles Lea to Dean Hoge's latest study, to present a competent history of celibacy's effects, and ends thus:

> Removal of the law requiring clerical celibacy in the Roman Catholic Church would not mean an end to priests being celibate, since many have in the past freely chosen such, and many in the future would do the same. Removal of that law would, however, remove one barrier in the conflict between the Roman Catholic Church and other Christian denominations . . . Though there would surely be failures in Roman Catholic Church clerical marriages as there are in the marriages of ministers of all faiths, that should be expected as part of a pilgrimage – the journey on which each person must seek and struggle to live up to ideals of faith.[94]

I feel that not many sixteen-year-olds could deal with such an issue as maturely and competently as Kelly Derden.

In a discussion I had in Texas, I asked two psychologists if there could be an empirical basis for my rather favourable impression of priests' children. They thought there might be. In his book, *Habits of the Heart*, Robert Bellah distinguishes three strands that are intertwined in the character of most Americans, which he calls biblical, jeffersonian and individualistic.[95] The biblical could be roughly described as the urge to do God's will. The jeffersonian is the drive towards giving everyone a fair deal – the humanitarian urge. And the individualistic is the me-first, I'm-all-right-Jack, get-rich-quick drive that is also in all of us. According to Bellah, the biblical and jeffersonian strands are surviving principally through America's churches, irrespective of creed. It would seem, these psychologists think, that a priest's family would be fertile ground for these two strands, and that priests' children are natural carriers of religious and humanitarian values. Such a hypothesis might be worth testing.

It would, of course, be naive to think that such children are immune from the natural shocks that flesh is heir to. Inevitably, some manifest the 'preacher's kid' syndrome that torments the families of Protestant pastors – the natural urge for a child to rebel against too-high expectations of a religious family. Nineteen-year-old Jennifer Zwick told me about her rebellion: 'When I was fourteen I went to this performing arts high school – I play the violin. Well it was a whole bunch of teenagers on an ego-trip. I met some friends, I got seized by Beatlemania. I got into drinking and smoking.

'Also, my parents were really strict. There were a lot of things I wanted to do, but wasn't allowed to, like staying out late or spending the night at a house my parents didn't know. I thought it absolutely ridiculous. I went through this for a year and a half, and it ended with me running away from home. My parents were frantic and called the police. Hours after I left, I got very upset: I realised I loved my parents and how much they loved me.

'So I decided to go to this Catholic school. It was a special kind of school, with Hispanic and black, and the nuns were just wonderful. They made me feel appreciated. That was the middle of my sophomore [second] year. I continued to be rebellious, and it really only stopped at the end of the eleventh grade. It gradually got better, my relations with my parents, and with God.

'I went to this music camp in North Carolina. I was absolutely miserable and homesick. Everything came to me again – how

much I loved my parents and they loved me. I could have come
home, but they had paid $1,000. My spiritual life began there. I
was so homesick I turned to God. I remember walking to the
Catholic church (it was in the Appalachian Mountains) and it
was wonderful.'

Jennifer was so inspired by one of the nuns in school that she
has seriously considered entering an enclosed order. 'But I've
always wanted to have lots of kids, eight maybe.' At the moment
she is studying, and is also in charge of a small satellite house of
her parents' Casa Juan Diego for caring for the homeless and
illegal aliens.

ANGER AND GUILT

Many priests who leave seem to go full circle, and eventually
arrive back at a balanced Christian life. As a married priest put it
to me: 'Somewhere along the line, we decided not to see the
Church as the enemy. It's just ourselves, anyway.'

However, one or both of the emotions, anger and guilt, can
trouble some of these priests for a considerable time. The anger
remains longest, anger at the institution, at the faceless ones, at
former colleagues who turned their faces away. And since those
colleagues too are often hurt and angry, as are those who
administer the institution, what is sorely needed throughout the
Catholic Church is reconciliation. But here let me say a little
about guilt.

Guilt can be a torment to a married priest. It need have
nothing to do with rationality: I know priests who left for the
clearest of reasons, on the advice of superiors and with their
blessing and encouragement, priests with full dispensations who
have married in church, whose lives are an example of prayer
and ministry, but who nevertheless deep down have suffered for
some time an irrational guilt.

It happened to me. Although the guilt is now long since gone,
it is still hard to write about. But I feel it may help someone if I
do.

In the early years of my marriage I would go through periods
of anguish, where the whole centre of my body, from solar
plexus to groin, would tighten up and throb in unison with my
heartbeat. It might continue, without let-up, for several weeks.

Sometimes I would go upstairs, bend over the bed and press my fists into my gut to massage it.

It would usually be triggered off by something I had read, or by something I might have heard on the news. I remember it hit me when Archbishop Romero was shot: if I rationalised it, I suppose I was telling myself he died a martyr and I was still alive with a loving wife. But mostly it was just a physical feeling of awful anguish. At times the only thing that helped was a little prayer that hung from a banner in the Portland church where I had been married: 'Turn your face to me O Lord, and give me peace.' I would repeat it over and over, and it was like cool water reaching the hot coals deep in my belly.

Then one bright day the anguish would be completely gone, dissipated. I would have months and months free of it, until some new thing would trigger it again. The biggest mistake I made was not to confide in my wife – I did not want to impose my anguish on her, and did not want her to think I regretted leaving and marrying – which was far from the case. I would leave and marry all over again tomorrow without hesitation, because it was, and is, right for me. It had been done with much prayer, and the encouragement and advice of respected colleagues and superiors.

A few years ago I confided in my wife what I used to suffer, and she said yes, she had known all along that there was something in me she could not reach, and had longed for me to trust her with it. I wish I had. She suffered more from my silence than if I had laid my suffering on her.

If only I had understood then what W. Robert Beaver says in his book, *Successful Marriage*:

> Guilt in individuals is related to hiddenness from others. The more I believe I must hide from my parents, my siblings, my friends, my lover, the more of me that remains 'not me', a source of guilt whether conscious or unconscious.[96]

On that passage John Dubay comments thus:

> These words seem to fit painfully for so many of the resigned priests whose guilt drives them to remain hidden with the consequences that hiddenness fosters more guilt.

> Over and over again, the hidden one recreates the scars of
> the past in a flood of guilt. From this flows the hiddenness
> which diminishes my awareness of myself and hinders a
> growth in intimacy with my spouse.[97]

Curiously enough, the time I spent writing a novel helped me
emerge from that suffering. The story was of a man who had
done a killing in Ireland for political reasons, had fled to the
United States, and there almost ruined his life through the guilt
and anguish that dogged him for years. Into that man I projected
my own anguish, and the very effort to describe it in detail was
incredibly healing.

With the passing of years, the guilt faded into the light of
common day. It had no basis in reality. I am totally free of it now.
But if the writing of this book can save any priest from what I
went through, it will have been worthwhile.

New Jersey's Dr Anthony Padovano, himself a married priest,
theologian, still an adviser to certain bishops and author of
twenty books, faced and dealt with the issue of guilt in an
address to a national gathering of married priests in Washington
DC, in June 1988.[98] In that address he asked point blank
whether married priests were men of broken promises: 'Are they
people who have abandoned their most sacred commitments,
men whose word is no longer trustworthy, Christians who do
not deserve to be entrusted with ministry because they have
betrayed it, selfish individuals who prefer their own interests to
the needs of communities for which they were ordained and
consecrated?'

Padovano goes to the Bible, to The Book of Judges (11, 29–
40), for his answer. There you find the story of the Hebrew
commander, Jephthah, who before the battle made a vow to the
Lord: 'If you give the Ammonites into my hands, then the first
creature that comes out of the door of my house to meet me
when I return in triumph from fighting . . . shall be the Lord's,
and I will sacrifice it as a burnt offering.'

Jephthah won the battle, and as he approached his house his
only daughter came out from it to meet him; she was dancing
and playing the tambourine. When he saw her he tore his clothes
and exclaimed, 'Oh, my daughter, my heart is broken! Must it be
you? I have made a solemn promise to God and I cannot break it.
I cannot unsay what I have said.'

She answered him: 'My Father, you have made a solemn promise to God. Deal with me as your vow demands. . . .

'But grant me this one request,' she said. 'Give me two months to roam the hills and weep with my friends, because I will never marry.'

'You may go,' he said. She and her girlfriends went up into the mountains and grieved because she was going to die and because she was compelled to be unmarried and childless.

After two months she came back to her father and he killed her, since he had made a solemn promise to the Lord. She died unmarried and childless. He treated her as the vow he had uttered bound him.

Padovano asked what kind of a God does Jephthah's action imply: a God who holds us to our word and to the law even if life is sacrificed to it, a God of legalism? Jephthah has made an idol of his word and sacrificed his daughter to it. This is in contrast with Jesus, who violated the law for the sake of life, by healing on the Sabbath, by touching a woman with a haemorrhage of blood, by putting his hand on the bier of a widow's son to raise him to life. Always Jesus chooses life, even when the law says no, and heals rather than destroys.

> There are three values [I am paraphrasing Padovano] which justify a change from one's earlier word, indeed compel the change so that, if it is not made, one remains consistent with one's word, but not faithful to God or to the inner life of the Church.
>
> The first of these values is life itself. Like Jephthah we must ask if consistency with an earlier promise enriches or diminishes our life and the lives of others . . . The context for the right answer is not a promise we once made but the effect of the continuance of the promise on our lives. To allow life to wither, as promises are stalwartly maintained, is an aberration.
>
> The second of these values is a sense of integrity. If I remain consistent with my earlier promise, will I be true to what is deepest and most authentic in me? Has the Church, which received my promise, been authentic in turn? If it refuses any discussion of the issue of obligatory celibacy, if it silences all honest and respectful dialogue, can one say the Church has acted with integrity and authenticity?
>
> The third of these values is intimacy. If I remain consis-

tent with my earlier promise, must I keep others at a
distance and close off my emotional life? Intimacy is our
vulnerability and sensitivity to others. This intimacy must
not be so discounted that one is unaffected by the needs and
the love of others for us. Clerical systems sometimes favour
ideology over people, abstract ideals over relationships,
promises of celibacy over commitment to others. . . .

Commitment is more demanding and enriching than
lifelong concurrence with an earlier word one may have
pledged. This word may not have been profound enough
when it was first spoken. Or, if it were indeed deep at that
time, it may have to be put aside now because even more is
asked of us. Jephthah's word was deep and serious when he
formulated his vow, but his daughter's life introduced a
more substantive reality into his life, one he refused to be
faithful to because he was blinded by fidelity to his earlier
word.

I have two points to add to this. The first is that only members of
religious orders make vows anyway. The hundreds of thousands
of diocesan priests make no vows whatsoever: it is simply
understood from canon law that celibacy is attached to the
priesthood, and they have no option but to go along with that if
they want to function as priests.

And secondly, the Church has the power to release from vows
and promises, which it does when it gives a dispensation.
Therefore those so released have no vows whatsoever, and are
free before God and man to marry. They are not unfaithful to
anything or anyone.

Let Padovano have the last word: 'Jesus once said, "If you love
me, I will come to you and you will be my disciples." Words of
such heart-breaking tenderness can never cease to echo in our
lives. We must hear them as we age and die, as we love and
prevail.

'My brothers and my sisters, your marriages brought love into
the world, a love which would have withered and died had you
turned away from it and not been faithful to each other. You
brought children into the Church and taught them of Christ.
You brought peace and joy and freedom into this sometimes
bleak and broken century. Nothing was ever broken in you,
certainly not the promise of your life.'

6

THE GIFT GIVEN BACK?

I can never be thrown away . . . In sickness, my sickness serves
. . . In perplexity, my perplexity may serve . . . A preacher of
truth in my own place.

Cardinal Newman

WHEN POPE JOHN PAUL II was in the United States in 1979 he
made a heartfelt appeal to priests to remain faithful to their
calling. 'We do not return the gift once given,' he cried. 'It cannot
be that God who gave the impulse to say Yes, now wishes to hear
No.'

A priest, now married, pondered these words during an
interview. 'But I don't want to give back my priesthood,' he told
me. 'It is possible to get more than one gift from a benevolent
God. I have also received the gift of marriage — I am a man of all
seven sacraments. Why can't I use both priesthood and marriage
for the glory of God?'

Does that mean that he would come running back into Church
employment if the celibacy rule changed? It does not. In an interview for this book, Dom Helder Camara, retired archbishop
of Recife, Brazil, mentioned he had heard that a lot of resigned
priests now wanted to come back. I told him I had not met many.
Certainly, there were few who simply wanted to return to an unchanged clerical institution. I said, however, that many felt a
strong urge to serve others, to act out Christ's words, 'I was sick
and you visited me; I was hungry and you gave me to eat.' In that
sense there is a very clear drive towards ministry, and it has led,
in fact, to many kinds of ministry being practised. But it hasn't
a great deal to do with the ecclesiastical system.

'I'm a Church rat,' says Frank Bonnike of Chicago. 'It's in me.' When Frank left to marry, he considered a career in business, but very soon realised ministry was his vocation and always would be. For nine years after he left, Frank was a general duty chaplain in a large Lutheran hospital. 'I'm simply a chaplain who happens to be a Catholic,' he said at the time. That meant counselling, being with the ill and the dying, caring for the bereaved. 'On occasion, of course, I baptise, hear a confession or anoint, but only when necessary and always according to the Church's laws [in cases of necessity].' He told me the late Cardinal Cody once promised him he would never try to get him fired from his chaplaincy work.

Bonnike is now involved in prison ministry, and is the administrator of PACE, an organisation that works to rehabilitate ex-prisoners.

Wasn't it Carl Jung who said that after the age of forty all questions are spiritual? Most priests who leave feel themselves lovingly pursued by the Hound of Heaven, and could not shake off their priesthood even if they would. As Terry Dosh puts it:

> The spiritual legacy that married priests continue to have after resignation, calls for to God and others. This can be exercised in many ways, but MUST be exercised. Those who do not, end up with some psychological, social, emotional or physical consequences . . . One cannot deny a legacy without severe consequences.[99]

But that does not mean going back into the system. Given optional celibacy, some might perhaps consider re-entering, but with their wives and families – a survey done in Spain indicates 23 per cent, and Corpus in the United States suggests up to one-third.[100] However, such priests invariably say they first would want to see very significant changes in Church structures.

'I'd want to renegotiate my way in,' an Irish priest says. 'I'd want to work out something I could give meaning to, not simply go back and take up passively where I left off.'

'I want to work for Church and people,' says a Chilean married priest in Valparaiso. 'But I detest the clerical style. And I'm doing apostolic work all the time anyhow. The only thing missing is the Eucharist. If I could just do that.'

'Going back in would be a terrible regression,' a Seattle priest believes. 'Could I in good conscience give the party line on

Humanae Vitae [the birth-control encyclical]? It was a monkey on my back when I was priest, and fifteen years later I'm still picking up walking wounded from the encyclical. And what they did to [Archbishop] Hunthausen was an absolute travesty. Do I want to be part of an institution that does that to people? On the other hand, maybe if I was inside I could cushion the blow for people.'

'I left because the Church didn't know how to use us,' says a German priest. 'If it couldn't use us then, how can it use us now?'

An Irish priest puts it in Irish terms: 'Do you think I want to go back to living over the shop, to *Humanae Vitae*, to no girl altar boys, to the Pope's notion of women, to taking money for Masses, to being a dispensing machine for sacraments, to blessing water with relics, to total control over my life and now over my wife, to being a full frontal cleric [that is wearing blacks and collar]? Not for all the tea in China. I just want to put something back, into the People of God, who ultimately put up the money for training me. They used to tell us the pennies of the poor supported us: well, now I work for the poor.'

Cardinal Lorscheider says it more gently, in more Brazilian terms: 'Married priests are not interested so much in celebrating Mass, but in asking themselves how can we, trained as priests, yet today part of the laity, how can we use our gift in this world? They are more interested in their own responsibilities in society. It is so different here from in Europe, where there is more a spirit of confrontation about ministry.'

I distinguish four different kinds of ministry among priests who have left. The first is the ministry on which Christ said he would judge all of us – 'I was hungry and you gave me to eat . . . I was naked and you clothed me.' – the ministry we are required to do from our baptism. The second involves giving the sacraments when necessary, even though outside formal Church structures. The third is voluntary part-time ministry in the official Church. And the fourth is a return to full-time Church employment, to which married priests are being recalled to a considerable degree in many parts of the world. Let us look at each of these four.

I. THE WORKS OF MERCY

'*Evert, waarom moest je weg*? [Why did you have to leave?]' The words of Father Gregory Brenninkmeijer, Provincial of the

Dutch Jesuits, talking to ex-Jesuit Evert Verheijden. 'What you are doing now, Evert, is all pure Jesuit and priestly work.' Evert told me they both became so emotional that they could not continue for a few minutes.

Brenninkmeijer is right. Evert is doing the same lecturing, counselling and caring that he always did. The only difference is that he comes home to his wife Else after work. The Verheijdens are approaching seventy, and have come a long way from that day many years ago when Evert became completely paralysed. 'The doctors found it was psychosomatic: I did not know where to go any more – in society, in the Church, in the priesthood.' The paralysis gradually lifted as Evert worked towards a decision to leave.

Twenty years later, Evert is a dynamo of energy. He is fulfilled, and his energy and happiness spill over into his counselling. Above his desk there is an oval black and white photo of a quite astonishingly beautiful child – a girl of about ten. She has bobbed hair, curling in under the chin. She is not smiling, but her eyes seem to be. I feel I would love to meet that child. It can't be a daughter: the Verhiejdens never had children. 'A niece?' I asked Evert.

'Take another look when Else comes back,' Evert said with a smile.

Else came in with the coffee. Of course. Her hair is grey now, and no longer bobbed, but the eyes are the same, and at seventy Else is still beautiful. She looks loving, and loved.

'That picture is always with me,' Evert said.

All over the world I found married and resigned priests continuing the works of mercy to which they had given their lives. Sometimes it is hard to see any break at all. Here I can pick out only a few instances from the hundreds in my notes.

There is, for example, Ed Kelly of Sapang Palay in the Philippines. In the early 1960s, Father Kelly was a newly-arrived Irish missionary when 25,000 squatters were forcibly uprooted from Manila. They and their dismantled scrapwood shacks were dumped 30 miles out, in the middle of a wilderness that lacked roads, sewerage, anything. The people simply sank into despair, drunkenness, dreariness and drugs.

Young Father Kelly volunteered to join them, without the language, with no plans, no training in community development. He just arrived, and, as he says today, 'God did the rest'.

He started a tiny school. He organised a march on the palace of President Marcos, a march that brought bulldozers and graders to build the promised streets in Sapang Palay.

The school grew, was destroyed by a typhoon, and grew again. Then Ed Kelly and the people started a high school. Eventually, after years of growing and developing, they had the temerity to start a college for higher education. And all the time organising the building, first, of 250 houses, then 400 more, then 400 more . . . and more and more, for an area growing to 100,000 from continued enforced relocations.

Today, Sapang Palay has those schools, as well as pre-nursery and nursery schools and kindergarten, three big libraries, a large farm to train locals in vegetable gardening, a medical team with several clinics, Christ the King Church and several chapels, a five-person guidance team, a six-person religious instruction and Christian-living team, free tuition for members of large families and for the poor.

It is not really Ed Kelly who has done all this – it is the people themselves, whom Ed has convinced, over years of persuasion and demonstration, that they have it within themselves to do it. He believes firmly in the principle of no free lunch: even the kids who receive free tuition are expected to spend summers helping to build new classrooms. Thus the most important thing constructed in Sapang Palay is the vibrant, self-confident community that thrives there today.

In 1982, with hardly a ripple, Father Ed Kelly married within the community he had served for eighteen years, and has simply gone on with his work in Sapang Palay.

People were delighted he had married a local girl (she was back home after graduating from Manila University). As one old lady expressed it: 'By marrying Minda you've turned your back on your own country and you've become one of us.' Recently Ed wrote a book which revealed that before he met his wife, he had gone through years of loneliness so desperate that it had almost driven him out of his mind.[101]

Today he continues his missionary work, his inspiring of the local community, the direction of Assumption College, and his unremitting dedication to the poor of Sapang Palay, who see him as one of themselves. The only two differences are that he now has a vigorous young wife to support him in his work, and that he may no longer celebrate Mass, which is a great grief to him.

And a third difference: he and Minda have a couple of lovely Filipino children.

In 1987 I spent a week with Ed and Minda at an international gathering of married priests. Ed is tall, silver-haired and gentle, and not particularly eloquent. Yet a kind of innocence and sincerity made his interventions compulsive listening. He is a man of unremitting daily prayer, and he gave us all a copy of a prayer he had written 'For the Coming of God's Kingdom through the Eucharist and the Bible'. Here is part of that prayer:

> O Lord Jesus Christ . . . the world needs the Eucharist, it thirsts for the Eucharist. Please give us more priests so that every remotest village will have its own priest, its own Eucharist, its own knowledge of the Bible. The Spirit has placed in the hearts of many married men and women throughout the world a secret longing and calling to the priesthood. Hasten the day when they will be accepted by your Church as priests . . . May the Bread of the Eucharist be in the hands and life of every human being on earth. . . .

I remember asking Ed and Minda what were their very first impressions of one another. Ed: 'I thought she was the most beautiful girl I had ever met. She turned out to be the most loving, too.'

Minda: 'I never realised a man could be so lonely.'

And now to Brazil, where ex-Oblate missionary John Burns runs Villa Serena, an unusually successful treatment centre for alcoholics. John was an alcoholic himself (one of nine children who all became priests or nuns, seven of whom later left), and in 1968 he walked out of his order, 'when the walls started closing in on me'.

Still drinking, he worked for the next ten years as US Peace Corps director in Brazil, until he was sent for a cure in Washington DC. It worked, and he came back to Brazil, where he persuaded some of the big international corporations to sponsor several badly-needed alcohol- and drug-treatment centres. Villa Serena is one of these, an oasis of green grass and trees outside São Paulo. John Burns has been running it for ten years, and his wife says he does more priestly work than he ever did in his life before.

The one thing that strikes you about Burns is his enthusiasm. An old Oblate colleague teases him about it: 'How come you're so excited about your work, John?' he says. 'We couldn't get you to say Mass in the old days. You were the last into the confession box – always out fixing the plumbing or something.'

Nowadays Burns hears confessions all the time: 'It's the fifth step of Alcoholics Anonymous. Yes, but I don't give [sacramental] absolution out of respect for the Church's wishes.'

Spirituality is the key to what happens at Villa Serena. Burns: 'The chief difficulty I had, and most who come here have, is the concept of God "up there". We have to bring Him down into very real immediate experience. If you want to know what your relationship to God is, check your relationship with the people around you.

'The God I had as a child was a God to help me die. But I need a God for surviving and living in the world. I feel comfortably part of the way God's working out His Kingdom in this time and place, and I'm very excited that I'm able to be part of God's plan. The world's like a clock running down, but plugged into God.

'You know, if the Church said, you can all come back, I'd say, why don't you guys come down here where I am? I'd try like hell to work with you. It's all here in the ministry of dependency – spiritual searching and action. We could have some nifty dialogues – I could bring a lot and I could learn a lot. So many things are coming together for them and us.'

Oxford married priest Peter Hebblethwaite explained to me how men like Burns are continuing something essential in Christian ministry, namely the ministry of the Word, even if they have to forego the sacramental ministry. He wrote me a letter following our meeting, which makes clear the distinction:

> One of the achievements of Vatican II, it was always said, was that it restored the balance between the liturgy of the Word and the sacramental liturgy. Word and Sacrament were complementary, and needed each other . . . It seemed to me that through the process of 'laicisation' one could say that although the sacramental ministry ceased (that was part of the deal), some form of ministry of the Word could continue, and I believe has continued. Communication is not an optional extra in the life of the Church. It is its essential life-blood. . . .

There are all kinds of ministries in the Church of which
the priestly ministry is only one. There is also the catechetics
ministry, the counselling ministry, and so on. This means
that there is no problem about talking about, and living out,
a continuing lay ministry of the Word which, like all
ministries, has to edify, that is, build up, the community.
That is what Paul has to say about gifts.

There are advantages in the lay ministry of communication: greater freedom and therefore greater credibility. The
more institutionally-tied priestly minister 'has to say' this or
that. Probably it would be going too far to talk of
'laicisation' as a sort of 'liberation for ministry', but it
would not be nonsense.[102]

A significant number of priests, when they leave, deliberately opt
for careers that are in fact a form of ministry. A few examples:
• Married priests Dennis Dooley and Stanley Gofron are both
adult probation officers in Texas, dealing daily with convicted
criminals. Snippets from our conversation together: 'It was our
founder – I mean, the Oblates' founder – who was always
saying, "Charity, Charity, Charity." That's what it's all about
. . . I try to present a Christlike image, dealing in a humane,
charitable manner, instead of a cold do-it-or-else. They can see
what we stand for by the way we deal with them. . . .

'We do a lot of problem-solving therapy. One suggestion I
sometimes make is to join activity at some church, for positive
peer influence. No priest could suggest that: he wouldn't be
listened to. I told a kid, you might enjoy being involved in
liturgy. He said, "Hey, my wife was saying, we should get
involved in church" . . . Criminals are an abandoned lot. The
Oblate motto is, "He has sent us to preach the gospel to the
poor" – well, you can't get much poorer than the guys we work
with.'
• Married priest Jednota K. is a funeral undertaker in a
Czechoslovakian town. 'Every funeral has to have an oration,'
he explained to me, 'and at civil [bürgerlich] funerals I'm called
on to give it. Even the Communists want me to speak. I try to
make it my ministry.' It is an infinitely delicate one, he says.
• John Flavin is a programme co-ordinator for AIDS education
and risk reduction, in the US south-west. 'I counsel people who
are infected. As a public speaker I address hundreds of groups.

My background as a priest has prepared me for it: I frequently have four or five talks to give in one day – it's like the four or five Masses I used to have on a Sunday . . . A lot has to do with death and dying . . . Compassion has something to do with it – it means to tolerate ambiguity, not to make a judgement. When you have compassion, you touch, you feel the dilemma. After I have touched a person physically, my compassion has grown.

'Many AIDS patients are forced into spiritual experiences, through social rejection and being left utterly defenceless. There have been AIDS patients who have ministered to me, with their courage, the way they see the truth about themselves. They have helped me to see how man is part of the universe, which can turn on the human body with such viciousness.

'This is a ministry of life and death: it is true ministry – as well as helping some people's bodies not to get infected, so giving them the opportunity to live longer and discover the meaning of life . . . I remember a telephone call at 9 a.m. from a man who had had sex with a prostitute, thinking he had AIDS and had he given it to his wife. So here was an opportunity to help – you're probably not infected, I told him, but you have to wait three months before testing. I could almost feel, as we were talking, the person making decisions, or re-evaluating his relations with his wife, with alcohol and so on.'

• In Cartagena, Colombia, Hugo Aceros and his wife Leonor have devoted the eighteen years since their marriage to the creation of an agricultural co-op and to the education of the *campesinos* in a village of the interior. Hugo: 'We base our teaching on Freire's "Pedagogy of the Oppressed". The Church did terrible damage in teaching resignation.' The Aceros teach the opposite – that the peasants can organise and make things happen.

Leonor: 'Our marriage proposal was, would we live and work together for the *campesinos*. It's been a reality for eighteen years. We are all accepted round here as priest and wife, and as a priest family we are honoured and respected.' (The Aceros have three teenage children, a boy and two girls.)

Hugo: 'People sometimes ask me to say Mass for them, but I say no. I don't want to confront the local bishop – I respect him, and his predecessor was my friend.'

• Jim Shannon, once auxiliary bishop of St Paul and Minneapolis, and now a vice-president of General Mills in charge of funding, has as his ministry the disbursement of over eight million dollars annually. Even more of a ministry is his immense personal influence for good in Minnesotan public affairs, greater than he ever had as bishop. And he was recently described as 'one of the outstanding people in philanthropy in America'.

By the time this book is published Jim Shannon will have retired, but everyone expects him to remain 'one of Minnesota's most respected movers and shakers', as a Minneapolis newspaper put it.

Jim is a daily Mass-goer, yet he will not even take communion, much less celebrate Mass, as he has technically been excommunicated since his marriage in 1969. 'It's formidable to go through the latter years of your life without communion,' he told me. 'But I am witnessing to my readiness to observe a legalistic requirement, and to live within the Church's rules.'

Once, when Jim was at a Mass in Peoria, Illinois, a nun took communion in her hand, came down to the back of the church and stood in front of Jim and his wife Ruth. With tears in her eyes she broke the Host into three parts, and gave one each to Jim and Ruth. 'We did not refuse,' Jim said.

● In the same city former Dominican Joe Selvaggio devotes his life to employing the hard-to-employ, and developing housing for the disadvantaged, especially underprivileged Native Americans. 'He's a moral force,' the local police chief says.

'Jesus told us to clothe the naked and house the homeless,' Joe says. Project for Pride in Living (PPL), which he founded and has continued with the help of three other married priests, builds sixty new housing units a year, and refurbishes dozens of old houses. It also runs a light manufacturing plant, employing people no one else wants. 'The aim is to give people back their dignity,' Joe says.

In 1983 a priest told Joe about a Filipino woman in danger of her life from the Marcos regime. The priest asked Joe to marry her so she could save her life by coming to the United States on a fiancée visa. Joe said yes. In March 1984 Joe and Rose Escanan got married. They planned on a brief marriage and a quick divorce. But they found they had a great deal in common, especially a concern for social justice, and began postponing the break-up. 'We got to know each other,' Rose says, 'and the relationship developed into what it is.' It looks as if Joe and Rose are going to stay married.

According to Dr Terry Dosh, over 60 per cent of priests who leave take jobs in some sort of social services – as teachers, psychotherapists, social workers, counsellors. One could argue that some simply choose a role close to the caring ministry they already knew. It is interesting, however, how many others who are in purely commercial or administrative jobs nevertheless seek out ministry during their free time.

Psychologist Don Conroy believes that many priests who left – himself included – were conditioned by their experience as priests, and, after leaving, proceeded to obtain further training, education and qualification to act as professionals. Thereby they were able to distinguish for the first time between their social role or profession and their personal life. To make this distinction is a step towards maturity.

These brief narratives, Conroy says, 'tell about men and women who are free to perform their "life's work", and have a personal, social life (marriage and family). So they are more free, more mature.'

These men, he continues, have confronted their need to be free to do their life's work, and have risked their security. 'The paternalistic Church does not want men who are that free and mature. It is a temptation for many of us to fold back into the security of the large institution, but in so doing we fear we would jeopardise our freedom to grow and express ourselves from within our conscience, rather than from within the "corporate" conscience.'

Bob Boler, former Maryknoll missionary in Japan and now an Arizona state official, spends much of his free time ministering to the dying. The local pastor has encouraged him, and lately Bob's three teenage daughters have started to accompany him.

French priest André H, married and now divorced, makes it his ministry to keep a permanently open door to others. *La maison du bon Dieu* [God's House], people call it. André is back to the dreaded loneliness he had as an active pastor, but he says he has a sense of caring he never had then. His nights are given to listening, consoling, counselling. 'My faith has never left me,' he says.

These are just a few items culled from over 130 detailed examples in my notes of this kind of ministry.

II. SACRAMENTAL MINISTRY

One night in Recife, Brazil, I went with married priest Brian Eyre to sit in on the regular Wednesday meeting of dwellers in a *favela*, which is one of those massive squatters' slums that teem in every corner of every Latin American city. These folk have formed a little neighbourhood group, which they call a 'base community'. We drove over dirt tracks swarming with children and dogs, past makeshift open-air shops with bare-chested men and bumped across a concrete slab ('it covers the sewer pipes we put in,' Eyre said).

They were handsome people gathered in the tiny hall, mostly black, neatly dressed, and in that sultry night air there was the smell of soaped, clean bodies. A fluorescent light lit the hall, and a fan whirred ('the electricity we brought in,' whispered Eyre). They were talking about the health clinic and some loquacious lady was boring the hell out of everybody – meetings must be the same the world over. My mind wandered: I found myself thinking, I'm sitting here watching a married priest who started all this only five years ago, and you'd hardly notice him, except for the pink skin. He's just one of the group.

One reason Brian Eyre is so accepted is that, like St Paul the tentmaker, he works for his living. He teaches English. 'I see no conflict between having a job and doing pastoral work,' Brian says. 'I could earn more than I do, but my boss knows that on two nights a week I work in the *favela*. That's a decision Martha and I came to.'

What does he do in the *favela*? 'Exactly what I used to do when I was a pastor,' he says. 'Most of my work then was with the poorest – it was raising their consciousness, their awareness, reflecting with them on the reality of no water, no sewerage, health problems, rubbish, rats . . . But reflecting in the light of what it says in the Gospels. Now they've reached the stage where they have leaders who can go to the prefecture and demand rubbish collections and rat killing.'

Why bother with all this? 'Because I'm happy doing it. This is what makes me tick. And Martha has reinforced this ticking – she was a nun. She hasn't in any way made me tick less.'

Like so many other married priests, Brian Eyre has been careful not to intrude on the sacramental area, reserved for celibate priests, particularly as he got word that the new ultra conservative bishop (replacement of Helder Camera) had expressly sent word that Eyre was to have no liturgical function whatsoever in church. But something happened lately to make him wonder about this: 'We moved recently, and where we live now is a place where no priest ever sets foot. It's abandoned. There's only Martha and myself – they call her 'a mulher do padre [the priest's wife]'. Well, there was a woman here 101 years old – born the year before slavery ended in Brazil. The people came to tell me she was dying and asked me to come. With the community we tried to improve her physical needs. That done, I said to the people, let's pray. We prayed. To me, what we did was the Sacrament of the Sick: the Church was present there.

'A week later there was a knock on the door. They told us she was dead, and the people said, would I do the funeral service?

'So while the bishop said I can't have service, the people came and asked me. I got a call from the People of God. I didn't ask them: they came and asked me.'

When I left Recife, Brian Eyre was still pondering his dilemma. People are starting to ask more of him. He wants to obey the Church: but the Vatican Council says explicitly that the Church is the People of God – that same People of God who summoned him to serve them. It is clear that they will be asking more and more of him soon in the matter of the sacraments. What answer should Brian Eyre give to them? Is he to say YES or NO to the People of God? To the Church?

All over the world I have found this phenomenon: the People are calling their married priests back to sacramental service.

Some of these priests still feel they must say no. A Columbian married priest described his anguish to me: 'We have so many abandoned towns, towns that don't have priests. It would be beautiful if, in such places, one of us could go there, preach, say Mass, in places like Santa Rosa. We are actually invited by the people, but we say we can't go because the bishop won't permit it. They say they don't understand the Church . . . If they only knew it – they are the Church. But there was one resigned married priest, in the Magdalina region, who did do it – did the Mass and sacraments for the people, and went to jail for it. He was accused of usurping the powers of the clergy.'

Others, however, are beginning to say yes, as in Madrid where Julio Perez Pinillos, activist of Spain's married priest group, declares: 'If a concrete existing community sends and asks us for the celebration of Mass and the sacraments, we simply do not have the right to refuse them.'

It happens all over the world: American resigned priests working in hospitals are regularly called on to hear confessions and administer the Sacrament of the Sick (and in danger of death they are authorised by Church law to do so); in a Pennsylvania small town, when an alcoholic pastor refuses to do baptisms, the people take their children to a nearby married priest; in Holland, France, Germany and Ireland, I have encountered or heard of people turning to married, resigned or suspended priests and asking them for Mass, baptisms, weddings, and the Sacrament of the Sick.

A memorable and beautiful instance of people asking for Mass occurred in 1985 when married priest Professor Adrian Hastings of Leeds University, England, was visiting a nuns' convent on America's East Coast. Hurricane Gloria was roaring up the coast, and was just reaching its worst. Professor Hastings told the story in *The Guardian* newspaper:

> I had been browsing in the library when a sister, of long missionary experience in Africa and of outstanding spirituality, hurried up to me to ask whether I would be willing to celebrate Mass. There was a special group of people gathered for the Eucharist but the telephone had just rung to say it would be quite impossible for the priest to come. Then, suddenly, someone had remembered that I was there. I was, of course, greatly surprised. The sisters knew well that I was married and they were far from lawless.
>
> Was she really sure the others would not be upset? She assured me that they would not, and eventually I allowed myself to be persuaded to do what I longed to do. It was a lovely Mass.
>
> For me this experience was a great joy: in fact [it was] the first time since my marriage in 1979 that I had actually celebrated Mass within a Catholic building. It had also a sharply illuminating and symbolic significance. In normal circumstances I would certainly not have received that invitation. It was Gloria that did it. A hurricane was sufficient, just for one hour to make the rigidities of canon law look as ridiculous as they truly are when faced with the realities of human and pastoral need.[103]

No marks for guessing what they called him when he got to England. Hurricane Hastings.

Events, particularly in Latin America, indicate that local communities are sensing they have a right to Mass and the sacraments, and that they have a right to select someone to minister to them, and to call upon that person to do so. While it seems to arise from a sort of community instinct, those communities might be surprised to find out that there are solid theological opinions underpinning their actions. The Second Vatican Council expressly refers to the right of a community to the Eucharist as the heart of the community, and theologians of high standing, such as Edward Schillebeeckx, hold that communities should be able to choose and call their ministers. In his book *Ministry*, Schillebeeckx suggests too that changes in the Church can come from the bottom upward:

> Thus from the history of the Church it seems that there is a way in which Christians can develop a practice in the Church from below, from the grass-roots, which for a time can compete with the official practice recognised by the Church, which in its Christian opposition and illegality can eventually nevertheless become the dominant practice of the Church, and finally be sanctioned by the official Church.[104]

I was informed that in the city of Bogotá, Colombia, every Sunday scores of married priests fan out across the city, celebrating Mass and giving the sacraments in the churches and chapels that have no pastors. My informant suggested to me that even Church law allows for a 'custom contrary to law', which, if it endures for about twenty-five years, could itself acquire the force of law.

When flying down from the Caribbean coast I stopped off at Bogotá to check this out. I had only one contact address, no telephone number, and only one day to spare. My contact did not materialise, and I had to resume my journey. So I still do not know if it is true.

III. VOLUNTARY CHURCH WORK

In 1987 I spent some time in west London. For Sunday morning Mass friends took me, not to the large and institutional parish church on the high street, but to a little community centre, dwarfed by battered and fearsome high-rise flats.

In that community centre everybody knew everybody. Children romped among the chairs and the trestle tables where coffee and home-made buns were being laid out. There were black families, Irish families, Filipinos, and Londoners of the old stock. Maybe 80 or 100 people all told. The young visiting priest knew everyone and was accepted as one of them. But it wasn't on account of any sort of unique personality of his – the love and care seemed to grow naturally out of the community.

The priest's short talk meant something to me, and I felt quite moved when he publicly welcomed me, and people turned round to smile and take my hand. It really was a sign of peace.

This is as close to being a base community as I have found anywhere in the world. It is having an impact. You can see it in the faces: these people are not lonely, not sour, not frustrated. They enjoy being there, and they relish the Good News they hear there. There is far more to it than the weekly Mass: this is a community that looks after its members, who are in regular contact throughout the week – a community that also reaches out to the many other Asian and non-Christian groups in the area.

In this particular part of London people remark on the distinct sense of community. It stems from many sources, such as the South Acton Tenants' Association and the Acton Asians' Association, among others. This Catholic base community is only one of many forces for good, but its effects are felt and noticed.

Among the small group of committed Catholic lay-people responsible for building this community spirit, I frequently heard mention of Luis and Margaret Ulloa. They are a married couple who seem to work closely and effectively with the local Catholic priests. Luis is from Ecuador, and Margaret from London.

What people did not mention, however, was that Luis Ulloa is a priest who resigned and married. I'm not sure if people were even aware of it, or if it simply did not matter. What did matter was the way the Ulloas were part of a group that was drawing the people and their local priests together in real community.

I went to see Luis and Margaret Ulloa. It was clear that they saw what they did as a normal part of life for a married priest and his wife, still dedicated to ministry. They told me many other married priests and wives would be similarly involved in their own local Church communities if they could. But they would need the kind of moral support that Luis and Margaret were getting from their local priests and bishop.

The Ulloas are but one instance of a worldwide phenomenon, where priests who left are being drawn back into involvement with their local church on a voluntary basis. Sometimes they offer their services; sometimes the pastor comes looking for them.

In many parts of the world there are now active pastors who are totally committed to involving their married ex-colleagues as far as possible in the life of the Church – pastors such as Father Frank Zapatelli of Phoenix, Arizona, or Father Joe Kramis of Federal Way, near Seattle, who has six priests married in the parish and has managed to get them all involved with the church. It is not a matter of Mass or the sacraments, but of the myriad other tasks and ministries a well-run Church community demands.

In Lima, Peru, former missionary David Molyneux took his family to live in a new parish, presided over by an old Belgian priest who had 60,000 people to care for. Molyneux presented himself to the priest and offered his services. The old man fell on his shoulders: 'Just what I need, dear brother. Could you do the seven o'clock Mass on Sunday?'

'Now, not so fast, Father,' Molyneux said. 'You see, I've left, I'm married and I've got kids.'

'Oh.' The old man's jaw dropped. 'I, uh, I don't know what anyone would think of my having a former priest working here.' Then he brightened up: 'Tell you what, come with me to one of my areas and I'll introduce you round. We'll take it from there.'

Dave started going regularly to that area, sitting in at meetings, participating in community, getting involved with education for the youngsters. 'They really want me there now,' he told me. 'They realise I have something to offer. I find I have risen to a position of leadership. The auxiliary bishop comes up now and then: he knows me from the past, and has no problem with it.'

By way of contrast, married priest Bernie Groom returned to Ireland and settled in the town of Kinnegad. He offered his services to the local parish priest, to help in giving out communion.

'Well now, I don't think we're supposed to do that,' said the pastor. And that was the end of that.

The pastor, of course, was referring to the various provisos that the Vatican still attaches to dispensations, which attempt to exclude dispensed priests from any liturgical function whatsoever in church. However, Cardinal Lorscheider told me those rules are to be interpreted in the light of the more tolerant statements from the 1971 Bishops' Synod and from the bishops' meeting in Puebla.

Much depends on the openness and the attitude of the pastor. Pastors have been known to treat offers of help with contempt ('You can clean up the church grounds,' said one), whereas others are glad to put every function they can within the reach of the married priest. There is a dilemma for a married priest who is offered work that seems humiliating or demeaning: should he insist on nothing short of real priestly ministry, thus stressing the reality of his priesthood, or should he show Christian humility and accept whatever crumbs of ministry are thrown to him?

Some bishops, too, are starting to reach out to their one-time priests, and you find married and resigned priests serving voluntarily on diocesan committees, acting as consultants to a diocese (if they have perhaps become specialists in psychology or finance), doing adult religious education, giving retreats. Married priest Bernie Henry of Chicago serves on Cardinal Bernardin's personnel board, and is a member of the Association of Chicago Priests. In San Diego Paul Dion teaches adult religious education for the diocese, and sits on the diocesan marriage-annulment tribunal.

IV. Church employment

A few years ago, after I published a series of newspaper articles on priests who leave (*The Irish Times* articles which led to this book),[105] among the astonishing flood of letters that came in was this one from a Mrs Purcell in Ireland:

> I have a son who left the priesthood after fourteen years working in Brazil. He would love to get in touch with you. He is married now, and left off for one year. His bishop is ever so good to him, gave him a new parish and a house for his wife and baby.

Two years later, when doing the research for this book, I went to Brazil, and one of my primary objectives was to meet this man and others like him. I shall not identify city nor bishop, and I shall use false names for some of the priests concerned, as there is a real fear that the Vatican could simply telex its nuncio: 'Get rid of those men.' I would not want any book to exact such a price.

My first sight of Matt Purcell was on a Sunday morning, after lurching over miles of red clay tracks with *favelas* on every side, some just clusters of hovels made from flattened oil-drums and plywood, others mutating into concrete-block settlements. My driver was a priest from the diocese. Finally, we stopped at what looked like a small garage with the doors open wide: a crowd clustered round the doors. A smiling Brazilian woman in her thirties greeted us, rocking a pramful of infant twins, and holding by the hand a blonde two-year-old girl who glared suspiciously up at us. 'Matt Purcell's wife,' my companion said. 'Used to be a nun.'

She handed over the pram to a nearby child, and led us through the little crowd to the top end of the garage. At a makeshift altar, a slender fair-haired young man, with a face of quite unusual serenity, was just ending a quiet-spoken homily in Portuguese. He wore an open-necked shirt and grey trousers, and a priest's narrow white stole hung from his shoulders. He came over and shook hands with us, then went on with the Mass. Suddenly, we were saying the Our Father together and it was communion time, and I realised there had been no consecration. This was a communion service.

I stayed with Matt Purcell and his wife Sandra for a week. Sitting in their kitchen I found the whole notion of compulsory celibacy shot to ribbons, watching Sandra breastfeeding one of the twins and Matt changing the nappies of the other one, while most of the time children from nearby shacks were tripping in to play with the two-year-old, and fearsome-looking moustachioed men came in to drink coffee with Matt, and women and wives dropped in and out to talk with Sandra (sometimes it seemed serious and sometimes just gossip).

'There's a place for a woman in all this,' Matt explained to me, 'where a man can't go. They ask Sandra about problems they would never have brought to me in confession. And they tell her about a lot of things they would never tell me.'

The Purcells live in utter simplicity, on a tiny income partly from the bishop, and partly from the Irish missionary order to which Matt was once attached. It is not a terribly secure existence, but Purcell says you have to take risks and have faith in God. 'You do worry, but if you opt out of the system, nothing will ever change. The thing is to stay, and make a space for what you are doing. You get more and more accepted. You keep working with these groups – after a while they forget you are married.'

Does the bishop forget it?

'He put us in here. If he could have married clergy tomorrow, he would have. A fair number of bishops here would do so, but there's no way they can go against Rome.

'Many of the Brazilian celibate priests here have women on the side. You see, any sort of social life is impossible – forget about golf or anything like that – so priests would have to live like hermits. And anyway people don't believe any priest is celibate.'

Matt says that even with a wife and family, the work itself can be lonely and sometimes heartbreaking. 'It's good when someone like you comes to visit. When a man has been here a while, you get so caught up in the whole question of rights for people, the distribution of wealth problem. Do you know that 1,000 babies die of malnutrition every day in this country? That's the yearly equivalent of five Hiroshima bombs. Did you ever hear of infants tearing their mother's dress looking for milk?'

What ministry do Matt and Sandra do? Their non-sacramental work consists of bringing people to an awareness that the gospel does not want acceptance and resignation, but that in the light of that gospel they can change things. And the sacramental ministry includes everything a celibate priest does – baptisms, weddings, annointings, funerals, blessings, preaching, retreats – everything, in fact, except the words of consecration at Mass and the words of absolution in confession.

And why not those words? 'That's because I'm married,' Matt says with a wry grin.

The nonsense implied in such a ruling should become increasingly evident as more and more married priests like Matt Purcell come back into Church service, and have to tip-toe round the words of consecration and absolution, just because they love a wife. In that one area of the city, there are eight other married priests now back in the diocese, running churches, chapels and parishes.

I went to see the auxiliary bishop who had brought them all back. I found a man who combined courage and subtlety. 'My overriding principle', he told me cannily, 'is, whatever a lay minister can do, a married priest can do. Now a lay minister can be a minister of baptism, can witness marriages, can be the driving force of a community, can instruct in religion, can be a special minister for the Eucharist. I don't go beyond that. And the final affirmation to justify this is Church law – the very final article in the Code of Canon Law is this: *In ecclesia, suprema lex, salus animarum* [In the Church, the supreme law is the salvation of souls].[106]

'We have to give a reply to the people when they look for priests. We have an immense country, where the majority is Catholic and is abandoned, without pastors. My own region has three million people. What I do, I do with tranquillity, as a successor of the apostles, and because of my pastoral responsibility.'

But, I said, the Vatican came down like a ton of bricks on Archbishop Hunthausen in Seattle, for doing far less than you are doing.

'Nobody has the competence to do that, to prevent what we do here. I have no right to prohibit the exercise of that part of a man's priesthood that comes from his baptism. Because that mandate he gets directly from Christ – his baptism inserts him into the community, and he has a duty to serve it.

'I believe that married men must be ordained priests, and I think it is a matter of urgency. Much more important than tying celibacy and priesthood together is to guarantee to the people that they'll have a priest, married or not.'

After such words the reader may understand why I do not want to identify this bishop or his diocese. Nor shall I identify other dioceses where similar things are happening, and they are happening in many parts of Latin America, in some parts of the United States, and in other parts of the world.

There is one married priest I can identify, because he is already well known. Bern Brown is pastor of Our Lady of the Snows Mission, at Colville, in Canada's Northwest Territories. As a young Oblate missionary, he singlehandedly founded and built the mission at Colville Lake, 50 miles above the Arctic Circle, where he had found a small group of Indians called 'The End of the Earth People'. It has grown into a settlement of sixty-five, with its own airstrip, and accommodation for sport-fishermen, where Bern has at various times hosted former Prime Minister Trudeau, as well as Prince Charles.

In 1971, Bern was dispensed from celibacy, and married Margaret, an Eskimo girl who was a former cross-country ski record holder. His bishop flew up to perform the wedding in the little log church. However, Bern still carries on as pastor, except that he may not celebrate Mass. A missionary from Fort Good Espe flies in once a month to fulfil that duty.

Bern also carries on as community doctor, dentist, secretary of the co-op, manager of the fishing lodge, and curator of the Indian museum he founded. He has become a well-known painter, and flies his own Cessna airplane 90 miles south every week for the mail. There is no other way to reach Colville.

In some places the wheel has turned almost full circle, and priests who left some years ago are finding themselves called back into Church work. In the United States the Corpus organisation publishes a list of the various ministries now performed by such priests. Some are voluntary, and some are full-time, paid occupations. Ministries of worship are first listed:

1. Minister for communion service, with readings, preachings and prayers, when no [celibate] priest is available for daily or Sunday Mass.
2. Preacher on occasion, either following the gospel proclamation or at a later point in the liturgy.
3. Eucharistic minister: communion to the sick and shut-ins [housebound].
4. Lector; commentator; liturgical planner.
5. Music minister; cantor; song leader.
6. Minister for prayers and blessings at wakes, funerals, burials.
7. Minister for annointing of the sick, and Sacrament of Reconciliation in emergencies.

Married priests also perform the following *pastoral* ministries:

1. Administrator of a parish with a resident pastor.
2. Administrator of a parish without a resident pastor.
3. University campus minister.

4. Hospital chaplain; director of pastoral care.
5. Secretary to bishop.
6. Chancellor of diocese.
7. Director of religious education on diocesan and parish levels. Religious education teacher.
8. Director of diocesan Family Life Bureau.
9. Diocesan director of social services; director of Catholic charities.
10. Diocesan ecumenical commission, and preaching in other Christian churches.
11. Director of specialised ministries: youth; mentally and physically handicapped; alcohol- and drug-rehabilitation; the elderly; hospice for dying.
12. Principal of Catholic elementary or high school; diocesan director of education.
13. Director of diocesan Justice and Peace Office.
14. Diocesan psychologist.
15. Director of parish catechumenate programmes.
16. Parish adult education, advent and lenten programmes.
17. Parish counsellor; diocesan counselling service.
18. Director of preparation programmes for parish infant baptism, confirmation, marriage.
19. Retreat master; director of days of recollection.
20. Lecturer at clergy conferences; moderator of priest support groups.
21. Theology professor in Catholic colleges and universities.[107]

Not everyone, however, even among the married priests, sees it as a step forward that some should now be returning to full-time Church employment. It can have its drawbacks.

A member of Britain's Advent group of married priests pointed out to me that some of its members keep a low profile and make no attempt to shift public opinion on married priests, because they are employed as teachers in Catholic schools. They have to keep their heads down if they want to keep their jobs. I certainly would not dare write this book if I were teaching in a Catholic school.

A married priest employed by the Church of today would be haunted by insecurity. He is dependent on good will, not on established rights. Even if the employer, whether priest or bishop, be a man of conviction and generosity, he must eventually resign or die, and could be replaced by a Pharaoh who

knew not Joseph. There are no guarantees of similarly fair treatment by the successor.

Some resigned priests who have gone back to work for the Church have spoken of low pay, stigma, humiliation, and of being treated with coldness, hostility or envy by celibate colleagues.

There is also the danger of exploitation. In a parish on the US East Coast, a married priest has been taken on as assistant to the pastor. The pastor happens to be a lazy man who plays golf all the time, and has simply dumped the whole work of the parish – bar the words of consecration and absolution – on the poorly-paid shoulders of his married assistant. It is an enormous load and includes answering sick calls to several nearby hospitals. With work extending into all hours of day and night, hardly any time off, and no help from his pastor, the man's home life is suffering, and his wife is growing angry.

Lastly, there is a feeling in some quarters that returning to full Church work, on less than equal terms, postpones rather than hastens the day when celibacy will become optional, when married priests will have equal place and status with their celibate colleagues.

As yet it is an unresolved issue and one that is getting increasing consideration among married priests as more and more are invited back.

There is, however, no discussion, nor any need for it, on the primary role of the married and resigned priest in the Church today. Echoing the words of St Theresa of Lisieux, it is to do the ordinary things extraordinarily well, so that the world will look at these men and their families and say, 'See how these Christians love one another.' As Carole Hegarty of Chicago puts it: 'Preaching was never any good without example. Now they only have example.'

While in Rome in 1987, I asked Don Franzoni, former Abbot of St Paul's-Without-the-Walls, what message he had for resigned priests. 'Tell them this,' he said. 'Not from me, but from St Paul. Who can separate us from the love of Christ Jesus? Neither sword nor death, nor suffering nor exile.'

Don Franzoni believes that a resigned priest has two duties: 'the first is to continue a dialogue with the Church, so it becomes a Church of service, not of power. Remember the centre of the

Church is not Rome, but Christ. And the second duty is to continue to meet the needs of men and to preach the gospel.

'Even if laicised,' Franzoni says, 'I am still responsible for the Word of God. Woe to me if I do not preach the Gospel, as St Paul said.

'Remember that even canon law gives me the right and the duty to minister to someone at the point of death. Well, I have a similar duty to the living. If I meet a young person without hope, I have the same duty to give him the Gospel.'

7

PRIESTS WHO STAY

To give and not to count the cost, to fight and not to heed the
wounds, to toil and not to seek for rest, to labour and to look
for no reward save that of knowing that I do thy will.

St Ignatius Loyola

A FEW YEARS AGO a professional killer was hired to assassinate
Dom Helder Camara, Archbishop of Recife-Olinda in Brazil. He
was paid by certain of the country's powerful landowners who
felt threatened from the way Dom Helder was raising the consciousness of Brazil's millions of poor.

Dom Helder lives in a small house with a walled garden in
front, and a door in the wall leading to the street. The man rang
the door bell and a frail five-foot man of seventy-nine came out
to open it. The visitor asked to see Dom Helder.

'I'm Dom Helder,' said the little man.

'You are Dom Helder?' stammered the assassin, his image of
the evil 'Communist' bishop immediately shattered.

'Yes, I am. What can I do for you? Why don't you come in?'

The Archbishop led his guest through the garden into the
house and gave him a chair.

'Now,' he said. 'What can I do to help you?'

'Nothing,' the man said, his hand trembling. 'I don't want to
have anything to do with you, because you are not the sort of
person I could kill.'

'Kill? But why do you want to kill?' asked Dom Helder.

'I was paid to kill you,' was the answer. 'But I can't do it.'

'If you've been paid, why don't you do it?' said Dom Helder reasonably. 'I will go to the Lord.'

'No,' the man said. 'You are one of the Lord's.' He got up and went away.[108]

Some years later, after I passed through that same garden to spend an hour with Dom Helder, I understood what the assassin had meant. Dom Helder Camara is one of the Lord's. By which I mean that the Lord has clearly answered his most frequent prayer, borrowed from Cardinal Newman: 'Lord Jesus, do not extinguish the light of your presence within me. O Lord, look through my eyes, speak through my lips, walk with my feet. Lord, may my poor human presence be a reminder, however weak, of your divine presence.'

Dom Helder Camara is a priest who stayed, and could be a symbol of many other priests who have stayed and truly lived their celibacy, and have grown in wisdom and grace before God and men. One cannot, of course, assert that all priests stay for the right motives, and it is clear that not all grow within the priesthood. But many do. And there is nothing quite like a priest who has stayed and has grown in his priesthood, or is striving to do so. 'Since I left,' an Irish married priest told me, 'I've known groups of teachers, media people, every kind. But the men I knew in the priesthood, I'd rate those men as above all the groups I've known since I left.'

If this book is to speak of men who have left the ministry and are still striving to grow in God's love, it would be churlish and inaccurate if it failed to salute those who, without ever leaving, have been so striving all their lives. That is why I write this chapter.

The great French Dominican, Henri Lacordaire, summed up the ideal of the celibate priesthood in a memorable passage:

> To live in the midst of the world, with no desire for its pleasures; to be a member of every family, yet belonging to none; to share all sufferings, to penetrate all secrets, to heal all wounds; to go daily from men to God, to offer Him their homage and petitions, to return from God to men, to bring them His pardon and His hope; to have a heart of iron for chastity and a heart of flesh for charity; to teach and to pardon, console and bless and to be blessed for ever. O God, what a life is this, and it is thine, O priest of Jesus Christ.

It is an ideal that has grown progressively harder to strive for, as the traditional supports for celibate priesthood have been steadily eroded in modern pluralist society.

It can take something akin to heroism to live it well: when the world no longer believes in celibacy, or that any man could be really celibate; when the wrongdoings of other celibate priests tarnish the image of all priesthood; when a man feels betrayed by colleagues who leave; when thousands of former colleagues seem fulfilled and happily married; when the priest himself believes celibacy should be optional; when overwork and stress are overwhelming, due to the growing scarcity of priests; when authority treats priests like pawns; when the comforts of the world seduce through television; when Church authorities seem to be turning their backs on the promises of the Vatican Council.

TRUE CELIBATES

Yet some priests do not merely endure, but grow through all of this. They are men of resurrection. I have been privileged to know a few.

There was my own uncle, Dominican Father Oliver Gabriel Stokes. I became a priest because of his example. Years later he did my wedding. When he died in 1983, he was friend more than uncle. A man with enough personality quirks to make him thoroughly human, and with enough humour to keep the Dominican Order chuckling for half a century, he made giving – of himself and the little he possessed – as vital as breathing.

He spent years as a missionary in Trinidad, and when he used to depart for Europe on leave, the people of the parish would charter buses to come to the docks or the airport to see him off. I am told people in Trinidad still talk about him, a quarter of a century after he left for the last time. At his funeral, other priests were seen weeping. A very old priest told me that is the rarest of tributes from one priest to another.

Like St Dominic before him, my uncle always had an eye for a pretty woman, yet I knew him well enough to say that he was chaste all his life. Today my clearest memory is of sharing a hotel room with him, and watching him kneel at his bed in prayer.

My very last memory is of him sitting up in his hospital bed, with a glass of Jameson's Irish whiskey in his hand, three hours before he died. Sitting round the bed were two young Dominican seminarians who were his friends, and me.

'Did y'ever hear,' said my uncle, 'of the two fellas coming out of the pub? "Better let me drive, Michael," one says to the other. "'Cause you're too drunk."

' "Whaddiya mean, I'm too drunk? It's my car, and I'm driving!"

'Well, they lurched along for about an hour. Then Frank says, "You must be getting near a town now, Michael."

' "Why so?"

' "'Cause you're knocking down more people."

' "Whaddiya mean, I'm knocking them down? I thought you were doing the driving!" '

Those were practically my uncle's last words to me. He died in his sleep later that night, at the age of seventy-four. I think maybe he died chuckling.

Then there was Paul Hynes, another Dominican, and the closest friend I ever had. We joined the Dominicans the same day, detested each other on sight, and fought like cats for two years. Then, inexplicably, we became friends for life. On one vacation after ordination we explored Europe with motorcycle and tent. People wondered how we could even stand each other, as Paul was teutonically efficient, and I was not.

I watched Paul Hynes grow, from an impatient, somewhat arrogant youngster, through an efficient and still impatient superior, to a priest in his forties who combined strength, sensitivity and love in a way that few could have predicted. He had a zeal to spread God's word, and a quite extraordinary concern for others even in the midst of illness.

After I left the ministry, he remained my closest friend. He remained genuinely chaste, too – I know, because he told me. He would be in his fifties now had he lived, but a terrible wasting illness took him.

For a while after he died, I used to pray for him. Now I find myself praying to him.

THE OPEN DOOR

It is not that the good priests are all dead. But two good ones are, and I miss them terribly.

There is one, however, who is very much alive. On visits to London I kept hearing so much about Father Michael Hollings, parish priest in Bayswater, that I went and interviewed him for this chapter. I am going to devote a considerable part of the chapter to him: I shall let him speak for the many other devoted and generous celibate priests who still grace the Church.

Michael Hollings was a young Guards officer in the Second World War. He had a girlfriend, lots of personality, and no religious faith whatsoever. Somehow or other he became a believer, and then told the chaplain he wanted to be a priest.

'But you don't even go to Church,' spluttered the chaplain. 'How could you want to say Mass?'

'I want to help people,' said young Hollings.

'Well, be a social worker, then!'

'No. I want to be a priest.'

Michael Hollings has been a priest for many years now – he must be touching seventy. He appears to be a very happy man. Wherever he becomes pastor he practises his notorious 'open door' policy, and there gradually accumulates in the parish rectory a sort of impromptu floating community. At the time of my visit, the following eighteen people were in residence in the Bayswater rectory: A West Indian, who plays the guitar and studies accountancy; Old Sister Joe, in her eighties; a Coptic Ethiopian; Emily, 21, who is studying the organ; a nun from Dublin; somebody called Antoinette; a man who tried to become a priest, and wants to try again, and meantime is working full-time with AIDS victims; a Dominican sister; an artist (no religion), who had been in squatters' digs, until Michael picked him up and brought him home, and got him into art college; a German friend of the artist, who has come to visit; an older women called Doris, who goes home midweek; a priest from Hyth; a girl from an old Catholic family; a drunk whom Michael brought in off the road, and after six months discovered was a priest; a lad from Northern Ireland who came for one night and stayed four years; a man just out of prison, who was released to Michael for a month; and another artist – a girl – who has set up her studio upstairs.

If that's not quite eighteen, it doesn't much matter – in the time it takes to write this, the kaleidoscope will have shifted anyway. And, by the way, there's also tea and sandwiches twice a day at the church door for all the poor in the district. So if you happen to find yourself near Bayswater. . . .

Margaret Ulloa spent a couple of wildly unforgettable years as a member of Hollings's impromptu community, which was then in the Southall parish house, where Michael was pastor (in fact, it was there Margaret met Luis, the priest from Ecuador whom she married).

'It's an extraordinary house to live in,' Margaret says. 'People come in and out of the house, youngsters wander in for a cup of coffee, and to read the newspaper. There are people of all sorts coming in to see Michael all the time with their problems.

'People mistake Michael as some kind of wonder-worker. In fact, his greatest gift is in perceiving what people are capable of. He has a way of asking you to do things so that you gain the confidence to do it.'

But lest she give a false impression, Margaret says, 'I assure you, life with Michael Hollings is no heavenly light. He'll have you working sixteen hours a day. But then he works twenty. If he realises he's wasting your time or his, he'll cut. And he can be harsh and critical and crotchety, and needn't appear at all charismatic. And he can put you in your place if you need it.'

There was that awful moment when Father Michael was addressing a group of very important nuns – it was at the annual taking of vows. 'Sisters,' said Michael in the homily, 'remember always you are looking ahead to Jesus, not behind to Mother General.'

Margaret says Michael Hollings seems to be living a totally fruitful life: 'Everybody's last resort is always Michael, when things go wrong.

'But there has to be some untouched inner bit, to make this possible,' she believes. 'A sort of hole in the middle. He does, in fact, do one hour of prayer, from five to six o'clock, every morning of his life. I know: I lived in the same house with him.'

This, then, is the priest I came to interview. I wandered through the enormous house and nobody seemed to mind. At length I found myself sitting in a room piled with what seemed to be boxes for the Vincent de Paul, a couple of frayed armchairs, and a poor smothered desk near which Michael Hollings had inserted himself. He is a big man, hair still dark, and has a habit of chuckling gently before he tells something that amuses him.

Did he ever think of leaving? I asked him. Nothing like getting to the point.

'There've been many times I've had total frustration with the Church, with individual bishops and clergy. But also with myself, y'see. Sometimes you wonder how you will survive without taking to the bottle.

'I was someone who wanted to go ahead and work on Vatican Two. I was in favour of the birth-control issue – that kind of background. But lots of conservative people didn't want to go forward. Although I'm a funny sort of a mix: I can see the value of the old as well as the new. I like the Tridentine mass, for example.

'Well, I knew Charles Davis well [who left the Catholic Church in 1967, saying it was corrupt]. I was in Wimbledon the day of the announcement that he was leaving, and we came up in the train together. Later he was to take me to task: "You just sit in the middle," he said. "You don't have the guts to go one way or the other."

'I said I thought it might be more valuable to stay in the middle – not so much with a foot in both camps, as sometimes attacking the progressives and sometimes the conservatives. But I suppose I could easily be seen as a colourless character. . . .

'But I cannot see myself as having any power or effect outside the Church's ministry. I felt, rightly or wrongly, that Davis lost more of his possibilities – he lost so much by coming out. Much of what he had to offer became useless. Bruce Kent too: he had great effect when he was inside. Certainly, he has far less limelight now than when he was a monsignor. Of course, that would not be a good reason for staying. And I have been in touch with many who left and are doing an awful lot of good now. I would not want it thought that when you leave, you are a lesser citizen.

'But I have no qualifications except the priesthood. I'd have to go for retraining. I suppose it comes down to celibacy: I always say I'd be an extremely poor husband – I'm so busy doing other things. My poor wife and children, they would fall by the wayside.

'Celibacy does give me freedom, but that's personal to me. Because there are married people who find more time to do things than I do. What I'd love to see is a situation where celibate and married priests could all be in the same racket together.'

Michael Hollings is not sure if celibacy is a charism, that is, a special gift from God. He thinks in more down-to-earth terms: 'In any work you find three kinds of people. I remember some people in Oxford, they wanted degrees, basically, so they could get married and settle down. They weren't interested in a great career. That's the first kind.'

The second type, Hollings says, are the people wholly dedicated to achievement: 'the people determined to get to the top of Everest. Actors and so forth. They marry almost on the side. The first thing is their vision. Now to some extent, that is what happens with the priestly vocation.

'Then there is the third kind, the sort of Universal Aunt. Like women who never get married, but look after everyone else.

'I don't see that any of them are charisms. They are just a natural development of man or woman.'

Michael Hollings sees himself as one of those Universal Aunts, and thinks there is a place in the priesthood for all three types. But if there is, there is a place for marriage too.

What does Michael Hollings see as his greatest strength?

'That would be a rather proud thing to say, wouldn't it? It isn't easy to say – maybe that one has to take risks. I mean, I find myself getting hauled over the coals by bishops, more than most priests. Especially if I do something on the progressives' side. As, when I do things like blessing a marriage for a divorced couple.'

Is he not then putting his judgement before that of the Church?

'I don't think the Church is always right. I mean, she changes her stance many times. For example, on a television programme in 1959, I was asked why the Mass was all in Latin. I said, there's no reason why it couldn't be in English. That came out in the Catholic press, and I was summoned to Cardinal Godfrey. He said, "Latin is the liturgical language, and you are never to say that again." I was then summoned to the apostolic delegate, as I had been denounced to Rome. He said that in future I ought to write down anything I was going to say in public.'

Hollings began to chuckle gently, and recalled how in 1964, as chaplain at Cambridge, he found himself landed with two somewhat incompatible guests – a monsignor from the Vatican, and the Vatican's *bête noire*, Hans Küng. 'I hid Hans on the top floor, and put the monsignor in another part of the house. I put Hans's book [*The Council and Reunion*] beside the monsignor's bed.

'Next morning, the Monsignor met me with the book in his hand: "If only I could meet a man like that," he said. "You know, canon law is strangling the Church. I think if Jesus Christ came today, he'd be condemned by the Curia."

'It's from things like that I get my encouragement. So when I do the things that I do, like blessing the marriage of David Frost to the Duke of Norfolk's daughter, I may be following my own judgement, but the Church has changed before. I try to balance it with prayer, and just be as obedient as I can.'

What about loneliness?

'I had had a girlfriend when I was in the Army: she eventually married somebody else. What I found most difficult in the early days [of my priesthood], was when all my contemporaries were getting married – some of them were getting me to do their marriages. I felt tremendous loneliness going back at night.'

How did he handle his loneliness?

'For me, very largely, it was prayer. I would get up early in the morning – at five – I'd have to put myself to bed early, of course. A certain amount is just discipline.

'The loneliest was in the early years. After that I was fortunate to be in a university situation. In the following ten or eleven years, I had youngsters in and out, morning, noon and night, as chaplains do. There was just no time for loneliness. They were so friendly and loving.

'Then, subsequently, I developed my notorious "open door" family. Since I started the open house in 1959, I've not nearly such problems with loneliness. And now that I'm so used to it, I'd find it very difficult to live in a shut-in presbytery with two priests or by myself.'

What message would Michael Hollings have for married priests, many of whom are his friends?

'I suppose it's patience. And I hope they can do the kind of thing that Luis and Margaret Ulloa do: that they can have a wide apostolic life in the situation where they are. Many, of course, are doing it under the frown of the Church, and cannot use their ordination. It's a terrible impasse. I am sure there will be married priests in the future, and I hope very much that the Church will see the way to letting these men back to using their priestly orders – those who want to do so.'

MARKS OF THE PRIEST

It takes God a long time to fashion a mature and holy priest. For many it's a lifetime of struggle. Some leave and grow to maturity in marriage and parenthood, and some stay and do that same maturing in their priestly life of ministry (and some, of course, never mature at all, inside or outside the ministry, but that's another story).

There are distinctive marks about the men who stay, remain genuinely celibate, and attain real maturity or are growing towards it. These marks are apparent in a man like Michael Hollings, but the same qualities recur over and over again in other such priests.

To begin with, they all seem to know how to pray. And they do quite a lot of it. Most have a sense of humour. God knows they must need it. They appear as men who have taken responsibility for their lives. They are givers rather than receivers. Irishman Father Andy Horgan, once my pastor in Aberdeen, Washington State, is now known as Seattle's 'waterfront priest'. He recalled for the *Seattle Times* his first visit back to Ireland as a young returned missionary.[109] 'There was a big crowd of relatives and friends out to greet me. We went to a pub and my brother bought the first round of drinks. When we downed that, my cousin bought a round. Then another cousin bought a round.

'Then my great-uncle, Connie Mahoney, looked at me squarely and growled, "Andrew, stand your round."

'I have never forgotten that,' Andy says today. 'Always stand your round. Don't be a leech, don't be a freeloader.'

That's about it. These men aren't freeloaders: they give rather than take.

Most of them are not afraid to show emotion. They are not afraid to weep, or to be angry. And their features do not have that neutral grey mask that hides the real feelings (always the give-away of a priest who is unhappy in his role).

They have tolerance and understanding towards men who leave, and want what is good for them rather than what seems good for the institution. Usually they want such men back working with them, and often go after them to invite them to do so.

Almost all seem to want priests to be free to marry, even

though they might not choose that option for themselves (a *New York Times* – CBS poll shows that of all US priests, 55 per cent would favour optional celibacy,[110] while a poll by Terrance Sweeney has 25 per cent of bishops in favour).[111]

Father Tim O'Connell, director of the Institute of Pastoral Studies in Chicago, notes four common elements in the life-style of most fulfilled and happy priests.[112]

Firstly, he says, they truly enjoy the work of priestly ministry, which includes 'caretaking', nurturing people in survival, growth and development, as well as relating flexibly to many different kinds of people in many different ways, as friend, confidant, teacher, leader, mentor. 'Men who don't like that work don't end up as happy priests,' he believes. 'There is no substitute for this.'

Secondly, he comments, 'I notice that these priests all have a private life which is clearly distinct from their professional, ministerial life. The job does not own them: they are not workaholics.' In other words, they have achieved individuation, the establishment of an identity and life that is separate from role.

Thirdly, O'Connell is struck by the fact that such men have distanced themselves from the issues and agendas of the institutional Church: 'These priests simply don't care about the internal politics of Church life, and, if they ever had them, they have abandoned their ecclesiastical ambitions.'

This distancing is accomplished by a single-minded commitment to the people of their parish; by shaping their ministry on the Gospel; and by a Sinatra-like tendency to do it 'my way'. 'They don't go out of their way to make trouble for the wider institution. But when it appears clear that the institution's agenda is something other than the good of the people, they opt for the people.'

Lastly, 'the happy priests whom I know have all dealt with the issue of intimacy in their lives.' Instead of moaning about celibacy or escaping into alcoholism, workaholism, abusive sex or endless hobbies, these men have taken steps to meet the needs of intimacy: 'In some cases they have done so through some sort of group life. There are members of religious communities who have made their community life an example of authentic and committed family life. There are diocesan priests who have formed prayer groups, support groups, deeply caring friendship groups. There are recovering alcoholics who experience a broad range of intimate sharing in their AA group.

'In other cases, these happy priests have developed individual relationships that meet these intimacy needs. The ways that these relationships define themselves, the specification of the partner (male/female, religious/lay, single/married), and the frequency of interaction, vary widely. But the common denominators are that it is a genuinely reciprocal, self-revelatory relationship, not a disguised occasion for ministry, and that it is a close relationship which does, in fact, meet the intimacy needs of the priest.'

RELATIONSHIPS WITH WOMEN

People were shocked when a novel by Father Andrew Greeley described a celibate priest, Kevin Brennan, loving Ellen Foley chastely.[113] Yet deep friendships, sometimes love, between celibate priests and women, have a long and honourable history.

There was a celebrated thirteenth-century friendship between St Dominic and Blessed Diana d'Andalo. According to the breviary, she became a nun, making her vows at the hands of St Dominic, 'whom she loved with all the ardour of her soul.'[114] St Francis de Sales, bishop of Geneva, had a famous friendship with St Jane Françoise de Chantal. I think priests and their house-keepers, who live together chastely for sometimes forty years, must frequently develop deep trust and friendship, and surely often love.

One of the best-known friendships of all was that between Pope Pius XII and his housekeeper, a nun called Mother Pasqualina. He met her in the 1920s when she was a quite beautiful young German nun, and he was a rising young monsignor in the Vatican diplomatic service. He asked her Order if she could become his housekeeper, and she remained with him until he died. He turned to her for help and counsel in practically everything he did.

When he became Pope in 1939, she too moved into the Vatican, where she proceeded to rule the papal household with a rod of iron. They called her 'the Popessa'. The Curia detested her, and French Cardinal Tisserant ordered her out of the Vatican the very day the Pope died.[115] (Although the late Cardinal Browne once told a friend that, after the Pope's death, Pasqualina had refused to hand over the keys to the papal apartment. 'Well now,' chuckled old Browne, 'you just don't do that to a former French cavalry commander like Tisserant!')

When the new Pope, John XXIII, was elected, he asked Pasqualina to come back.

Psychologists tell us that most people are unable to mature without some kind of intimacy at some point in their lives, or at least a very deep relationship. Tragically, too many priests have been deprived of it. It has its dangers, of course (and I shall return to these in the chapter on celibacy), but a life without love or a deep relationship, a life to which clerical training has condemned thousands of priests, is far more dangerous, far more stunting to growth. Love is less dangerous than no love at all.

'I, for one, love women,' Archbishop Pat Flores told me in San Antonio. 'I also love men, children, little boys, girls. I just love people, period. The question is, where does a relationship, just in a Christlike way, stop being virtuous and become dangerous? Spiritual direction, I guess, would come in here, for many priests.' And prayer.

The great French thinker, Father Teilhard de Chardin, loved three different women at different times in his life. While in Beijing in the early 1930s he was deeply in love with an American woman, Lucille Swan. The intensity of his love drove him to ponder his celibacy more than he had ever done. A brief paper, 'The Evolution of Chastity', records his thinking at the time.[116]

Teilhard wonders why he does not make love to Lucille. Is it just that he is conditioned from childhood? Or by a desire to be faithful to a long history of moral duty and respectful admiration? No, there has to be more than that.

Teilhard always sees the material world as evolving towards something spiritual, and love is one of the greatest forces leading to God. There are two kinds of love: sexual love and love of God. How can they be combined to lead to God?

There are two possible ways. The first is complete sexual union, with its enormous release of energies that can lead to God. The second way, Teilhard says, is that of the celibate: to keep only those elements of the mutual attraction that can lift up the partners in their mutual approach; to fly to each other in an upward movement; to love one another, and to deflect that love up to God. The spiritual power of the flesh remains, but it leaves room for virginity.

Teilhard: 'Two solutions. Two ways. On this point individual testimonies oppose and contradict each other. By birth, I can say, I find myself committed to the second way. I have followed it as far as possible. Of course, I have known difficult passages on this journey but I have never felt diminished in it, or lost.'

The fact is most men, celibate and non-celibate, will encounter romantic love at some point in their lives. Jungian analyst Robert Johnson calls it the single most powerful experience most of us will have. Celibate priests are not immune from this experience: in fact, priests are particularly attractive to good women because of their well-developed anima, the gentler side of the male.

It takes enormous discipline and commitment to know and experience a caring woman, to encounter the power of romantic love, and nevertheless to remain celibate. Relatively few seem to be able to do it, and they are inevitably those who have made a free choice of celibacy, rather than those who have had celibacy imposed upon them. And the suffering is invariably great.

Teilhard's 'difficult passages' are an understatement. I know a priest who fell in love with his housekeeper. Maggie was a handsome young widow, mother of a flock of teenage children. Let Maggie herself tell the story: 'A month after he said he loved me, all of a sudden he started wearing full blacks and collar the whole time. He could hardly say hello. He'd been to his spiritual director who said "dump her". We went for a walk: I was crying. He started to cry too.

'He got himself moved to another rectory. I knew what he was doing: walking away so I could have a life.

'There was one Sunday I was at home alone—all the kids were out. I started to drink. Then I remembered the Phenobarbitol. I went to the kitchen to get it: I must have made five trips before I found it. I felt almost the presence of evil.

'I cried out to God for help. I broke down hysterically. Then I realised I couldn't die and leave the kids alone.'

When Maggie's children returned, they were pretty shocked at the state she was in.

'It's got to be a man,' one of the boys said.

'But she's not seeing anybody,' said one of the girls.

'Then it's got to be Father Jack.'

Maggie did not deny it. The elder kids were furious: their mother had always been a pillar of the Church 'and there was I telling them I loved a man who was a priest.'

The next day the kids asked their mother how could she ever have got involved with a priest.

'We've been very respectful of the law,' she told them. 'There's been no sex. But we can't help the way we feel. I'm very happy when I am with him.'

One of the daughters hugged her: 'All I want is for you to be happy,' she said. 'I'm just sorry it has to be this way.'

'You're nuts. You must be crazy,' said one of the other daughters.

One day Father Jack came back to that church on a visit, and Maggie saw him celebrating Mass. He waited for her after Mass.

'Why did you go away?' she asked him.

'I wanted you to have a life,' he said. 'The Church isn't going to change the celibacy law.'

Maggie says they had already talked about his leaving, 'but I couldn't be comfortable with that, and neither could he. He's a very good priest, well loved by the people, and a very spiritual man.

'He drove me home that morning. He said he was sorry, and he'd never leave me alone again. He told me he had picked up the phone many times, but always put it down. Why? I asked him. "I was afraid of what you might say." '

Maggie and Father Jack have been in love for a good few years now. Father Jack is still celibate. He is a regular visitor at Maggie's home. The kids have grown very fond of him and regard him as one of the family.

'I'm comfortable with the relationship,' Maggie says. 'So is he. We're grateful for what we do have.'

That's not quite the end of the story. There are two more things to tell. One is that Maggie began to read about celibacy to see if she could understand why it's an obligation on all priests. 'There have been times, up to fifteen hours a day, eating peanuts and pounding the books – Aquinas's *Summa* and *Contra Gentiles* – I studied history, psychology, theology, patristics, scripture.' A gifted researcher, she has amassed an enormous file of documentation on celibacy, and is now a regular writer on the subject. She is convinced that celibacy, as an obligation on all priests, has outlived its usefulness, if it ever was right. She believes its real value is as a freely-chosen option.

And the second thing? Father Jack has cancer now. Cancer of the throat. And Maggie is caring for him with a love that is moving to watch. He is still active as a priest, and continues his parish ministry. But a few times a week now he comes to Maggie's home for his food, all of which has to be liquidised.

'I never chose celibacy,' he told me. 'It was just an offer I couldn't refuse.'

One Sunday after Mass I was with Maggie in the supermarket. I saw her buying a jar of baby food.

'But you don't have any more babies,' I said.

'I do.' She smiled. 'It's for my baby in the Roman collar.'

8

THE SHADOW SIDE
OF CELIBACY

Deprive the Church of honourable marriage and you fill her
with concubinage, incest, and all manner of nameless vices and
uncleanness.

St Bernard of Clairvaux

FATHER HANS M. LIVES in a calendar picture. His little white
church with its onion-domed tower nestles in a hauntingly
lovely German valley; timbered houses cluster round the church
as if for protection; green pastures ascend the valley slopes on
either side, to disappear intriguingly into the dark woods above.

One of the timbered houses is the rectory. It is a Sunday
afternoon and I am sitting with Father Hans in the tidy living
room, as he tells me of the woman and child he keeps hidden in
a city 100 miles away.

Father Hans is of medium height, gentle except for a powerful
handshake, with a trimmed, reddish beard and bright blue eyes.
He is a young-looking forty-five.

'My son is eight years old,' he tells me. 'And he's getting
restive. Gretchen is having a hard time with him just now. You

see, he keeps asking where his father is, and she tells him his father is gone, she doesn't know where.

'He thinks I am his uncle. I drive to see them a couple of times a month. And sometimes I bring them down to stay here for a weekend, round Christmas or Easter. I tell people it's my sister-in-law and her child.

'But it's getting harder and harder all the time.'

So why not leave? I ask.

'It's the priesthood. It means so much to me. I cannot leave the priesthood, not for anything. Besides, what would I be fit for, now?'

The room has the bleak neatness that a man achieves without a woman. There is a kind of airless, bachelor smell. The armchairs are functional rather than elegant, and seem little used. On the left wall is a crucifix made of two gnarled and twisted branches, on which an anguished Christ arcs his body and writhes. Beside it is a group photograph of Pope John Paul II, with some men in black cassocks and purple sashes.

'It's getting harder and harder to keep this a secret,' Hans said. 'And it's getting to us both, more and more.'

There is a long pause.

'And worse things have happened.'

I notice his knuckles are white and tight, fists pushed together in his lap.

'Last year she got pregnant again. But there was no way we could keep one more child a secret.' His fists are grinding together.

'So we had an abortion.'

Hans opens his fists and puts his head in his hands. I look up at the gnarled Jesus, saying nothing. An Alpine clock is tock-tock-tocking somewhere out in the hall. I want to say, 'Is the priesthood worth this?', but I can't find the courage.

Father Hans looks up and his eyes are liquid. 'Someday,' he says, 'I must stand before God and answer for what I have done. But those men', he points to the picture, 'will stand beside me. Their rules drove me to this.'

It's just 3.20 on a Sunday afternoon. There is to be a baptism in the church at 3.30. Germans are punctual, so Hans has to get ready. May I come and watch? I ask. But certainly. I would be most welcome.

It is a country family waiting in the church – proud young

papa in unaccustomed blue suit, neck tight against collar and tie. A rather hefty girl holding the baby. Grandparents ever so proud. All gathered where the altar-rails used to be. From a distance, at the far end of one of the front seats, I watch the joy in every face but one.

Father Hans smiles, leans forward to make the sign of the cross on the new little forehead. As he straightens up, he catches my eye for an instant. I doubt if I have ever seen such anguish in the eyes of a smiling human being.

BREAKS IN THE CHAIN

Three days later I was visiting a woman called Anne Lueg in her home at Solingen, Germany, where she lives with her three children and her priest-husband, now a prominent figure in Germany's Christian Democratic Party. Anne runs an organisation to help women who are sexually involved with priests, and has 300 names on her books. I asked her how many children does she personally know, who have been fathered by active priests.

'How about fifty?' she answered promptly.

And how many abortions? I asked.

'Ten that I know of, at this moment,' she said.

Anne has already published a book, *Ein Sprung in der Kette* [A Break in the Chain], in which the story of some of those fatherings are told.[117] She has enough more for a series of volumes, and similar books have been published in both Germany and France, for instance, *Unheilige Ehen* [Unholy Wedlock], by Ursula Goldmann-Posch.[118]

Three thousand miles away and three months later, I found myself at Canadensis, Pennsylvania, in a house deep in the woods, from which one Cathy Grenier runs a non-profit-making orgnisation called Good Tidings, also to help women who have become involved with priests. She has over 700 women on her books.

Cathy took over as director of Good Tidings from Maggie Olsen, who had founded the group after a woman friend took her own life when dumped by a priest-lover. Cathy is a young woman with a loving and a caring big enough to embrace all those 700 and their men (who include three bishops). Her husband Joe, French Canadian and priest, backs her every step of the way. And a feisty five-year-old daughter makes it clear to visitors that she wishes Mum would get off this kick and be like any other mum.

Cathy Grenier cries sometimes, because of her knowledge of grief untold, heaped up, full measure and overflowing. She has her own troubles too: she and Joe are poor as church mice. Joe is not doing well at estate agency, and so many women make reverse charge calls that their phone bills are hundreds of dollars a month. Yet they keep open house for the women who need help, and these women frequently come to stay.

Could they be just crazy, I ask, women with a crush on some unwilling priest? No, says Cathy, because upwards of a hundred of the priests themselves have been in contact with her. Sometimes they too come to visit: it is sometimes the only place they can turn to. There is a rough and ready monthly retreat at the Greniers, for any who want to come. Somehow there are camp beds or floors to lie on, and somehow there is food on the table.

'We even have baby showers by mail,' Cathy says. 'Some of the women are just desperately in need of baby clothes. We get cheques by mail to pass on to women expecting babies. We get calls from priests, like from the guy whose spiritual director had told him he didn't choose fatherhood. I said you did, as soon as you pulled down your pants.'

> Priests who father children in the United States seem to be above the law [Cathy has written]. Cases of paternity drag on for ever and those who admit to paternity oftentimes do not care for their children.
>
> This is not corrected by the superiors of the priest, and the women/mothers are not cared for as sheep of the shepherds. Instead the women are scorned by Church members (both laity and clergy) and the man is permitted to 'go free' without fulfilling his obligation to fatherhood. . . .
>
> Priests who have children seem to be above the requirement of making restitution in order to receive absolution, and the continued public humiliation of the woman and child is overlooked. The women are intimidated by the misuse of God-given authority and are often offered a sum of money which is a tenth of what it takes to raise a child in today's world.[119]

In December 1988, Tineke Ferwerda, a Dutch woman who had had a clandestine relationship with an active priest, placed advertisements in the national press, asking other women with such relationships to write to her. She did it as part of her research for a diploma thesis on the topic. It was widely featured in the Dutch Press, and Cardinal Simonis said in an interview that he guessed there were no more than a hundred such cases in the Netherlands.[120]

However, Tineke already has nearly a hundred letters from such women, and these would only be the few willing to come forward.

THE LONG SHADOW

I called this chapter 'The Shadow Side of Celibacy'. When I was a boy, my father used to recite a ditty to my kid sister:

> There was a little girl
> Who had a little curl
> Right in the middle of her forehead.
> Now when she was good
> She was very very good:
> But when she was bad, she was horrid.

Celibacy is like that little girl. When it works, it works very well indeed, and redounds to the glory of God and the salvation of souls. But when celibacy does not work, it can be horrid.

The trouble is that celibacy is not chastity, as already pointed out in Chapter Two. Celibacy is merely the permanent state of being unmarried. Chastity, for any unmarried person, means abstaining from genital sexual activity. The tragedy begins when a priest is celibate but not chaste (which can easily happen when celibacy has not really been freely chosen by the priest).

That is when it becomes horrid. Celibacy without chastity is a failure, and it is horrid in the grief it brings to thousands of women around the world; horrid in the lifelong damage to children begotten and then denied by priests; horrid in the remorse of those priests or – more terrible still – in the seeming indifference, cowardice or hypocrisy of some of them.

But what has this to do with the story of priests who leave? And should it not be quietly passed over for fear of scandal? Firstly, it has everything to do with priests who leave: it is, in fact, an option they are rejecting when, in marriage, they publicly declare their relationship to a woman and their honest intention to become parents and to found a family.

Secondly, when one realises the sheer enormity of rejection of compulsory celibacy by clergy around the world, it becomes evident our Church is living a lie, and that compulsory celibacy simply does not work. The hundred thousand priests who left and married are simply the tip of the iceberg: figures given later in this chapter suggest perhaps twice as many again may have left inwardly, at least in the matter of celibacy. An American psychologist, a practising Catholic, wrote to me as follows:

> I have mentioned your book to a few trusted friends and all encourage you to deal with this issue. One priest said to me that the book would have 'no validity' if you did not address this concern.
>
> The more I think of it, it is 'the secret everybody knows about'. Some incidents have got a lot of publicity and Catholics are 'scandalised'. It used to be that priests leaving the ministry were the ones who were accused of 'scandalising' the people. There are times that homosexual priests, sexually active priests, priests having relationships with married women, and priests who are sexually abusive of children, are more acceptable to the institutional church than those who legitimately leave and get married.
>
> A recent case in one diocese of a priest sexually abusing several boys was settled out of court by what they call a 'bag attorney' – one with a bag of money going around trying to buy secrecy or settlement. Several attorneys were enraged at the implications of the Church implicitly protecting such criminal offenders.
>
> It is inevitable that if you address this issue you will have those who stand in judgement of you, criticising you for recognising the problem, the reality. You will inevitably be labelled a muckraker.
>
> But you may want to remember judgements come out of fear, insecurity, vulnerability, and feeling threatened. Judgement is a form of projection – a way of coping with information we are very uncomfortable about. We project on to the other person a label, judgement, or criticism, in a

way that we can more comfortably deal with the reality and
our own discomfort and fears.

But the reality of the 'shadow side of celibacy' is obvious:
priests with one or several sexual relationships with women
or men, active priests who have children, priests who
sexually abuse boys or girls.[121]

The abuse of children, aggravated and abetted by secrecy, is a
story in itself, but beyond the scope of this book. Here I am
concerned rather with what has happened to women, as this is so
obviously celibacy's shadow side – the hidden cost of imposing it
indiscriminately on every priest. It is the price paid, or exacted,
by some priests who choose not to leave, yet do not, or cannot,
observe celibacy's demands. Some priests? How many? How
long a shadow does celibacy cast round the world?

• Germany's Catholic News Agency (KNA) on 30 January
1985, released the findings of a questionnaire administered to
the clergy in the Archdiocese of Cologne and answered by 27 per
cent of priests. No. 13 of the questionnaire asked if these men
believed 'a certain number of priests live celibacy only
outwardly, and that, hidden from public view, they evade
celibacy through numerous compromises [*die Zölibatsverpflich-
tung durch zahlreiche Kompromisse umgehen*].' Seventy-four
per cent of the diocesan priests and 88 per cent of the order
priests answered YES.[122]

• From Stephen Pfürtner, writing in the Catholic journal
Concilium: 'It is no longer a secret that at least part of the clergy
can no longer – for a variety of reasons – accept compulsory
celibacy. Have a few men, such as the Pope and bishops, really
the right to dispose of the lives of thousands of other men, even
against the convinced consciences of those men?'[123]

• Father William Wells, an active priest now fourteen years
ordained, writing in the Franciscan magazine, *St Anthony
Messenger*, says that 'mandatory celibacy has become the
millstone round the neck of the priesthood and is threatening to
destroy it.'[124] The law of celibacy, he says, is routinely flouted by
many priests, some of whom have secretly married and pass off
their wives as live-in housekeepers in the rectory. Others, he
reports, have taken lovers. The law, he feels, has also led to
'rampant psychosexual problems', including a huge increase in

reported cases of child molestation and a 'noticeable increase in the number of gay seminarians at Catholic divinity schools'.

• A committee of bishops has been established by America's National Conference of Catholic Bishops to examine the problem of sexual abuse by priests.[125]

• From an editorial in Britain's *Catholic Herald*, 8 May 1987: 'What is clear is that a blind eye is being turned to the large, indeed increasing, amount of unhappy priests and the very high incidents of homosexuality and drunkenness among clergy due, ultimately, to loneliness.'[126]

• From a letter by a former US military chaplain: 'In 197–, my endorsement as chaplain was pulled by the Military Ordinariate. I went through a lengthy battle . . . In one of my conversations with my military lawyer, he told me that this investigation of whether I was married or not had been broadened to determine whether other Catholic priests in the military were secretly married . . . My lawyer discovered that the general investigation of all Catholic priests showed evidence that some seventy Catholic priests in the Service were most probably secretly married . . . When this information was presented to the Chief of Chaplains' Office and to the Military Ordinariate, the OSI was told to dump the evidence and information.'[127]

RAMPARTS CRUMBLING

In the Netherlands, Father Pieter cycles home each evening from his pastoral assignment in the Diocese of Rotterdam. He wheels his bicycle up the pathway to the two front doors of the semi-detached where he lives. The doors are side by side, and his name is on the left-hand one. On the right-hand door his neighbour's name is clearly written: Jolanda van Rijn.

Father Pieter puts his key in the door and lets himself in. Inside, the walls are down and it is one house. Jolanda is already home: he kisses her on both cheeks and they start preparing supper together.

While researching this book, I stayed a week with Jolanda and Pieter. They reminded me of a wooden weather house I had as a child, where the Dutch boy with umbrella came out of his front door in wet weather, and the little Dutch girl came out her door in fine weather. But both doors opened on the one house.

I also talked with one of the Netherlands' most distinguished priests, a household name in his own country and a familiar name abroad. I shall call him Father Jan. Father Jan has given a great deal of himself to the Church and to other people. He has also had a relationship with a woman for nearly fifteen years.

'Karen and I decided not to share a house', he explained to me, 'and we both do our own housekeeping. We see each other five times a week, and we have Sundays together. We eat together Wednesdays and some other days. Nights together at either place.'

The relationship of Father Jan and Karen is fairly well known, but not spoken about. 'People tend to ignore things that they cannot put into categories,' Jan says. 'They can understand clear, fixed social forms like monastery or marriage. Anything else they sort of look past it, without seeing or wanting to see.'

I listened as Jan and a priest colleague discussed how many other priests had relationships with women. They agreed on between 10 and 20 per cent – 'but that's just guessing,' said the colleague.

How many couples do you know personally, I asked Father Jan?

He started counting on his fingers. I watched him move down the fingers of one hand, then across to the other hand. He paused. Then he started on the first hand again. He looked up: 'Could I write to you later about this? I'd like to get the figures right.'

Later I got a letter from Jan, giving a total of twenty-five.

'But let's not call them clandestine relationships,' a celibate Arnhem priest said to me. 'It's insulting: to say that, is to deprecate both persons, and to use the oppressive language of Rome.' Another Dutch priest, himself unattached, believes it is a lot better to have a steady relationship with one woman, than to be messing about with several, as is not infrequently the case, he says.

Yet it is perceived as far from ideal. It is natural for a woman to want to be acknowledged publicly as a man's spouse. And if children come, the situation can often become intolerable.

Some priests leave and marry when a long-standing relationship reaches the point where a child is conceived, or when a woman has had enough of secrecy and tells her man to acknowledge her or break it off. 'There is a very deep feeling in most women that the relationship should be public,' Father Jan says. 'I think there comes a point not to live beyond, or to marry.'

One of the most famous secret relationships in the Netherlands is that of Father Willem Berger and Henriëtte Röttgering. So how could a secret relationship be famous? Simple: it used to be secret; now it's famous.

Father Berger is a priest of the Diocese of Haarlem. Until he retired a couple of years ago, he was professor of the psychology of religion at Nijmegen University, where he also taught pastoral psychology. For the past twenty-five years Father Willem has lived in an intimate relationship with Henriëtte Röttgering. She was presented to the world as his housekeeper and secretary. If the relationship was a secret, it was an open sort of one. 'It had been known to all the leading priests and people of my diocese,' he tells me. 'There was a kind of silent agreement – we know, but without speaking about it. A lot of the priests came to our home for meals.' And for years he has been a consultant to his diocese.

Then suddenly in 1981, Willem and Henriëtte went public about their relationship. In an interview with *De Tijd* magazine, they told their whole story from start to finish. 'I'm sticking my neck out,' Berger told the magazine.[128]

Why did they choose to go public after all those years? Berger tells me it was the 1980 Special Synod of Dutch bishops that changed his mind. The bishops had come back from three weeks with the Pope and had announced that, since the reasons for compulsory celibacy were self evident, there was no need for further discussion. Celibacy was the only possible life style for priests, they had said.

'To me, the Dutch bishops were breaking a solemn promise,' Berger says. Ten years before, they had undertaken to continue to press the Dutch case for optional celibacy, so Berger now decided to speak out in the most effective way he knew.

I heard in the Netherlands that it was Henriëtte who finally pushed him to go public. In an interview at the time, she said she had suffered terribly from the secrecy. 'If you love each other, you want to share it with everybody,' she said. She described those early years together as 'a black time, of which I prefer not to think again. It's past.'

Willem and Henriëtta are now married.

ALL SUFFER

More than anyone, it is the woman who gets hurt. But a priest
too can suffer hugely from remorse. Take this letter, from a
dying French priest to his bishop:

> Forgive my miserable cowardice in writing to you anony-
> mously, but to do so otherwise would cost me enormous
> effort. . . .
> I am now a seventy-two-year-old priest, seriously ill and
> condemned to die with a cancer – one or two months to live,
> they tell me. So I *must* write this letter to tell you the
> truth. . . .
> Father, I am a wretched man: twenty years ago, in the
> name of my vocation and in accordance with our consec-
> rated way of life, I abandoned a woman in a cowardly
> fashion. Despite great difficulties in her life, she found a way
> to help me . . . My priestly pride, my cowardice before the
> rule of the Church, meant that I broke everything off, not
> wanting even to offer her a word or a sign of friendship.
> Today, lucid and imagining what suffering my action
> must have caused her, I regard myself as the most unworthy
> of priests. Furthermore, I have never been able to retract
> this cowardice because the person concerned died four
> years afterwards. Since then I have been a bad priest, torn
> between the words that I preach and my own conduct. . .
> Many people do not want the Church to remain rigidly
> adhering to rules which have nothing in common with the
> Gospel of Jesus Christ. You have sacrificed generations, but
> the present generation cannot be thus annihilated – men
> and women loving the Christian life, concerned for the
> value of human love and friendship. The greatest gift
> written in the hearts of men, above all for the future.
> Father, in the name of obedience and the rule of celibacy,
> I am dying with the greatest distrust for myself and for my
> priestly life. I haven't borne loyal and faithful witness for
> Christ Jesus, from the very moment when I behaved in such
> a cowardly manner towards another human being who
> trusted me.
> Father, pray for me. Help those others who are in the
> same position as me, to have the courage to be honest men –
> the only way to find the Lord and peace for the soul, while
> waiting for the Church to revise her position on imposed
> celibacy.
> This letter will make amends. A very tiny reparation at

the end of a life, and a duty that I owe to this person's family
and her son, who have, in spite of everything, maintained a
charitable contact with me. This confession cannot tarnish
all the respect that I have for you. My extreme physical
tiredness cannot diminish the faith that I have in you –
despite our rare and rather distant meetings.[129]

● Missionaries in Peru tell me they estimate that 80 per cent of
local priests live with women. But, one says, there is no way it
could be otherwise. 'The whole Andean culture is built around
the concept of the *pareja*, the couple. Everything goes in couples
– animals, the sun and the moon. There are even two mountains,
male and female. The word for a single guy is *mula*, a mule.

'And up in the mountains, authority depends on having a
family. You can't be celibate and be a community leader: you
can't be established if you don't have a wife and children. The
culture does not respect celibacy, because a man is expected to
shoulder responsibility, and that means the responsibility of a
family.'

● In Brazil a group of native priests inform me they estimate
that between 60 and 70 per cent of native Brazilian priests have
some sort of liaisons with women. A great many of those would
be permanent relationships. A missionary told me he thought
one in three missionaries would have their women.

● Journalist Tim Unsworth, who writes in the *National Catholic Reporter*, informs me that Cardinal Sin in the Philippines is
closing his eyes to 50 per cent of his priests living with women. I
myself met with a group of Filipino priests who thought this a
conservative estimate.

'In my deanery,' one of them told me, 'practically every priest
is involved deeply with women.' He explained that rural priests'
houses are always full of relatives and extended family. 'When I
was newly ordained, I always took for granted that the kids
playing round the rectory were the priest's nieces and nephews.
It was only later I realised they were his children. They are not
introduced as the priest's children, and the wife is never
affirmed. She is introduced as an aunt or a sister. It's a pitiful
situation for her and the children.

'The parish sends the children to the local school, and
supports them. The people are hesitant to give to the collection,

because they know its going to support the children. That's why collections in the Philippines are so small.'

One Filipino priest told me he asked his bishop why he tolerated what he knew was going on.

'What else can I do?' the bishop replied. 'I need these priests. They are all I have.'

• A missionary, returned from working in Zaïre, tells me that all local priests in the diocese where he worked have fathered children. All have their women. 'I would not say a woman, but women,' the missionary says. 'In African culture, if you are somebody you have two wives. Sometimes four or five. Now a priest is a man of honour: if he has two or more wives, no problem whatsoever. But the problem is, the priest cannot marry officially. The women usually stay on the mission, have little huts near it. Everyone knows it – the bishop, the chief – it's common knowledge.'

Some of the missionaries also have their women, this priest told me. There was one priest who returned home to Holland, leaving behind a native woman and their child. One winter's day, some years later, she arrived unannounced at Brussels Airport, with her eight-year-old son. This simple African woman, who had never been outside her village, must have been of sterling character. She had collected money from all her relatives, to enable her to go and seek out her man. She had negotiated the various airports and airlines to reach Brussels, and had managed to contact him in Holland when she arrived.

He found mother and son shaking with cold in their wispy cotton clothes, and sent them right back where they came from.

He continues to minister as a priest in Holland.

• Luis Kaserer, native of Bolzano in Italy, was a Mill Hill missionary priest working in Zaïre in 1982. He was living on his own at the mission station. Then came Brigitte, a Dutch nurse, who was also sent to live and work at the mission station. 'I was very much afraid,' Luis told me. 'How were we going to survive in the middle of the forest, me with a person as beautiful as that?'

They were left alone together on that mission for one and a half years.

'Yet I must say, when we found a baby was on the way, it was a big shock,' Luis says.

The couple went to break the news to the bishop, and to ask if they could stay on at the mission. The bishop said that Brigitte would have to go. Tell the mission her parents in Holland are seriously ill, and she has to return home, he suggested. 'Don't let yourself be troubled by a girl like that,' was his private counsel to Luis.

A few days later the couple got back to the mission. 'All the villages had heard Brigitte was pregnant,' Luis says. 'They had prepared a big reception for us. Everybody had come from miles round: there were lots of gifts, and congratulations for Brigitte and me.'

Then the elders of the village took Luis aside to inform him of his change of status, due to fatherhood. 'You are no *mwana* [child] any more. You are *ngolo* now,' they told him. That meant he was now a real adult, a person of weight in the village. If a *ngolo* talks, people are supposed to listen.

The villagers held a meeting of the parish council, which wrote a letter to the bishop, asking him not to send the couple away, as they were doing so much good in the district. 'To have a child in Africa is the most essential thing,' the letter said.

But Luis and Brigitte were sent away. They are now married in Holland.

A couple of years later Luis's identical twin, Konrad, also a Mill Hill missionary in Zaïre, met and left to marry an American girl who had come to work on the mission.

• I know of an Irish woman who went to Galway Races, and had a fabulous week-long affair with a handsome middle-aged man whom she met in her hotel there. Some years later she was passing through a town in the Irish midlands, and attended Sunday Mass. Presiding at the Mass was that handsome stranger – the local monsignor.

• We are told that the Church in Poland is flourishing, and it is a fact that one in three priests ordained in Europe is Polish. About this flourishing Church a young Polish woman spoke to a meeting of the Advent group in London. I quote from the group's bulletin:

> She recounted that her experience, back home, was that any priest who decided that he would marry the woman he loved, was banished, along with his loved one. But if he said nothing, life went along as before, and his children went to school with all the other villagers' children. Everybody just accepted the situation. With Vatican 'intelligence' superior

even to the CIA's, no one can say that John Paul II is
unaware. *Qui tacet, consentit* [Silence is consent]. Or, how
double can your standards get?[130]

My own experience bears out what the woman says. A few years
ago I became friendly with a small group of young Polish priests,
who were studying in Ireland. Although I had long been married,
these men were amused at what they considered my naivety
about celibacy. Their attitude was, quite simply, that no one
takes celibacy seriously nowadays. You stay in the priesthood,
do whatever good you can, and discreetly avail yourself of the
readiness of devoted, admiring women to make themselves
sexually available.

That was several years ago. However, I have just completed an
interview with another young Polish priest who ministers in a
city diocese in Poland. He explained to me why he and some
colleagues have no problem with breaking the rule of celibacy.

'Compulsory celibacy is just a human law,' he said. 'Everyone
knows it's going to change eventually. So why should our lives be
spoiled by something that's going to change in twenty years
time? Also, in our case here in Poland, the [civil] law is corrupt
since the first day we are born. Equality, for example, exists only
on paper. What you can do, what you can get away with, that's
the main thing. Celibacy is no different.'

But, I asked, could not a woman get hurt when a priest
behaves like that?

'The woman knows what she is getting into. Just like a woman
who gets involved with a married man. She knows we cannot
leave to marry, and she goes into it with her eyes open. So she
deserves what she gets.

'For us, it's far more seriously wrong to leave and marry, than
to have your woman. That's something that has come down to
us from the partisans during the war. When people's lives
depended on you as a partisan, it was treason to leave just to
marry a woman. But to have a woman on the side, when you're a
partisan, no trouble.

'It's the same for a priest today. We're still fighting a war.'

My Aunt Mary, who disapproves of my writing this book,
responds to items like the above by saying, well, some of those
foreign countries are a bit peculiar. Especially America – they've
been daft there for years, my aunt believes. In America, they say,

well what can you expect from places like Brazil? In Brazil they say the Europeans never had any morals anyway.

The fact is, as the above items will bear out, that no place is virginal in this matter. And it would be a mistake to lay most of the erring at the door of native clergy, wherever in the world. Peruvian mountain attitudes may explain Peruvian habits, but how can we explain similar habits in squeaky-clean suburban dioceses of, say, the United States?

FIVE LEVELS

In talking with active serving priests in many parts of the world, I have found five levels of relationships with women.

Firstly, there is the priest with a deep and lasting friendship with a woman, but without genital sex. Such friendships can bring immense consolation and maturing to the individual priest, and benefit to the Church.

The second level of involvement would be like the previous one, but with occasional physical sex. In totally celibate friendships, sexual attraction would be a normal and healthy development, even when not acted out. But the best people are human, and sometimes things happen.

Thirdly, there are priests with a permanent sexual relationship with one woman. A lover, a mistress, a common-law wife – call it what you will. Sometimes it's hidden for years. Sometimes the whole world knows, even the bishop, but chooses not to notice.

Fourthly, there is the priest who, from time to time, has sexual friendships with different women. Such various liaisons can run (to use a term from jail-sentencing) consecutively or concurrently.

Lastly, there is the priest who uses his Roman collar as a tomcat uses his miaow, to charm all the women he can, and to lure them to bed – and then uses his collar a second time round, to break his relationship or evade his responsibilities ('I'm a priest and I've got to end this' or 'I'm a priest, so you'll have to look after that brat on your own'). These are the Elmer Gantrys of the Roman Catholic Church.

A prolonged encounter with priests in this last category is described here by a young married woman, somewhere in the United States. She had been in an unhappy marriage for some years, had two children and an unfaithful husband. The local pastor, whom she calls Father X, gave her a job as housekeeper, and became her lover. She put this on paper for me after I had met and interviewed her.

Father X took good care of me. Besides my salary as housekeeper, I received quite a bit of extra money from the Church collection. He took many small bills from the Sunday evening Mass collection when the money counters were not round. He bought me clothes, took me to nice restaurants, anticipated needs that I had forgotten I had. On days off we went camping or, if the weather was bad, went to motels.

When Father X was away I was the pastor. I gave out the information for the bulletins, wrote the parish letters, stole the $1 bills from the 6.30 collection, opened and took care of his mail, etc.

In our parish there was an assistant pastor . . . Father Y. He always made passes at me but I never returned the favour. One time when Father X was in another state, Father Y had just been dumped by a true love. He was extremely depressed. I tried to cheer him up by cooking for him, reading to him, playing cards . . . whatever. One day we were playing gin rummy and he made the bet that if he won he would rape me and if I won I would rape him. I thought that was real funny. He won. He raped me.

When Father X came back I told him about it. He got on the phone to the personnel board to have Father Y removed. I heard him say, 'Get rid of Jacko – he's up to his old tricks again.'

It wound up that we all stayed. I made love to both of them (at different times). I separated from my husband. He took my older child and I stayed in our home with the baby. Somehow, the two priests became friends. X didn't know I was 'seeing' Y; Y knew I was seeing X, but didn't care. We became a threesome.

There were parties. All the priests of the inner sanctum would have parties at least once a month – sometimes in the rectories – sometimes in their mistresses' houses. I noticed that there were different types of relationships. Some were truly married in spirit and would never think of being unfaithful. Most were stringing along many women.

It was an exciting time for me . . . and it was a lie. I discovered that Father X was seeing other women when he was [supposed to be] making hospital visits or playing golf.

I called the other women. It was ugly. Some very hurtful things happened.

Father X came out of the whole mess unscathed. I came out with nothing – no parish, no reputation, no money, no love.

I accept responsibility for my involvement with these two priests. I needed love and took it from the wrong people.[131]

With this woman's permission I asked her psychotherapist what credence I could give to the above document. He said it was to be believed.

When I read my five categories of relationships to a respected monsignor in that woman's diocese, this was his response: 'Your categories are accurate. But the last category is far more prevalent than we'd like to admit. I wonder if 25 per cent or so would not be abusing women genitally in this diocese. But there are many ways of abusing the collar to hurt women – by its authority, as much as by direct sex. I wonder if another 25 per cent of them are using the collar to abuse women by lording it over them.'

In one US city, I interviewed a Catholic psychologist who does a large amount of advisory and counselling work for the local diocese, and allowed me to use her information on the understanding the diocese be never identified. The following are extracts from several conversations with this woman, later confirmed by a monsignor of the diocese and by a seventy-year-old priest, also of the diocese.

Q. I have heard a great deal about priests being involved with women in this diocese. Are you aware of it?

A. 'I am personally aware of a considerable number. I had a girl in this office this week who told me she had had sex in every rectory in this city.'

Q. Did you believe her?

A. 'Yes, I did. From what I have learned professionally elsewhere, yes, I have reason to believe her. From what I learned in terms of comment to me here in this office, at least 50 per cent of the priests in this diocese have ongoing relationships with a woman. I have no doubt about that. And other priests here have confirmed this for me.'

Q. Do you have direct knowledge of this?

A. 'Over the last few years, I have had many priests and their girlfriends in here for counselling. So I do have direct knowledge. Also it is recognised that certain priests come to public functions now with their women. People do not judge. But it hurts me deep down, because I know. I have an opportunity to know these priests' loneliness, but what has surprised me in the last few years is how public it has all become.

'I see a lot of priests and nuns, and I can tell you that there are many priests with one, two or three relationships going on at one time. And there is a trend now for priests to get their own apartment away from the church. A part of that may be their need for privacy, but from what I now know, it can imply other things.'

That is just one diocese. Perhaps others are different. I wonder, however, because of the amount of grief I have encountered among priests and women in the twenty-three other US dioceses I visited. Nor was it hearsay. I have had the children on my knee, and talked with their mothers – and their fathers. Mostly I found them good and dedicated priests, shattered, along with their women, by the rule of compulsory celibacy.

Statistics are understandably hard to come by. But there are some. Richard Sipe is a married priest who holds a teaching appointment as lecturer in the Department of Psychiatry at Johns Hopkins Medical School, Baltimore. He has concluded a twenty-five-year study, using 1,500 informants, of the practice, process and achievement of clerical celibacy, which is to be published in mid-1990.* Celibacy, for the purpose of the study, was defined as 'a freely chosen state, usually vowed, that involves an honest and sustained attempt to live without direct sexual gratification in order to serve others productively for a spiritual motive (in response to grace)'. Sipe obviously takes celibacy as meaning not just unmarried, but being chaste as well. However, he believes his definition allows for human frailty, without compromising essential integrity by denial or rationalisation.

In an address delivered in Washington DC, 17 June 1988, Sipe summarised the results of the study as follows:

> I estimate that at any one time no more than 50 per cent of American priests practise celibacy. No more than 2 per cent

---

*From Sipe, A. W. R. *The Search for Celibacy: Practice, Process, and Achievement*. To be published in New York by Brunner/Mazel. Used with permission.

of clergy have, with certainty, achieved celibacy without any major impediment, with an additional 3 to 6 per cent relatively well enough established in celibate practice to say they have achieved it.

These figures are not an indictment of good men struggling to reach an ideal. Nor are they a critique of that minority who may not give a damn and use their priesthood as a cover for sexual indulgence. What they form, rather, is a serious invitation to the Church to face important questions. What is celibacy? How is it practised? What is the process? How does one achieve sexual identity without sexual experiences? How does one remain celibate after sexual experience? How is celibacy achieved?[132]

Sipe's study also indicates that about 20 per cent of priests have ongoing sexual liaisons ('this is low', Sipe says, 'compared to some other cultures where the estimates run above 50 per cent'). Another 8 to 10 per cent have occasional affairs.

If Sipe's figures were to be matched on a worldwide basis, we would be talking of well over 200,000 priests failing to observe celibacy, to add to the 100,000 who have already left and married.

Until recently, Sipe reports, fewer than 20 per cent of clergy were of homosexual orientation or undetermined in orientation, of which one-fourth, or 5 per cent of total clergy, had a regular homosexual partner and another seven per cent had periodic sexual acting out with a number of partners. However, Sipe comments, reports of homosexual activity have increased significantly since 1978, in some areas closer to 40 per cent, if one isolates the figures from 1978 to 1985.

This growth in both homosexual orientation and activity, particularly in certain seminaries and among some newer priests, I have found to be a talking point among clergy throughout the world. Two different bishops acknowledged their awareness and concern about it to me – one of them being Dom Helder Camara. No one quite understands the reasons for the trend, but it cannot be too glibly blamed on compulsory celibacy, since some Protestant denominations, even with married clergy, are encountering the same phenomenon.

But there are connections. As Richard P. McBrien puts it in the review *Commonweal*: 'It is not inconceivable that the ordained priesthood is attractive to certain people precisely because it excludes marriage. To put it plainly: as long as the Church requires celibacy for the ordained priesthood, the priesthood will always pose a particular attraction for gay men who are otherwise not drawn to ministry,' because, he says, it gives them, 'occupational respectability and freedom from social suspicion.'[133]

In this regard I have in several places encountered a fear of what is called the 'snowball effect' – young heterosexuals entering the seminary, and then being turned off by the gay culture they find there. So they quit, thus leaving the field to the gays. And while a truly chaste homosexual ought not to be barred from ordination, a Church that became overwhelmingly homosexual in its clergy would hardly be acceptable to the heterosexual population.

DEVIL'S SIEVE

This is a sad chapter, but it has to be written. The material collected here surely points to one thing: compulsory celibacy does not work. And it is being rejected by priests all around the world. Silence has been imposed by Rome, but these men are voting with their feet, or whatever.

Heinz-Jürgen Vogels has written a treatise on compulsory celibacy entitled, *The Devil's Sieve*. It is an apt title.[134] And it is a sieve through which relatively few pass.

'By their fruits you shall know them,' Jesus said, and the fruits of compulsory celibacy are those thousands of men leading double lives, thousands of women leading destroyed lives, thousands of children spurned by their ordained fathers, to say nothing of the priestly walking wounded, the psychiatric cases, the alcoholics and the workaholics, the grey lonely faces, the cars, the bars and the whores that make wretched the lives of so many priests of Jesus Christ. Only Satan could invent such a sieve for the priesthood.

The good and wonderful men, described in the previous chapter, who have achieved true celibacy in their lives, are no justification for compulsory celibacy. They do not even need it: their celibacy is a free choice, and such men, and women too, will always be with us.

To see compulsory celibacy as justified by its relatively sparse successes is to make the same mistake that Haig, Joffre,

Ludendorff and all the rest of the generals made in the First World War. From the trenches they cheerfully sent hundreds of thousands of men over the top to their deaths, so that a few survivors could succeed in taking the enemy placement. They had no problems with a massive casualty rate. Their proportions were wrong, their hearts were hard, and history has branded them as brutal buffoons. And so will history – and God – judge us, the Church, and our general staff in the Vatican, if we indulge in the same kind of thinking.

But do our men in the Vatican know?

• A document prepared for the bishops at the Second Vatican Council, by one of the Council's experts (or *periti*, as they were called), which has come into my possession, told the Council fathers of the large-scale abandonment of celibacy throughout the world, and that was over a quarter of a century ago. The document, still stamped SUB SECRETO, uses some graphic images:

> Rightly or wrongly, a good number of priests who are in the ministry are not free from accusations of immorality, have conducted themselves so notoriously that it is a torture and a trial to be a priest in some parts of the world. In the cases of at least some priests in all dioceses, not allowing them to marry is like not allowing them to go for their essential needs. They stifle the whole atmosphere with a bad and suffocating odour. 'Celibacy is like Prohibition in India,' said once an elderly priest to the writer. This may be an overstatement and yet how many can throw the first stone?[135]

These words were written for the bishops of the Vatican Council, and read by them. And then stamped 'secret' and quietly filed away.

Yes, our men in the Vatican know, and not from that document alone. They could write this chapter for me. Yet they are silent, and they seem to be very frightened.

It is not so certain how much is known to bishops around the world today. I shared Sipe's figures with Cardinal Hume when we met in November 1988, and it was clear to me that he was deeply shocked and distressed. I mentioned at the time that I was worried whether I should even publish such figures, for fear of the scandal they might cause. He thought for a few moments and then said quietly, 'Be objective. That's really all you can do.'

If bishops do not know, it is because no one is talking enough. 'Celibacy has become a lot like cancer,' says one US bishop, quoted by the *Chicago Tribune*. 'Too many bishops just don't want to talk about it, and hope that the problems associated with it will simply go away. But the conspiracy of silence is doing all of us more harm than good.'

According to Catholic psychologists I have worked with while researching this book, the silence of the Church can be understood in terms of **denial** and **secrets**.

Denial is one of the classic ways of dealing with unacceptable reality. It is, however, a primitive, immature and dysfunctional way of doing so. Refusing to recognise the 'shadow side' of celibacy is tantamount to such denial, which can occur not only in individuals but in organisations. The collective denial, by ourselves and our Church hierarchy, of the reality of celibacy's shadow side, is quite simply an immature response. The wretchedness and misery it brings down on the Church cannot be faced or cured as long as this denial continues.

The other way to understand Church silence is in terms of family secrets, as outlined in Napier and Whitaker's classic treatise, *The Family Crucible*.[136] There are certain kinds of family secrets that are bad for the family. Some secrets reflect a whole family in trouble, and those problems cannot be dealt with if kept under wraps and never discussed – problems like a parent's alcoholism, sexual abuse of the children, an extramarital affair, homosexuality in a parent or child. It is like having an elephant in the family room, with everyone walking round it and no one saying the elephant is there. There is the fantasy that if the secret or embarrassment is not discussed, it will go away. Instead, it makes things worse.

We have maintained secrets for many years about popes, bishops, and priests, and we hold on to those secrets until forced to deal with them by public outcry. But secrets in this great Family that is the Church, the Family bonded by Christ, are particularly destructive. They interfere with family communication, withhold essential information, and deny problems. The problems never get resolved, and the seeds of Church pathology, disturbance and discontent grow.

It was Carl Rogers, one of America's most respected psychologists, who said that to solve a problem one has first to own that problem and take responsibility for it.

It was Jesus who said, 'Woe to you Pharisees, who bind burdens on men's backs and will not stir a finger to lighten them.'

It was Pope John XXIII who said in 1963, shortly before his death, in a conversation with his old friend Etienne Gilson:

> Do you want me to tell you what is my greatest worry? I do not mean as a human being, but as a pope, I am continually vexed by the thought of those young priests who so courageously carry the burden of ecclesiastical celibacy. For some among them it is a martyrdom. Yes, a kind of martyrdom. It often seems to me that I hear a sort of complaint – from here, but from much farther – as if voices were asking the church to take that burden away from them.[137]

And it was Marianna, a young lay missionary working with Maryknoll in Brazil, who said, 'Anyway, if all those priests around the world were suddenly to acknowledge their relationships with women, compulsory celibacy would be a dead duck overnight.'

9

IN SEARCH OF A ROOT CAUSE

A Church that bears the name of Jesus, heeds his word, and is impelled by his Spirit, must never be identified with a particular class, caste, clique or bureaucracy.

Hans Küng

WHEN COLUMBUS SAILED for America, the Black Abbey in Kilkenny, Ireland, was already over 250 years old. Today, after almost eight centuries of existence, it still functions as a church. There is now a tiny oratory built on to it, which has a window looking down over the altar. This is where the priests of the church can come to pray.

During the late 1960s I knelt at that window, hour after hour, day after day, looking down at the tabernacle and praying for deliverance. Deliverance from what, I did not know. Often the only prayer I could think of was the one from the Garden, 'Let this chalice pass from me,' which I would literally say over and over. Nor, in my aloneness, did I know what I know now — that while I knelt there, thousands of other priests were kneeling in anguish in every corner of the world, most believing themselves totally alone in their unthinkable thoughts, and also praying for deliverance.

I have met hundreds of these men, and heard their stories of why they left. We now know from Chapter Two that there are as many reasons as the men who leave. Some sought deliverance from smothering authority; some could no longer preach certain things they did not hold; some left to marry.

But is there common ground? Just as scientists keep looking for some one thing that would unify and explain gravity, electromagnetism, the weak and the strong force, as a sort of key to the universe – on a more modest scale, I am seeking a key to the mutiny. In this chapter I want to ask if these can be reduced to one underlying reason, whereby so many thousands left in such a brief span of time, and are still leaving. Is there a root cause?

Terry Dosh believes it is the mid-twentieth-century discovery of freedom, the need for liberation. But from what are they seeking liberation?

Is it from a celibate life? Certainly, the desire to marry permeates many a decision to leave, and a loving relationship with a woman often seems to tip the scales. But there are indications of more underlying reasons.

An investigation by Father Andrew Greeley and Richard Schoenherr, published by the US bishops in 1972, found the most frequently mentioned, very important reason for priests leaving was 'a feeling that they could no longer live within the structure of the Church'.[138]

The English Dominican, Father Conrad Pepler, champion and friend to many priests who leave, would substantially agree with Greeley and Schoenherr, but appends an insight on why it is happening at this particular point:

> The fact that all these men are quite suddenly asking for dispensation must have a root cause and, as far as I can see, that cause is, indirectly, Vatican Two. The Council had raised hopes for a new, or at least a renewed, dynamism in mission and ministry. But they did not see much change in the general structure of the Church, so that instead of a new drive, an uncertainty about the nature and mission of the priesthood developed. The possibility of dispensation from the commitment to priestly vocation, hitherto practically unknown, seemed to offer an escape from these painful uncertainties.[139]

In sum, priests leave because they perceive the changes in thinking at Vatican Two have not been made concrete through parallel changes in structures. I would take this one step further, and suggest that the particular structure that irks most, and drives these priests out, is something called clericalism. It is a hypothesis that would need testing, but it seems to me, nearly two decades after Greeley's report, that almost all the reasons people give for leaving can be reduced ultimately to clericalism. And it explains why so many of these men insist they have not left the Church, nor the priesthood, nor even the ministry. The only other thing they could have left is the clerical condition. In this chapter I shall try to explain my theory.

CLERICALISM

What is this clericalism, and is it separable from the priesthood? Father Yves Congar describes it as a caricature of what priesthood should be.[140] The late Father Thomas Merton called it a caste: 'The discipline of the medieval church required a celibate, clerical caste,' he wrote. 'It can be argued that in the modern world such a caste is a liability. . . .'[141]

Clericalism is an elusive concept, hard to define, and it is easier to describe a lot of things about clericalism than to say what it is. Let me sketch a picture or two.

Once in the 1960s, when I was a priest in Kilkenny, Ireland, I returned late from Dublin. It was a long drive, and I had not eaten, so I went down to a stall in a nearby alleyway to buy fish and chips. The pubs had just closed, and there was a line of about twenty people waiting at the little mobile stall. The street lights in the alley had gone out and it was quite dark. I fell into conversation with the man in front of me. We exchanged the usual remarks on the weather, he told me a simple joke he had just heard in the pub, and I told him one in return. Just two men passing a few minutes in a friendly way.

As the line moved forward, the light from the stall suddenly fell on my Roman collar.

'Oh God,' said the man, 'I didn't know you were a priest, Father. I never knew priests liked chips, Father.' There was a long and painful pause. Then: 'Father, I hope I didn't say anything that, uh – well, I didn't know you were a priest, y'see, Father. Sorry about them jokes, Father.'

I tried to revive the conversation, but the rapport was shattered; the man was so embarrassed he could not look me in the eye. My collar had fulfilled its function superbly: once again it had cut me off from an ordinary human being.

That is the essence of clericalism: it is a kind of ecclesiastical apartheid, whereby priests are isolated from the rest of people. Whereas Jesus walked the roads among people, ate in their houses, sat by the well talking to a woman, the cleric is deliberately cut off from people and formed into a special caste.

The cutting off is accomplished by a number of different means. The most obvious is by dress. The wearing of black suits, skirt-like cassocks, the powerfully symbolic collar – clothing cuts the man off in several distinct ways.

Firstly, it sets very distinct limits on his behaviour. Secondly, it controls how people perceive him and thus controls their behaviour towards him. The lack of that powerful symbol, the tie, says much to people. So does being dressed in skirts (remember the term, 'unfrocked'?). I remember hearing that in Ireland, when men first began wearing buttoned flies on their trousers, priests' trousers had no flies for many years. That must indeed have created certain ambivalent perceptions about the priest.

But more than anything else, his dress controls how the priest perceives the world round him. People's behaviour changes the instant they recognise the cleric in their midst, which means that he can never see people as they really are, except if he happens to queue for chips in a dark alleyway. 'Say goodbye to the truth, M'Lord,' someone said to an Irish bishop on the day of his consecration. 'You'll never hear it again.' But, sure, he hadn't heard it since he was ordained, anyway.

Let there be no doubt that apartheid was intended for all clerics and religious – priests, brothers and nuns. The Christian Brothers' rule prohibited them 'from frequent and unnecessary conversations with seculars', and 'from engaging in political conversations with assistant [lay] teachers'. The Sisters of Mercy required their members to avoid 'unnecessary secular intercourse', and the Presentation Sisters had this rule: 'When spoken to by men, of any state or profession, they shall observe and maintain the most guarded reserve, never fix their eyes on them, nor show themselves, in conversation or otherwise, in the least degree familiar with them, how devout or religious soever they may be.'[142] If Mary and Martha had been Presentation Nuns, they'd have had a hard time dealing with Jesus.

The seminary was the great breeder of clerical apartheid. In the wake of the Reformation, the sixteenth-century Council of Trent set out to make the priest a creature apart, and education was the means. The child was to be got before the world had tainted him, and he was to be raised totally apart.

In many parts of the world, boys as young as eleven, sometimes even nine, were taken into the seminary, dressed in little cassocks, and reared apart from the world. 'Cradle-snatching' was the contemptuous term we Irish priests reserved for it — hardly realising that entering seminary at sixteen or seventeen, as we had done, was not much better.

Cradle-snatching is not ended: Don Razotti, rector of the seminary in Reggio Emilia, Italy, told me in 1987 that they still accept eleven-year-olds: 'They end up clearer about what a vocation is, and clearer about the function of a priest,' he explained to me.

'Then I question the validity of their ordination,' was Mary-knoller Father Dan McLaughlin's comment when I told him about it.

Leo Bartemeyer, who was president of the International Psychoanalytical Association, and later president of the American Psychiatric Association, Catholic and friend of many churchmen, had this to say about slightly less extreme practices:

> We take promising young men from thirteen to twenty years of age, feed them well, educate them diligently, and eight to twelve years later we ordain them, healthy, bright, emotional thirteen-year-olds.[143]

Seminary education results in a phenomenon called foreclosure, whereby the life choices open to the young person are closed too soon. Psychologists believe that this can halt personal development, both emotional and intellectual, resulting in a too close identification of the person with his clerical profession. 'The seminary aim,' says psychologist Don Conroy, 'is to draw the person and his role so close that they cannot be separated. That's damaging.' I have already chronicled the consequent agonies when a man leaves the clerical state and attempts to separate person and role for the first time.

Military academies throughout the world have used seminary techniques (segregation from outside, fostering an elite mentality) to create officer castes.[144] But even officers can marry, and none of these castes depends on the incredible isolating factor of compulsory celibacy. That, more than anything else, is what sets the clerical caste apart. As Richard Sipe says, 'There is no other class . . . where part of their identity is defined by the sacrifice of their sexuality.'[145] The mechanisms necessary to preserve celibacy, at least in those for whom it is unsuited, serve to create barriers and defences against one-half of the human race, resulting in a quite horrendous apartheid.

CONTROL SYSTEM

What then is the clerical caste, and why has it come to be? All professions develop a distinct style: doctors have a recognisable way about them; lawyers have their own special way of talking. But clericalism is more than a style: it is something that enervates and suffocates and even destroys. It seems to be a kind of unintended growth upon the Church, a sort of cancer on the Body of Christ. It was not perpetrated by evil people, but crept up on good people.

A corps of professional ministers is, of course, necessary. 'Beliefs evoke structure,' as sociologist Max Weber pointed out.[146] All religions evolve some kind of administrative structure: a group of selected persons who are the guardians of the sacred event (which for Christians is the Resurrection), and who have the authority to teach and to defend it. Without them, there would be a chaos in beliefs.[147]

However, another sociologist, Robert K. Merton, has shown that professional groups, and especially bureaucracies, usually degenerate. They end up defending their entrenched interests, putting their own existence and, above all, the extension of their own power, before the needs of those they were founded to serve.[148]

I believe clericalism is such a degeneration. It is that part of our Church, of ourselves, that has turned away from serving God's people, from helping them reach God, and has set up the golden calf of power and control over others, before which it now bows down and worships.

Priests who leave are renouncing precisely that. And the men who stay, those who grow into mature and holy priests, spurn it with equal vehemence. When people perceive that the structures are impeding instead of helping them to reach God, then some sort of shattering of structures occurs. It happened to the Anglicans a couple of centuries ago, when John Wesley turned away from structures he regarded as holding people back from God.

Clericalism is, first and last, apartheid for the sake of control. The Turks once had their janissaries, Christian children taken by force, brought up in special seminaries to be fanatical celibate warriors for the Koran, never permitted to marry, totally controllable, going forth 'to slay the enemies of the Sultan and of Allah with the inflamed and contracted fanaticism of a monk,' as H. A. L. Fisher described them.[149] The Zulu King Chaka had a corps of celibate warriors, equally controllable and formidable. It works. And clericalism, likewise, has delivered total control, from the top to the bottom of the Roman Catholic Church.

Firstly, there has been control over the laity, by the elite corps of clerics whose apartheid both placed them on a pedestal and swathed their humanity in secrecy and mystery, and who could exact conformity by the fear of social disapproval, but even more by the fear of hell, diligently fostered in sermons at retreats and parish missions that were long remembered.

Far more importantly, within that corps there has been immense control by the higher over the lower clerics. The means of that control include fear, rewards, a tradition of unquestioning obedience and, above all, celibacy. The promise of obedience to the bishop made at ordination, combined with the belief that the superior's will was invariably the voice of God, left hardly any room for individual conscience. The cruelties and injustices chronicled in Chapter Four often stemmed from this – from what one active priest calls 'Eichmann theology'. The fears ranged from fear of hell for disobedience, to fear of unacceptable assignments and denied promotions, to that of destitution and of becoming a pariah if one left the ministry. An honours system, with titles like canon and monsignor, and a promotion system with ladders reaching to the highest level of hierarchy, took care of rewards. It had little to do with Christ's counsel about seeking the lowest place at the table, but it had a great deal to do with control.

Celibacy, of course, has been the control factor *par excellence*. Bachelors are, quite simply, easier to manage. There is no family to care for or to pay for; there is no wife to counsel disobedience or to stiffen resolve; there is no danger of nepotism or of children inheriting Church property, which was a very real problem for the Irish Church during the centuries after St Patrick. 'Clerical celibacy', says John P. Dolan, in his *History of the Reformation*, 'was in many respects the final phase in the moulding of a sacerdotal caste system, that came to identify the Church with the clergy rather than with the entire body of believers. It formed an inseparable barrier between the layman and the clergy.'[150] Divide and conquer. And control.

It was Eugene Kennedy who said, if you can control a man sexually, you can control the whole man. Eunuchs have been around for centuries, and even the Turks knew they made for easier administration. There is nothing to get caught in the ecclesiastical machinery.

It is little wonder that a famous book on management reckoned the Roman Catholic Church as one of the three most efficient organisations in history – the other two being General Motors and the nineteenth-century Prussian Army. But at a price higher than anything ever paid by the people of Detroit or Prussia: at the bottom, a clergy submissive, fearful and solitary; at the top, a hierarchy and Curia answerable to no one.

BY THEIR FRUITS

There is a scene in *Barchester Towers*, Trollope's satire on nineteenth-century Anglican clericalism, where the simple and godly old pastor asks Archdeacon Grantly what Jesus might say about certain local ecclesiastical shenanigans.

'This has nothing to do with Jesus Christ!' snaps the Archdeacon.

Right he is. And neither has clericalism anything to do with Jesus Christ: although it has a lot to do with the Pharisees he denounced for seeking to lord it over people instead of serving them.

Christ provides the ultimate test, 'By their fruits ye shall know them.' What are the fruits of clericalism? And while assessing them, let us remember that clericalism is not the Church, but rather something that is trying to hijack it. The following are some of its fruits:

I. **Clericalism first, Church second.**

The clerical institution puts its own survival first, and the needs of the People of God second. Just one instance: because of a

shortage of priests, thousands upon thousands of parishes round
the world do not have the Mass, the centrepoint of the Faith. If
priests could marry, sociologists estimate that vocations alone
would quadruple. But faced with a choice between the Eucharist
for which people are crying out, and obligatory celibacy, which
might shore up clericalism, the institution opts for celibacy, and
will not permit even discussion on it. Bare altars, priestless
communities and hungry sheep are thus among the fruits of
clericalism.

Northern Ireland yields another tragic instance of this phenomenon. In that unhappy province, Protestant and Catholic
children still attend separate schools, thus ensuring they never
meet each other. It almost guarantees a perpetuation of mutual
incomprehension and tribal hatreds. Yet Catholic Church authorities resolutely oppose mixed-religion schools, even refusing to
appoint a chaplain to an experimental non-denominational
school. Of course, mixed-religion schooling would bring inter-
marriage, and that would mean a loss of Church control. (In
fairness let it be said that Protestant Church authorities are
equally opposed to mixed schooling, for the same reasons.)
II. **Suppression of truth.**
Both suppression of truth and of the freedom to think and
communicate, in the end drives out many priests. Galileo was
only the most famous case of such suppression: today we have
Hans Küng, Leonardo Boff and Charles Curran. The late Karl
Rahner, accepted now as one of the century's greatest theologians, was ordered to submit his every word for scrutiny by the
clerics of the Vatican: 'these ghastly bonzes,' as he called
them.[151]

Only a couple of years ago, Jesuit Terrance Sweeney wrote to
all US bishops to ask their views on optional celibacy. One-
quarter of those who replied were favourable, but Sweeney was
ordered by the clerics of Rome to drop his research *and suppress
his findings.*[152] He resigned rather than do so. In Brazil, Eduardo
Hoornaert has been compiling a summa of liberation theology;
Rome has attempted to suppress it.[153]
III. **A paranoidal secrecy.**
Many priests say this has driven them out of the clerical corps.
'You cannot have both secrecy and accountability,' as I. F. Stone
says. Just as civil regimes use official secrets acts to cover up
ineptitude or wrongdoing, citing state security, the clerical

institution cites the danger of scandal, and shrouds its every deed and misdeed in the deepest silence. Christ's Church is not a nuclear power: what need has it of security and secrecy?

After the 1987 Synod, Canadian Archbishop Donat Chiasson spoke of 'Vatican civil servants obsessed with secrecy. What do we have to hide from people with whom we feel communion?' he asked, adding that he felt deceived by a system that makes real dialogue impossible.[154]

IV. Legalism.

The clerics have replaced the Bible with the Code of Canon Law: in the past it has often been the Church lawyers, who creep and intrude and climb into the Fold, who are the quintessential clerics. Legalism is the sin of the Pharisees – putting mechanical obedience to regulations above the human needs of people, whom those rules were meant to serve. Many a dedicated priest has been alienated by such legalism and by the little games of the lawyers, as was Anthony Kenny, now a distinguished philosopher and Master of Balliol College, Oxford. In his autobiography, *A Path from Rome*, he describes the legalism surrounding Mass offerings:

> If a lay person wishes a priest to offer Mass for a particular intention, he should offer the priest a stipend for doing so. Canon lawyers explained, in a way that was again mysterious, that though acceptance of a stipend was not simony (the exchange of money for a spiritual benefit) it did set up contractual obligations . . .
>
> Most of the Masses said by priests in Rome were offered in return for stipends from distant and anonymous sources, especially in America . . . To avoid the complicated bookkeeping which would be necessary if the intention of each benefactor was spelt out, we used to offer the masses . . . 'for the intention of the giver'. . . .
>
> I began to ask myself the question: since the donor's name was not preserved, nor the actual dollar bill he had handed over, was there an identifiable donor, known even to God? The more I thought about it, the more obnoxious the whole practice began to seem.[155]

It was similar legalism that led the Archbishop of Lund in 1213 to ask Pope Innocent III whether a man who had two concubines was ineligible to be ordained priest.[156] He was told that concubinage did not stand in the way of ordination.

It is a comparable legalism today that says that absolution by a priest is invalid if he moves a couple of yards outside the boundary of the diocese where he has permission to hear confessions.

Surely, it is legalism to say that the marriage of two Catholics is no marriage at all if the local parish priest or another priest sent by him is not present as witness (even though the essence of marriage is a public exchange of vows).

It was legalism too that allowed priests in the thirteenth century to live with a woman provided they paid a 'whore-tax'[157]; it was legalism that in our time allowed meat on Friday in Spain, on payment of a money offering.

It was legalism that invented limbo for infants who had not had water poured on their heads – a limbo now quietly closed down again.

It is legalism today that is playing games with priests' lives and declaring their children bastards by withholding dispensations even after years of marriage, and it is undoubtedly legalism that is the cause of those violations of human rights, which were outlined in Chapter Four.

However, in fairness it must be said that today some canon lawyers are in the forefront of change. In a few instances they are ahead of theologians and bishops, even if there are still others who remain steeped in legalism (see Chapter Twelve).

V. **Anti-feminism.**

The clerical caste is notorious for its hostility to women. It ranges from the quite pathetic banning of girls from serving Mass, to the refusal even to discuss the ordination of women, to the cow syndrome mentioned earlier, where women are used sexually and then discarded for the sake of the institution.

There is still the exclusion of women from any power position whatsoever outside of convents. There is the totally male domination of the Catholic Church, where males make the rules even in what concerns women most intimately. This is sexism: it is rooted deep in the need to defend celibacy, and has a long clerical history. It goes as far back as St John Chrysostom, who said in the fourth century, 'Among all savage beasts, none is found as harmful as woman', and St Thomas Aquinas, who said in the thirteenth, 'Woman is defective and accidental . . . a male gone awry . . . the result of some weakness in the father's generative power.'

Sexism has been roundly condemned by US Bishops Balke and Lucker in a 1981 pastoral letter:

> When anyone believes that men are inherently superior to women . . . then he or she is guilty of sexism. Sexism is a moral and social evil. It is not the truth of the biological, sociological or psychological sciences, nor is it the truth of the Gospel. Sexism is a lie. It is a grievous sin, diminished in its gravity only by indeliberate ignorance or by pathological fear.[158]

The sexism of the clerical caste is, of course, rejected by many priests. Some have left on account of it. Others have stayed and formed an international group to combat clerical sexism. Called Priests for Equality, the group has publicly asked pardon of the Church's women, adding: 'Our personal apologies for the gender discrimination of our Church cannot remedy the hurts and anger which you feel when a community that proclaims its following of Christ clings to discriminatory, authoritarian and patriarchal structures that violate the spirit and witness of Jesus. We understand, in our own way, the feelings which might urge you to leave the community and seek other, less painful, ways of worshipping God.'[159]

VI. Thinking from the top down.

Clericalism does much of its thinking purely from theory, deducing from first principles, without putting it to the test of experience. It then imposes its conclusions on ordinary people, trying to control their behaviour in ways that their everyday experience tells them are wrong. Thus we find a celibate male clericalism dictating what behaviour should or should not take place in the bedroom, which would be funny if it were not for the misery it causes. Archbishop Rembert Weakland of Milwaukee, writing in *America* magazine, expresses an awareness of this danger:

> Among the many practical concrete options open politically and socially at a given moment of history, it cannot be assumed that the choice of the morally most acceptable solution will be easy and self-evident, even if the theory is clear. In other words, the debate cannot cease at the transition point from theory to praxis. Such a neat deductive kind of moral process is idealistic and does not corres-

pond to life's experiences. New circumstances can call into
question aspects of existing theory.

To understand what is going on, the 'teachers' (the
clergy) must be a part of the whole process, otherwise their
positions will always be taken too late to be helpful . . .
Moreover, the Church that employs this model often loses
credibility, since it is too slow to condemn concrete and
clear cases of injustice (Nazism in Germany or Fascism in
Italy).[160]

VII. Fear of sexuality.

The clerical caste is steeped in Gnosticism, one of the oldest and
most persistent of all heresies, which sees the body as evil and
only the spirit as good. It results in a hang-up about people
taking their clothes off, instead of a concern for putting clothes
on those who have none, which is what mattered to Christ.

The hang-up can reach ludicrous levels, as in 1987 when a
married man, Ivo Schmitt, was ordained in Brazil by special
Vatican permission. Before his ordination, Schmitt was required
to sign a Vatican document vowing to refrain from intercourse;
his wife, Adulina, also signed papers renouncing her rights as
wife, although they would continue to live in the same house. It
is called Living as Brother and Sister. After the ordination,
Adulina was heard to say, 'From now on, all he gets from me is
kisses.'

What does this say but that sex is dirty? But it says something more sinister: it hints at the old notion of a superior caste,
above the needs of the flesh, that is expressly called to rule.
We're getting close to the Master Race.

One of the results of this fear of sexuality, according to
Richard Sipe, is that the Catholic Church has failed to develop
a credible theology of sexuality. Sipe calls it the 'black hole' in
Christian theology, which has been made more and more obvious by progress in psychology, medicine and clinical and pastoral experience. This, again, is basic to priests' leaving: celibacy
is hard enough to live at the best of times, but harder still when
its theological basis becomes doubtful, and when one suspects it
is really about clerical control of one's life.

VIII. Sexual ambivalence.

Clericalism is surrounded by an infinitely subtle hinting that its
members are not quite fully men. Ordinary people are well

aware of this: it shows in their expectation that the 'good' boy, the gentle or studious boy, the boy who is not interested in girls, becomes the priest. Docility is even one of the criteria for accepting seminarians in some institutions.

Most priests, of course, are far from being wimps, and it is this subtle hinting that is hardest for them to bear. They sometimes react by being extremely macho, or by becoming superb sportsmen. Yet even admiration for their sporting successes is tinged with: 'How marvellous, especially for a priest.'

This sexual ambivalence, an inevitable spin-off of compulsory celibacy, is undoubtedly one of the most repulsive and unacceptable characteristics of clerical life. It is also undoubtedly what drives men to leave the clerical condition: many of the reasons given for leaving can be boiled down to precisely this. I wonder, too, if the tragic clerical exploitation of women, chronicled in Chapter Eight, is not a despairing kick against this perceived sexual ambivalence.

IX. Colonialism.

It was Brazilian Eduardo Hoornaert who made me realise that clericalism is a wholly European phenomenon, and quite out of place, even offensive, in certain other cultures.

'It's a Roman import,' he told me. 'As a clerical structure the Church is purely European. For Europeans, the Church is principally the clerical institution. But for us, especially for the Indians, the Church is the *Povo* — the People. The People of God.'

In trying to force clerical structures on Brazilians—structures such as celibacy, Roman legalism, European-style hierarchy—the Vatican is committing the same crime as any colonial power in forcing its customs and mores on the natives.

And it will fail, as the colonial powers did.

X. Love of the rich and powerful.

Father Bernard Häring, in a lecture in São Paulo, Brazil, December 1987, denounced what he called, 'the irritating history of the sacred alliance between the throne and the altar: a hierarchical and clerical Church pleased to get wealth, honours and privileges from the powerful for favouring an unequal order which enriched the wealthy few at the expense of the impoverished masses.'[161] That is clericalism at its ugliest and most blatant.

And these are the things that priests are renouncing when they leave. In Chapter Two, almost all the reasons cited by priests for leaving can be reduced to one or other aspect of clericalism. Vows growing meaningless as a community ceases to challenge society; seeing kids eating from priests' rubbish bins; Don Franzoni forced out after denouncing military parades and saying that poverty was not wished by God but by rulers and oppressors – all these have to do with a clericalism facing towards Mammon and away from the People of God.

Priests who leave because they feel trapped, or because they feel excluded from human life, or because they feel perceived as sexually ambivalent, are breaking out of clerical apartheid. Those who leave from loneliness or for love are doing the same, or are reacting against that great bulwark of clericalism – enforced celibacy.

Even marriage is often seen as the way to re-enter the world of real people.

And priests who leave over doctrinal matters like the ban on contraception are instinctively rejecting clericalism's way of putting people's needs last, and the institution's survival first.

Lately, such priests are finding how accurate their instincts were, for it has now been revealed that the ban on contraception was renewed by Pope Paul VI in 1968 (against an overwhelming vote in the Papal Commission on Birth Control) precisely because Cardinal Ottaviani warned in a letter that a change in teaching might undermine the credibility of the institution, and endanger confidence in Church teaching.[162] So this was allowed to outweigh the desperate need of millions throughout the world. Ironically, it was this action that brought the Church its greatest loss of credibility for several centuries.

In the prologue I wrote of the lack of an accurate term for priests who leave. They are not 'apostates', as they have not left the Church. They are not 'ex-priests' or 'former priests', as most have not left priesthood or ministry. But I think they would gladly accept the term 'ex-cleric', or 'non-clerical priest', and perhaps those are the words we have been looking for.

It is not only priests who leave who reject clericalism. Some of the most eminent Churchmen also do so. Father Leonardo Boff calls for the emergence of 'another form of being Church', as opposed to 'the expansion of an existing ecclesiastical system, rotating on a . . . clerical axis'.[163]

'Think,' says theologian Father Yves Congar, 'of the Church as a huge organisation, controlled by a hierarchy, with subordinates whose only task is to keep the rules and follow the practices. Would this be a caricature? Scarcely.'[164] But it would be clericalism.

Bishop Kalilombe, in an African context, speaks of: 'what should be called clericalism, that is, the sorry fact that basic ministry and effective leadership and responsibility are concentrated unduly on only the ordained type of ministry.'[165]

The attitude to clericalism of many active priests is summed up in a rather unkind remark made at a gathering of missionaries in a Latin American country. There was a small knot of Irish missionaries at the reception, and one of them kept glaring across at the Vatican's representative, the Apostolic Nuncio. 'Would you look at that little so-and-so,' the missionary was heard to growl. 'With his beady eyes, checking up on everything we do. Y'know what, lads? If there was no God, that fella would still be a priest!'

When I think of clericalism I think of the famous Greek sculpture, the Laocoön, in which a father and his two sons are engaged in a struggle to the death with loathsome serpents, the coils of which are entwining thighs, locking arms and torsos and tightening inexorably upon throats. Aptly enough, that sculpture is in the Vatican.

Yet it would be a mistake, I believe, to see clericalism as some sort of wicked 'them', as opposed to a noble and upright 'us'. Clericalism may be a structure, but it is also a state of mind, like Phariseeism, and the virus is in all of us. We relapse into it whenever we put power and control before the service of God's people, and even layfolk, members of confraternities and knights, are capable of that. Jesus told us not to lord it like the pagans, but to be the servant of all. His washing of those feet was the ultimate gesture against clericalism.

Anyway, the Laocoon may be in the Vatican, but the Holy Spirit is there too, as everywhere else in the Church. And we were promised that the Gates of Hell would not prevail.*

---

*Theologian Heinz-Jürgen Vogels disagrees with my hypothesis that clericalism is the root cause of priests leaving the ministry. He says the root cause is compulsory celibacy and nothing else. I paraphrase here a letter he wrote to me after reading this present

Ecclesia semper reformanda

All human things degenerate, even the human side of the Church, and are in constant need of renewal. But our Faith tells us, and history demonstrates, that the Church has some extraordinary power of self renewal.

Perhaps that is what we are seeing now, as clericalism starts to crack. It is being assailed from all sides. The clerical attitude to women is being met by a powerful feminism: as woman's status rises, it becomes harder and harder to see her as the medieval temptress, the Eve to be guarded against. And as woman takes her full place in society, she is demanding it too in Church.

Mutual love and support now have equal status with procreation as the purpose of marriage, and marriage is no longer seen as being inferior to celibacy. So the clerical downgrading of sex is being confronted, and priests everywhere are asking what is the justification for enforced celibacy, or are simply rejecting it, either by ignoring its demands or by leaving to marry.

Liberation theology and the 'option for the poor' has led many of the ground-level clerics to look again at their role. This especially when they are ordered to stay out of politics, whereas the higher clerics are seen as being deeply involved in it, too often on the side of the right-wing big battalions.

And the old cruel legalism is being more and more ignored: as one priest put it, the Curia is still pushing the buttons, but the lights aren't going on any more.

The priests are crying out for the freedom that clericalism filched from them. Another of those Vatican Two documents, prepared for the Council bishops by a *peritus*, and still marked 'secret', bears out the reality of this cry for freedom. It summarises priests' problems under three main heads, paraphrased here:

The first is **alienation** in the priest. He feels he has lost his place

---

chapter. 'The charism [gift] of celibacy is not given by God to every priest, so that many of them are simply 'incapable' of celibacy, though definitely called by God to the priesthood. Here we have the most simple, most general and most convincing explanation of the failure of celibacy throughout history and plainly in our times: vocation to priesthood and vocation to celibacy are not identical and do not always coincide. The Second Vatican Council took over this reasoning and states explicitly three things: (1) 'Celibacy is a *gift* from God.' (2) 'Celibacy *is not required* by the essence of priesthood', and (3) thus you can only 'pray that God may generously grant this gift to all obliged priests'. (Presb. Ord. No. 16). This implies that you can no longer demand it from all priests. This is not your or my personal opinion, but the one of the Church. It is *the* 'root cause', explaining both the success of celibate priests who stay, and the impossibility of celibacy for so many others who leave.

in modern society. In older societies he felt needed, his education was valued, his theology was accepted. The modern world values him less; he no longer feels adapted to it and with little to offer it. The fact that he is not free to participate in the workplace, rear a family, or share in normal burdens and anxieties [i.e., fact of apartheid], increases this alienation.

The second problem, outlined in the document, is **affective conflict** (which in modern terminology would probably be called 'affective disorder'). The requirements of celibacy, as fostered in the seminary, could erect defensive and repressive attitudes in the acceptance and expression of affection, as well as emotional immaturity. The document says that confrontation with reality can lead to alcoholism, workaholism, sexual deviance and exploiting of women. Arrival at maturity, or the experience of the first mature affective relationship, can occasion abandonment of celibacy [and perforce of the ministry, simply because of present Church rules].

The third problem is **conflict with authority**. Confrontation with superiors; lack of dialogue between superior and subject; authoritarianism; Church authorities seen as warm to outsiders yet insensitive and uncaring to its own priests; treatment of priests as pawns, children or delinquents – all of this has been widespread.[166]

Note that these are not my conclusions, but those of documentation prepared for the bishops of the Second Vatican Council. What I add, however, is the conclusion that all of this is part of a clerical apartheid, which is beginning to shatter.

And I append, too, the question of whether an end to compulsory celibacy would speed the shattering and meet some of the above problems. Family life, and the need to get out and work to support a family, are an antidote to alienation. A good and devout wife can sometimes bring renewed prayer and an increase in the spiritual dimension in a man's life. A spouse and children can help stabilise a man's life, and lessen those affective disorders, which stem from a solitary and unnatural lifestyle. And the coldness and harshness of clerical existence could be replaced by the warmth and support of family life.

It is interesting that many of the above symptoms have also been identified in police life by novelist Joseph Wambaugh. But one of the things that keeps them in check, makes police work bearable, and helps people remain within the police force, is the support of family life.

In this sense the celibacy issue could be seen as intimately tied in with the issue of clericalism, in the whole matter of priests leaving the ministry. If indeed this exodus is a cry for freedom, then maybe the first freedom sought is that to cleave unto a wife. That is what the next chapter is about.

But meanwhile, back at the Vatican, for the moment clericalism still rules okay. Priests and people around the world, and even some bishops and cardinals, are well aware of the lengthening cracks in the clerical mould, but that awareness has not yet penetrated the Vatican.

Those great Bernini colonnades in front of St Peter's had always seemed to me a symbol of the Church, arms open to embrace the world. But if you pass under them, you encounter the walls of the Vatican, sloping Kremlin-like ones, unthinkably thick.

Now when I think of the Vatican, I no longer see those arms embracing the world, but the high, dark walls. Not Vatican City but Vatican Citadel. Inside are men of good will, some of goodness, some perhaps even of holiness. Yet you could hammer on those walls until kingdom come, and no one would hear you. Like Kafka's man, waiting at the castle gate until he dies. Come O Holy Spirit.

10

THE GATHERING

Take care what you do with these men . . . For if this plan or
this undertaking is of men, it will fail; but if it is of God, you
will not be able to overthrow them. You might even be found
opposing God.

Acts of the Apostles, 5, 35–39

THE LITTLE ONES must have had it up to here. Grown-ups talking, talking and talking, and sometimes laughing and crying
too, and then talking some more, for a whole week. And in all
the funniest foreignest languages you ever did hear.

But whatever it is, it seems to be something awfully important
to the grown-ups. They have come in cars, boats and airplanes
from all over the world to get here. Getting together seems to
make them very happy. Of course, the kids are having fun with
each other, too, except you have to use your hands to talk to the
ones with the funny languages.

Well, this is better: at least the grown-ups are singing now,
instead of talking. Look at that big, tall Belgian lady standing
out in front of them all, getting them to sing together, arms
going like windmills: *Alleluia. Loue le Seigneur,* that's what
she's getting them to sing. Whatever that means.

Hildegaard, two and a half, stares up at the Belgian lady. *Was
ist's? Weiss nicht.* Well, whatever it's about, looks as if they're

having a good time – if grown-ups can. And singing so hard. And all in a big circle around a sort of a table, with the evening sun slanting across the flat roof and a warm Italian breeze plucking at the men's shirts and the women's bright-coloured dresses. Then one of the men at the altar raises something up for everybody to see. And there's a couple of men with tears on their cheeks; never thought that happened to men.

Little Hildegaard, child of a German priest who has not acknowledged her, trots across to her *Mutti* – a slender, young woman who is a respected lawyer. *Mutti* lifts her on to her shoulders, and Hildegaard surveys the scene, eyes wide as saucers.

She is gazing out over the flat roof of the Casa della CGIL, a trade union building in Ariccia, set high in the cool hills outside Rome. The Pope can almost hear the singing, as his Castelgandolfo residence is just about on the other side of the hill. It is 27 August 1987, and this is the closing Mass of the worldwide congress of the International Federation of Catholic Married Priests and their Partners.

Well over a hundred of them have travelled here from Germany, South Africa, Britain, Argentina, Austria, Belgium, Canada, Brazil, Spain, United States, France, the Netherlands, Ireland, Italy, the Philippines and Czechoslovakia. Argentina is represented by an outspoken bishop, Jeronimo Podestà, with his wife Clelia. Not all the priests are married, of course, and there is also a sprinkling of active diocesan and religious order priests from Spain and Italy.

It has been a week of prayer, planning, debate, resolutions, and sharing, with the world's press and television peeping over one's shoulder and giving an astonishing amount of coverage. It is also the week in which this worldwide movement – in its self-confidence and in the maturity of its resolutions – has come of age. The days of the Shepherd in the Mist are gone for ever.

LOST, AND IS FOUND

Only a few decades ago the priests who left were the *Desaparecidos*, the Disappeared Ones, of the Roman Catholic Church. Their role was of solitary, shuffling pariahs, from whom Christian society asked only that they should disappear off the face of the earth. And disappear they did, not only into anonymity, but into an aloneness that engulfed even the women courageous enough to share their lives.

Three years ago, at one of the early gatherings of the Irish married-priest group, Leaven, I saw a woman weeping uncontrollably, while another had a reassuring arm round her shoulder. I asked what was wrong. Between sobs the woman managed to say: 'I have been married to a priest and living in Dublin for fifteen years; I have a teenage son – and this is the first priest's wife I have ever met. And these are the first married priests I have even seen in my life, apart from my own husband. If you could only know how much this means to me.'

So the old ways can take a while to die. Yet everywhere they are yielding to a new phenomenon: all over the world the ex-clerics are emerging from their purdah, to take their rightful place in their Church. They are forming associations that will speak for them to the People of God, and to Church authorities if these will listen, and where they can support and help each other.

It often begins when the married and resigned priests of an area start to cluster in small groups, such as Connections in Texas and Louisiana, or the Social Umbrella in Oregon, and has evolved to the point where many countries now have national organisations of ex-clerics, their wives and families. Some of these have acquired considerable clout, as well as skill in the use of the media.

Most groups share certain principal aims: mutual support of the members, spiritual, emotional and physical; help in finding employment; liaison with the people and with Church authorities; consciousness-raising in the Church, by putting the case for optional celibacy and a married priesthood; and working towards a renewal of all forms of ministry in the Church.

The emphasis, of course, can differ from one group to another. For instance, the Brazilian group, MPC-Rumos, sets great store by hospitality, and publishes a catalogue of priest families willing to offer a bed to a travelling brother, which is important in a country of vast distances and great poverty (the catalogue contains the old Latin warning: 'Post dies tres, vilescunt pisces et hospes [Guests are like fish: after three days they start to stink!]').[167]

Some groups are broad-ranging enough to include everyone, from those who long to return to formal ministry to those who would never dream of doing so.

Why are such groups emerging at this particular time? One reason is that people didn't have time until now. For many priests who left, those first years were usually a struggle to hold down a job and found a family. It is only now, with children growing up, perhaps security achieved, that they are beginning to get time to do things. And to do some more thinking, and to organise and put that thinking into practice.

There seems to be a kind of evolutionary process in these groups of resigned priests. In the early stages, members find all they can do is to share their feelings and talk, perhaps for the first time, of their hurts and anger. Then there is a veteran's reunion phase, with the customary recollections of boot-camp. Then the wives start coming to the fore, and there is emphasis on helping those in hard times. Next comes the high-profile stage: invitations from the media for interviews, with a will-I-won't-I-go-public dilemma. Many individuals decide to go public, and with that comes a euphoric sense of walking tall. From then on comes a new confidence in the whole group, and the group finds itself functioning partly as a lobby.

A striking example of an effective lobbying group is the Corpus organisation in the United States. Corpus explicitly promotes the aim of optional celibacy and a married priesthood in the Catholic Church, including the return to full ministry of those who had to resign in order to marry. Its members declare their willingness to resume such ministry.

Corpus began back in 1974 when a US bishop declared that priests who resign and marry have no further interest in the Church. At that time there were 10,000 such priests. In Chicago two married priests, Frank Bonnike and Frank McGrath, replied that a great many such men would dearly love to serve the Church again, even in an active role as priests.

That same year the National Opinion Research Centre (known as NORC) conducted a nationwide survey, which indicated that 79 per cent of Catholics would prefer a married priest as their pastor.

Encouraged by all this, Bonnike, McGrath and two other Chicago married priests founded Corpus (Corps Of Reserve Priests United for Service). Within ten years the four Corpus facilitators had asked 3,000 resigned priests if they would be willing to function again – in a situation analagous to the reserve corps in the military. About 1,000 said yes, and this pattern of one-third saying yes has been consistently repeated in the intervening years.

At the time of writing Corpus is in its fifteenth year: the organisation has grown to be a powerful voice in the US Catholic Church, with over 4,000 members, a mailing list of 8,000, unofficial financial support from some of the bishops, and a highly professional approach to the media.

Corpus's full-time national coordinator, Dr Terry Dosh, is a former Benedictine monk. His television skills are awesome: cool and quite unemotional, he uses statistics like a Gatling gun.

'Do I call you Father, Father?' asks an interviewer.

'I'm your brother, not your father,' smiles Dosh. Next question.

He was invited to Ireland in 1986, for a twenty-minute interview on the *Late, Late Show*, the country's premier television talk show. I have heard it said that in those twenty minutes Terry Dosh changed the Irish attitude to married priests.

Dosh is the first to point out that Corpus still has a long way to go. The number of resigned priests in the United States has now risen to 18,000, and it will be a formidable task to locate and make contact with many of them. Dosh is working with Corpus to build a national infrastructure of area representatives and resource people, and there are 175 such key people, including seven in Canada. A special information letter goes to all of these, six times a year, over and above the bi-monthly *Corpus Report*, which is sent to the 8,000 on the mailing list.

Dosh travels relentlessly to keep contact with married priest groups throughout the country. He conducts what amounts to a dialogue with the media – in one two-year period he was interviewed seventy-one times, for television, radio and Press, with an additional fifty-five interviews from his home by telephone.

He uses important Church events to catapult Corpus into the limelight; when the Pope visited the United States in 1988, Corpus was featured on six national television shows, and on three more in Canada.

When further change finally comes to the Catholic Church, in the matter of ministry, priesthood and celibacy, Corpus will certainly have had something to do with it, if only because it is a huge and effective operation in the most powerful province of the Catholic Church. Things happen earlier in the Americas,

both North and South, and they rattle Rome's cage more –
simply because what happens in the American Church today
happens in the World Church tomorrow.

Britain's national group is called Advent. It traces its origins to
1969, when a group of married priests in the Midlands began
getting together. Father Conrad Pepler, against the wishes of
some bishops, lent them Spode House, a Dominican conference
centre and retreat house. These meetings, which included the
families, were for spiritual sharing and prayer, and led eventually to the formation of a national association.

Advent is primarily a support group, offering counsel and
friendship to priests and their families. It has developed cordial
relations with some of the English bishops (not all), and its
members are gradually becoming more assertive and confident
of their role as married priests in the Church.

A deeply-appreciated gesture was a letter that Advent sent to
Ireland in 1986, when Ireland's married priests were just on the
point of forming their national association (subsequently called
Leaven). The letter offered encouragement and whatever help
Advent could give. It ended thus:

> We feel certain that you will come together to be Ireland's
> voice, as well as giving each other mutual support. Until
> then, can we help by offering our love and support, along
> with any information we may have or can get for you?
> Don't remain isolated. . . .
>
> So take heart, the ministry of married priests is coming –
> in some places it is already here. Let us console one another
> in the sure knowledge that Christ the Eternal High Priest
> loves us and supports us in this new but difficult era of His
> Church's history. We now need to hear the voice of
> Ireland's married priests and their wives – you have been in
> the wilderness too long.
>
> All our love and all God's blessings. Yours in Christ.

The letter was signed by secretaries John and Angie Crawford-
Leighton, on behalf of the Advent group in Britain.

Besides Advent, Britain has other organisations which do not
necessarily have a married-priest membership, but which share
some of Advent's aims.

One such is New Bearings, founded in 1969 by a group
including Norman St John-Stevas (now Lord St John of Faws-

ley), who were concerned about priests and religious leaving and disappearing, and felt they, as part of the Church, should be supportive. Since then it has been dedicated to helping priests in transition. It is a first contact point for such people, offers referrals to counselling services, and to other agencies that can help with financial or legal advice. New Bearings offers its services also to pastors and religious from other faiths. Donations from some of the English bishops help keep New Bearings going.

One of the best-known associations is MOMM, the Movement for the Ordination of Married Men, which consists principally of active priests and lay people dedicated to a change in the Church's compulsory celibacy law. Run by Father Michael Gaine from Liverpool (where Gaine is head of the sociology department at Christ's and Notre Dame College), the efficacy of MOMM lies principally in its disinterestness: the priests and the lay-people involved are not looking for anything for themselves, but are convinced that the Church itself is in urgent need of married priests.

Chile now has a similar organisation to MOMM: it is called *Siete Sacramentos* (Seven Sacraments), and was founded by a layman to press for married priests in a Latin American church that will hardly survive without them. Its founder, Patricio Molina Molina, farmer of Los Andes, Chile, has dedicated his life to this goal. He is in contact with groups all over the world, and conducts letter-writing campaigns in the newspapers, (although he told me the Bishop of San Felipe said he should keep all such discussions 'in the interior of the Church, and not ventilate them in the daily papers').

There are now national or nationwide organisations of resigned/married priests in Germany, Austria, Belgium (two separate groups), Spain (three groups), France (three), Italy (three), Ireland, Britain, the Netherlands, Portugal, Switzerland, Czechoslovakia, United States, Brazil, Argentina, Colombia, Haiti, Canada, Malta, Sri Lanka, Puerto Rico, El Salvador, Chile, South Africa and the Philippines.

The tenor of these national organisations understandably reflects their countries of origin. Belgium, predictably, has two groups – one French-speaking, the other Flemish. A Spanish group, CO.SA.RE.SE, is engaged in an energetic campaign to have the years of active priesthood count towards retirement pension, as many of its members face an old age of poverty. From the bishops the campaigners have so far had 'fine words, but nothing effective'. Now they are talking with the state's *Defensor del Pueblo* [Public Defender].[168]

Brazil's group, MPC-Rumos, has a good working relationship with some of the country's hierarchy, including Cardinals Arns and Lorscheider, both of whom have attended the group's meetings. Bishop Luciano Mendes, president of the country's hierarchy, on returning from Rome in 1987, held a conference with Rumos members to brief them on developments. Cardinal Lorscheider has set aside an office in his seminary for the use of Rumos.

The atmosphere is considerably different in the Netherlands. There the national organisation (called GOP, or Union of Married and Unmarried Priests) is inclined to be confrontational towards bishops, and especially towards Rome, as most Dutch Catholics are. GOP is also somewhat impatient of its counterpart in West Germany. Dutch group president Evert Verheijden disagrees with aspects of the German association's approach: 'Imagine,' he snorts, 'their president Klaus Thoma sending out 16,000 letters to the German bishops and priests, asking them for support for optional celibacy!

'If you wait for the bishops, you'll get nowhere,' he says. 'But that's the German way of working, for you: they're locked into thinking authoritarian and idealistic. They're stuck in the clerical way of thinking.'

The Germans don't agree at all; they see their function as spreading the good news of married priesthood in the most efficient way possible.

The Irish group, Leaven, arose almost spontaneously, out of what must have been a long-felt and crying need. In 1986 I had published in *The Irish Times* the series on priests who leave. Among the remarkable number of letters that came in reply, many said, in effect, 'if only we had an association for priests who leave. . . .'

So when Corpus's Terry Dosh came to Dublin, we called a couple of public meetings to hear him, and asked how many listeners wanted to form a resigned and married priest group. In no time there was a president, a secretary and a lively association, which called itself Leaven.

The Italian penchant for left- and right-wing polarisation is reflected in Italy's two main national groups, Vocatio and ORMA. There is now also a fledgling third group, Hoc Facite. Undoubtedly the most assertive of the groups, Vocatio was founded in Bologna in 1976, and became a legally constituted society in 1981. Aldino Ricci, one of its three founders, told me they now have 3,000 members, of which 1,000 are resigned priests, the rest being spouses, priests still in active ministry, and supportive layfolk.

Vocatio is hardly a comfortable association: its handbook calls it, 'a disturbing and critical voice, sharing with all men and women of good will the hunger and thirst for justice.' Vocatio has little interest in reinstating married priests in the Church as it is, but looks for a new kind of Church based on liberation theology and new concepts of ministry. As its 'Declaration of Identity' expresses it:

> We leave behind the notion of a citadel-church, secure on the mountaintop and separated from the world, with a rigid hierarchic structure, absolute holder of the truth, that saves only whomever takes refuge within its walls, separating themselves from the others – and we pass to the idea of a Church as the communion of the People of God, that realises its mission by walking with men and women, particularly the most marginalised and powerless, in a full sharing, without privilege or separation, in the joys and hopes, sorrows and anguishes of people.[169]

Vocatio's president Gianni Gennari, one-time Roman university professor of moral theology, and now a journalist, is probably one of Italy's most influential married priests, by virtue of the acerbic and quite brilliant column he writes in the *Paese Sera* newspaper. He has been writing it for years, since long before he left the ministry to marry in 1982. Not much escapes Gennari's eye, and few high ecclesiastics are safe from his acidic pen, not even Pope John Paul II, who, Gennari maintains, sometimes reads the column.

When two seminarians committed suicide, Gennari's column began: 'In six days two suicides. I want to know why.'[170]

When the Bishop of Pistoia said celibacy could some day become optional, and later retracted his statement in a somewhat grovelling way, Gennari was on to it: 'This bishop is constrained, I don't know by who, to call himself a liar, saying he did not mean to scandalise, that he professes unconditional obedience to everything and everybody, and that he did not want to say anything new. And, above all, that his statement should not be seen as expressing a wish. How pathetic: in this day and age a bishop not even free to express an opinion on a simple problem of pastoral discipline. What pressures he must have had, the poor bishop. It's autocracy, like in Stalin's time.'[171]

Again and again he returns to the theme of optional celibacy and justice for married priests and women. In the eighteenth century the Church lost the intellectuals, he said in a recent column. In the nineteenth -century, it lost the workers. And in the twentieth century it is well on the way to losing the women.[172]

The Vocatio people have little time for ORMA, which is Italy's other main group of married priests. They regard ORMA as far too conservative, content with the Church as it is, and wanting only to have married priests ministering in an unchanged church. 'More papal than the Pope,' a Vocatio member growls.

ORMA is its popular name (taken from the title of its bulletin, ORdinatio-MAtrimonio). Strictly, it is the Union of Catholic Family Priests, or USFC. Its members have their own misgivings about Vocatio. ORMA's founder, Paolo Camellini, speaks concernedly of the danger of 'stepping outside Catholic orthodoxy'.

'If you don't recognise the Church hierarchy,' he said to me, 'if you say that pope and bishops don't matter, if you question whether ordination is a sacrament, you're in danger of making a *chiesa acefala* [a headless church].

'Whereas we say, of course we want to renew this Church, but let's stay faithful to the Catholic Church that Christ founded. I mean, the Pope as successor to Peter; the bishops as successors to the apostles; unchangeable dogma. We want to renew this church, not to make another one, not even a better one. No, if we had wanted to do any of that, we could have become Protestants.

'What we're looking for is pastoral reform, not reform of dogma.'

As he told me this, we were sitting in the summer twilight by the window of the Camellini flat in the old part of Reggio Emilia. Directly across the street are the massive Renaissance windows of the Bishop's palace and offices.

'You didn't move very far when you left to marry, did you?' I asked. 'The men across there, do they see you as a threat?'

'I meet the Bishop in the street and he nods to me,' Paolo replied. 'And we still have celibate friends in the diocese. They are delighted to be in our company, and to find how our work is going. But these same men, when we meet them in Church circles or on the street, are different people – more distant, because they don't want to be involved.

'I tell them so. They give embarrassed smiles. In their houses they'd give you their hearts, but not in public. They are afraid of their confrères, superiors, hierarchy. I call them hypocrites, in a joking way, but it seems just.'

Paolo Camellini is a smallish man, with dark curly hair, in his late fifties. He is gentle, not angry, even though he works as a labourer in a plastics factory, having been the author of a number of published books. Carla, his wife, had been in the next room all afternoon, sewing a wedding dress. She does it for a living. Now we could hear her in the kitchen, and the smell of something delicious and very Italian wafted in. Their little Down-syndrome boy took us by the hand to lead us into supper.

Carla served the meal. She is rather tall, well-groomed, friendly and matter-of-fact. She could be in her forties, but says she is more.

'How did you two meet?' I asked.

The two exchanged glances. 'It's a long story,' Carla said. 'Too long for now. We'll tell you the next time.'

'I've got all evening,' I replied. 'And there may not be a next time.'

'Very well,' Carla said, 'but promise not to laugh.' Then she told me her story, which I repeat here without comment.

Carla is charismatic. She said that for eighteen years Jesus has talked to her during prayer. Father Conrad Baisi, seminary professor and theologian, was her spiritual adviser and studied her case for ten years. He thought her charism was similar to that of Teresa of Avila.

Don Paolo Camellini was parish priest of a mountain village in the Apennines, where Carla used to take her two children for holidays, before she was widowed. She knew Don Paolo only slightly.

One day Carla went to Don Paolo and told him she had had a revelation that they should get married, so as to dedicate themselves to the cause of married priests. Jesus had told her that he wanted married priests, but only in holiness, 'holy as priests, and holy as spouses.'

Carla: 'Paolo was devoted to his celibate life. He actually cried when this was presented to him. He loved his role. But he wrote out his request to marry, and brought the documents to the Bishop.

'He was called to Rome, and asked why he wanted to marry. Paulo replied, "Because this woman says Jesus asked her to marry me."

'One month later, came the dispensation from Rome.'

There was silence around the supper table. The little boy reached over and patted my arm. I asked, what were Jesus's exact words?

Carla: 'This is the first time I have ever told them to a journalist. Maybe it is time they were printed. Jesus said, "Do not fear this choice, because it [the married priesthood?] is a spot of oil that grows always bigger, and that no one can ever stop. I wanted this mission for a renewed Church. Because too much blood has been poured out for this my work in you."*

Carla paused. 'That last bit frightened me. I thought of past cruelties, of abandoned kids of priests, maybe. Or of the priests who have perhaps died or killed themselves. I still don't understand the meaning of those last words.'

I turned to Paolo. Did he believe all this at the time, I asked him.

Paolo: 'Yes, I did. I had always loved my celibacy. I had always lived it, and had never once betrayed it. But I understood, I am a child of God, and God can do with me whatever He wants. I said to God, "I once offered you my celibacy. Now you want me to marry. *Va bene*."'

They married in 1970, and they are convinced their subsequent history shows the hand of God. In 1979 they met Giustino Zampini (who had resigned and married over fifty years before,

---

**Non temere di questa scelta, perchè è una maccia d'oleo che si allarga sempre più, e che nessuno più fermera. Voleva questa missione per una Chiesa rinnovata. Perchè troppo sangue è stato versato per questa mia opera in voi [Carla's actual words].

suffering frightful privations in those days), and together they founded ORMA.

In 1980 the Camellinis had the idea of an international gathering of married priests. They went ahead with it, and it took place at Chiusi in 1983, bringing together married priests, mostly from Europe, and for the first time in history.

This was the beginning of the most remarkable development in the whole saga of resigned and married priests. For years thousands of resigned priests had lived in isolation. Then suddenly all over the world, almost spontaneously, they had begun to cluster into groups.

But for some years, those groups themselves were isolated, each thinking it was the only one in the world, not realising that it was part of something happening simultaneously in many countries. Then came the gathering at Chiusi, the word spread, and the groups around the world found themselves saying, 'We are not alone.' Other international gatherings were to follow.

The Camellinis suffered for their efforts, of course. Carla: 'I was a teacher of catechism, but as soon as I began my campaign, they fired me. And the Bishop gave orders that Paolo was not to teach catechism either, as soon as he got his dispensation. Not only was he out of the parish, but out of teaching as well.

'One of the arguments for celibacy is that it would cost the Church more to keep a family. We reply, we don't want Church upkeep: we just want to keep our jobs. I say, leave us the work. But the first thing they do when we marry is take away any work.'

How did the Camellinis get the idea of that first international synod?

Carla: 'Jesus told me it was time to go out and talk to everybody, in any way possible. Like at Pentecost. At that moment Paolo was down in the courtyard, praying, walking up and down. Suddenly he got an idea – let's start an international gathering.

'He came up and told me. We talked, and decided to call it a synod. Later we suggested it in the ORMA bulletin. Then the Press took it up . . .'

Later, as I waited at the station for my train to Turin, Paolo Camellini had a final word for me. 'Write your book with love for the Church, not with rancour,' he said. 'If you write out of love, you will do good.'

Going international

The Chiusi synod was followed by another one in 1985, this time held at Ariccia, outside Rome. A consequence of this was the setting up of an International Federation of Married Priest Groups. The federation, headquartered in Paris, has gone on to bring worldwide recognition to the movement. Belgian Bert Peeters is its president, and Pierre and Micheline Lautrey of Paris are the movement's secretaries.

In 1987 came the international Congress of Married Priests and Partners, also held at Ariccia. In the summer of 1990, there is to be a further international congress, this time in the Netherlands, just 12 miles from Amsterdam. Its theme: 'A New Ministry in a New World'.

The gatherings so far have been seen as milestones in the movement towards a married priesthood and a renewed ministry. Each has had its own particular flavour and emphasis, as experience accumulates, thinking matures, and goals are refined.

The 1985 Synod at Ariccia concentrated on the desirability of a married priesthood, and produced a schema of the biblical, historical and theological data that support the compatibility of the two sacraments of matrimony and ordination to the priesthood.

Belgian delegates stressed that Rome's unwillingness to face the questions of celibacy and ministry had retarded development in the whole Church. Others pointed out that the heart of the problem is not celibacy, but a defective attitude towards marriage and sexuality, and a narrow one to priesthood: a priest is not primarily someone who gives up marriage, but a ministering person who gives himself to others, spouse and children included. The point was made that married priests are ideal for base communities, where close union between priests and people is of the essence.

It became clear during the session that some bishops around the world had encouraged married priests to attend, a few even paying travel and accommodation for them and their families. Others bishops were requesting the documentation, but were asking that their names not be mentioned, because of the Vatican's attitude.

This Vatican attitude was made explicit in a meeting where three of the synod's co-ordinators, Paolo Camellini, Father

Lambert van Gelder and Heinz-Jürgen Vogels, met with Monsignor Canciani, unofficial mediator appointed from the Vatican's Congregation of the Clergy. The following is from a report on that meeting by the three synod representatives:

1. The Congregation does not want to deal with us as a group or organisation, but only with us as individuals, about each personal case. (This is the old advice: *Divide et impera* [divide and conquer].)

2. The Congregation have 'quite precise instructions' from the Vatican Secretary of State, Cardinal Casaroli – Canciani said – 'not to give you status nor an official character [*non dare importanza, non dare ufficialità*]'.

3. We would have the right to gather as a civilian corps, like a trade union, but we are, for them, 'outside of the Church [*fuori della Chiesa*]'. It seems they mean: 'outside the clergy'. The expression tells much about the concept of church that the Congregation has.

4. If the Congregation would concede to us, Canciani said, everything would break down [*crollerebbe tutto*], because it is a matter of principle. Probably they mean: the priestly celibate discipline would break down (the Church itself cannot break down from married priests, since there are already such in East and West. It shows that there are irrational fears behind the attitude).

5. They observe a 'convergent strategy' working in different initiatives throughout the world, said Canciani (strangely enough they do not observe that all those spontaneous movements cannot have been started by one man, but must originate finally from the Spirit). . . .

6. We should not expect the Congregation to speak, Canciani said. We, however, should speak ourselves and give a testimony of a 'historic faith' and a 'lived faith' [*fede storica e fede vissuta*], which means a faith that respects the grown tradition and which is active in our new condition of life (this is exactly what we are doing in our documents: they are historically proving our claim to minister as married priests and speak of the present life of the priests in their communities). It appears that with this testimony of faith they would accept us as full members of the Church, or would even expect a changing of the situation (which was not actually said, but why else should they expect such a testimony from us?)

> Monsignor Canciani himself added: Even the Roman
> congregations are groaning under the present general
> 'stagnation' – they 'only repeat what has been said ever
> since, without uttering anything new.' But: 'When doors
> are closed, all mouths are open [*A porte chiuse, tutte
> bocche sono aperte*].'[173]

An American document, prepared for the synod by Dr Anthony
Padovano, was entitled, 'Send Us'. It argues that the movement
toward a married priesthood is irreversible, and that even the
present Pope has allowed more married priests in the Western
Church than any other pope since the twelfth century (despite
the fact he ordains only converted Protestant pastors who are
already married). The document cites a growing number of
bishops, cardinals and national hierarchies who are publicly
asking for a married priesthood.

'We confess our faith in Christ and our affection for the
Church,' the document says, 'in its width and breadth, its
mystery and structure. Send us . . . We are here in Rome with
memories of all we were, and with bright shining hopes of all we
can be, with you.'[174]

ISSUES CLARIFIED

By the time of the next international gathering – the Ariccia
Congress of 1987 – a considerable evolution in thinking had
taken place. Two distinct schools of thought were developing
within the national groups preparing for the congress: whether
to concentrate simply on pressing for a married priesthood and
optional celibacy, or whether to work towards a far wider
renewal of the concept of ministry in the Church.

The differences were clearly spelt out among Britain's married
priests when Scotsman Joe Mulrooney, provoked by a prelimi-
nary questonnaire circulated by congress organisers, passed
around a paper of his own, entitled, "Some Reflections on the
Forthcoming Congress'. To which Adrian Hastings made
answer meet, with his 'Comment upon 'Some Reflections'''.[180]

Writing with Lowland bluntness, Mulrooney attacked the
pre-congress preoccupation with abolishing compulsory celibacy as 'inward-turned and too concerned with its own affairs'.
He said it showed a narrowness of aim and vision that was

totally unrepresentative of the experience, aims and aspirations of members of the Advent group in England. 'Not all left for reasons of celibacy,' he said. 'There are many other motives . . . and we can lump them all together under the term "institutional incompatibility". The congress must take the whole picture on board, or its documentation will read like a Roman document, in seeing marriage as the only reason for leaving.'

Not everyone aspires to return to priesthood, in the sense of a full sacramental ministry, Joe Mulrooney went on. 'Many aspire to fulfil their "mission" vocation, or indeed are already doing so, in a variety of roles other than the sacramental.' He took the documentation to task for using the words 'priest' and 'priest-hood' in an uncritical fashion: 'There seems to be, in the light of current theological discussion, an unwarranted confidence that we know what this means. The content comes through as narrowly sacramental.'

He said preparations had lost touch with complete areas of ministry and responsibility, stemming directly from baptism rather than from ordination; had lost touch with the emergence of a committed laity to perform such ministries, a laity no longer content to be passive and subject to the clerical caste as sole repositories of authority.

As for the ministry of the sacraments, Mulrooney called for a study of 'how we find, train, and ordain' its ministers. Should they be chosen by the community itself? 'The autocratic impo-sition on a community of someone (be he celibate or married) from outside the community, will no longer suffice.'

Beyond this broader context, Mulrooney insisted, the question of 'Priesthood, married or celibate' is just a red herring, which will totally fail to respond to the ministerial needs within our communities. 'If we simply adopt as our aim, in isolation, the abolition of the law of celibacy, we will appear to outsiders as a self-serving group, seeking its own interests,' he argued.

In replying to this, Professor Adrian Hastings conceded that the congress's preparatory materials 'clearly do not point to-wards a far wider reform of the ministry', and it would be extremely unsatisfactory simply to have married priests minis-tering in an unchanged Church.

But, he said, it is a matter of tactics. 'It would be far, far easier to change other aspects, and the wider understanding of the pattern of priestly ministry if this one great change were made –

"the abolition of the law of celibacy for all secular priests". It is that law which has imposed rigidity all across the board, which so divides clergy from laity, professionals from the rest, and so on. And, being grossly unjust, it has led to lots of other related injustices.

'A campaign has to have a sharp focal point, and I am quite convinced that our campaign should remain sharply focused on the issue of celibacy – rather than on the vaster, deeper issues of a more "missionary stance", the relationship between the priesthood of all and the ordained priesthood, the autocratic character of the present system, etc.'

Anyway, continued Hastings, the law of compulsory celibacy is far from a red herring. 'Deep down, the law has itself produced one context, and its abolition will ipso facto go very far to abolishing that context: it will immediately allow and encourage, especially in many Third World countries, a radical alteration in the shape of the ministry, for example, in regard to basic communities . . .

'It is not true that the celibacy issue in itself is just a red herring. It is, on the contrary, the major point at which the Roman tradition went wrong. It is unscriptural, indeed antiscriptural, deeply unjust, and immensely wide in its impact upon past and present.

'It also has the sheer clarity, in terms of theology, law, spirituality and pastoral need, which make it a very good point to target.'

Two positions, clearly defined, and they ran like threads through the congress. A consensus gradually emerged, where people began to realise that compulsory celibacy, while perhaps not a red herring, was far from being the whole picture.

I recall that August week in Ariccia as a stimulating and enthralling debate, with votes won on the narrowest of margins.

The two threads, optional celibacy or a totally renewed ministry, became the warp and the woof of discussion. It became clear that since the previous synod, many of the delegates had found fresh ways to minister, without waiting for a nod from Rome. And their whole concept of ministry was expanding vastly.

Belgian Jesuit Father Jan Kerkhofs, sociologist, rector of a college in Louvain, and head of the Pro Mundi Vita Institute, gave what amounted to a keynote address to the assembly. More than half of all Christian ministers, he said, are married men and women. The Latin rite is the exception. He spoke of the rapid evolution of newer forms of ministry, and of a move away from the pyramid structure of Church [pope at the apex, bishops right under him, clergy halfway down, laity flattened out at the bottom of the heap – my description, not Kerkhofs's]. The new idea of Church is of concentric circles, with pope and hierarchy in the middle rather than on top, and where service rather than tyranny prevails.

With nearly half the world's parishes now without a priest, unless there is some change, there will be NO church left in the Third World. Bishops from all around the world are telling Rome this, and begging to be allowed married priests. Priest councils everywhere in Europe are likewise asking for change.

The theology of priesthood and ministry is evolving, Kerkhofs said. Theologians stress that ministers and leaders should be drawn from the community, rather than sent in from outside; that ministry could be temporary, and not necessarily concerned about sacramental character. And there is no first-rank theologian today who says women should not be ordained.

It is women, in fact, who will change the Church in the coming years, more than cardinals or bishops. If they are not allowed to, Kerkhofs fears, they will leave the Church, and take their children with them.

We should always talk of ministry rather than priesthood, he counselled – ministry which can be either sacramental or non-sacramental: ministry of the sacraments or of service.

The most effective way to change attitudes is by the good example and credibility of married priest groups, Father Kerkhofs considered. Individual bishops will begin to trust these priests, and will invite them to take on pastoral care [precisely as is happening in Brazil].

It is no use trying to contact Rome: Rome is hopeless. When pressed on this point, Kerkhofs was adamant: Rome is hopeless. He knows his history, and has dealt much with Rome. Leave Rome alone he said, and spend your energy locally or nationally. Support your own bishops, especially those who go out on a limb, and give courage to the slower ones to move.

Father Kerkhofs – no wild man of the Catholic Church, but a distinguished Jesuit – believes there will be married priests in ten years and women priests in twenty.

SEEK FIRST THE KINGDOM

In the end, what emerged from the week's discussions was a consciousness that 'life after leaving' was not about sitting round, waiting for Rome to do something or permit something, like the scriptural handmaiden with her eye on the hand of her mistress. Life is too short. There are massive amounts of ministry within reach, crying out to be done, and many of the married priests and their spouses are already deeply involved.

As one delegate put it, there's no need to tilt at Vatican windmills, like Don Quixote. 'Let's be more like Sancho Panza, bypassing the snapping curial sails, and plod serenely forward.' Let us do whatever ministry we can, and let the Holy Spirit take care of optional celibacy and married priesthood.

It was a few days after the congress ended that I went to see Don Franzoni, former Abbot of St Paul's, and he said almost the same thing. He earnestly cautioned against concentrating efforts solely on attaining optional celibacy.

'I don't believe in the liberation of the priest outside the liberation of man,' he said. 'A Church that struggles for liberation, that fights racism, exploitation of women and apartheid, will take on a new shape. It will have a wider horizon, will be a Church of service, not of power.

'And within that process there will also be resolved the question of married priests and celibacy. It will happen en route.' Seek first the Kingdom of God, and all these will be added.

'Most important, and hardest, is to be a believer, to become a disciple of Jesus. But in a Church of such disciples, will it matter who has the gift of tongues, who presides at the Eucharist?'

11

CELIBACY, FORCED OR FREE?

The struggle between the sacred old and the prophetic new is
a central theme of the history of religions.

Paul Tillich

AMONG THE FIRST blasts of the trumpet on behalf of women's
liberation is a remarkable epic poem in the Irish language from
two centuries ago. 'The Midnight Court', (*Cúirt an Mhean
Oiche*), written in 1780 by the County Clare poet Brian Merriman, not long after the ending of Ireland's religious persecu-
tions, is laced with that mixture of bawdiness and belief so
natural to Gaelic.

It tells of a young man who falls asleep in a field, and dreams
he is dragged off by the fairies, to answer court charges against
all Irishmen of failing the women of Ireland by neglecting to
mate and propagate. In the course of these assizes, a lovely
female accuser turns her ire upon Irishmen of the Cloth:

> The object of my fond research
> Is my own old ancestral church,
> Why are its clergy women-free
> And given to celibacy? . . .
>
> We women see what we require,
> And what our lonely hearts desire,

And what might mollify our itches
Shut off by those black broadcloth breeches! . . .

The isle of saints lies waste indeed
All through this waste of saintly seed
Which foolish laws forbid to breed . . .

Say what authority induced
Such celibacy mass-produced?
Who had authority to tell
The natural feelings not to swell
But starve and sicken as they dwell
Imprisoned in this dungeon fell?
Paul never told one man he must
Not marry, but forbade all lust;
Give up your kin and family
However great your love may be
Cleave henceforth solely to your wife
One with her for the rest of life . . .

O let the Lamb damn lies and say
Out truth that shall not pass away;
It was no spinster made God human,
God's Mother was a married woman . . .

No one said it better than Brian Merriman.* Compulsory celibacy was a problem then, as it is a problem now, as it has always been a problem since it was first forced on a screaming and kicking People of God many centuries after Christ.

Compulsory celibacy, that is. Not celibacy freely chosen, which has earned the heartfelt respect of Christians. In fact, the only real celibacy is that which is freely chosen: compulsory celibacy is a contradiction in terms – not celibacy, but more akin to castration.

And it cannot be argued that every priest chooses celibacy freely. A man called to priesthood by God is hardly free to ignore that call: but if other men have tied on celibacy as part of the package, then it has been forced upon the man.

Chapters Two and Nine have shown how the celibacy obligation runs like a thread through the saga of priests leaving – if not invariably the primary reason for leaving, nevertheless permeating the whole decision process, making unbearable what

---

*Translated by Canon Cosslett Quin, and reproduced by permission of The Mercier Press, Cork & Dublin.

might have been bearable, and often tipping the scales when a man leaves primarily for other reasons. And whatever the role of enforced celibacy in priests leaving, it is certainly the primary reason today why men are refusing to become priests, as this chapter will show. So it behoves us to look at celibacy.

GIFT FROM GOD

True celibacy, freely chosen (or freely accepted) for the Kingdom of God, is a many-splendoured thing in man or woman. And it is one of the easiest things to discern: you know it by the love it generates. One would surely see it in Mother Teresa, in Dom Helder Camara, in Cardinal Lorscheider, in Brother Roger of Taizé. One would have seen it in Gandhi, in Pope John XXIII, in Dorothy Day, in Padre Pio. I encountered it in a nun who was a hospital matron; in a man who once taught me; in certain priests who were my colleagues and in some priests whom I lately met in missionary lands. There is a translucence about such people, and a goodness and energy which are unmistakable.

Psychologists suggest that such goodness and energy comes from the deepest roots of sexuality. In an address to the National Guild of Catholic Psychiatrists, 8 May 1988, Richard Sipe quoted Eknath Easwaran on Gandhi:

> It was in South Africa that Gandhi learned to translate . . . tremendous ideas into effective action . . . Night and day, carrying . . . stretchers across the vast deserted hill country of Natal, he plunged himself deep into prayer and self-examination in a fervent search for greater strength with which to serve.
>
> The intensity of his desire led him to the source of power itself. Deep in meditation Gandhi began to see how much of his vital energy was locked up in the sexual drive. In a flood of insight he realised that sex is not just a physical instinct, but an expression of the tremendous spiritual force behind all love and creativity which the Hindu scriptures call *kundalini*, the life force of evolution. All his life it had been his master, buffeting him this way and that beyond his control. But in the silence of the Natal Hills, with all his burning desire to serve focused by weeks of tending to the wounded and dying, Gandhi found the strength to tap this power at its source. Then and there he resolved to be its

master, and never to let it dictate to him again. It was a decision which resolved his deepest tensions, and released all the love within him into his conscious control. He had begun to transform the last of his passions into spiritual power.[176]

Such free celibacy serves a very special purpose in a priest who is so endowed. Fathers Gallagher and Vandenberg, in their book, *The Celibacy Myth*, point out that celibacy does not only free the priest for more duties. The unique thing about priesthood, they suggest, is not just service or ministry: 'What a priest has to offer his people, that no one else has to offer, is the unique relationship he can have with them as their priest. Just as a couple's activity takes on a deeper significance and even a new meaning to the degree that there is genuine commitment and bonding between them, so priestly activity becomes truly "priestly" to the degree that it reflects a genuine commitment and bonding between himself and his people.

'Enter celibacy. As a catalyst speeds up and enhances the chemical reaction of two elements without being essential to that reaction, the charism of celibacy deepens and enhances the relationship of the priest with his people, without being essential to that relationship.'[177]

And that is what we perceive in a priest who is truly gifted with celibacy. Such a gift, by the way, need not mean ease – it could involve day-to-day struggle, and reiterated choice, as with Gandhi. Celibacy is not bachelorhood, nor simply a contentment with solitude. If it is a charism, as some maintain, then a charism is a gift from God, not for oneself, but for the benefit of others. Like the gift of tongues. It does not have to be comfortable.

'You don't just promise celibacy on the day you become deacon,' Cardinal Hume explained to me in an interview. 'You have to renew it every day. Profoundly I believe in the two creation chapters of Genesis, in which we are told to increase and multiply, and that it is not good for man to be alone. Now celibacy is saying No to both of those – it can only do that if it is saying Yes to something else. To being open to the love which you come to understand in God, and through that, to try and give love to all the people you are involved with.'

It is that love that bonds the celibate priest to his people as few things can.

Compulsory celibacy

A celibacy, however, that is externally and indiscriminately forced upon every priest, whether willing or not, whether capable of it or not, is light years from the celibacy described above. And such compulsory celibacy has rather strange origins in history. Let us take a brief look at a few moments in that history, bearing in mind the dangers of oversimplification, and that these are indeed but moments in a long and complicated evolution extending across 1,200 or more years. But Cardinal Doepfner did warn the Fathers of the Second Vatican Council that they should try to know something of celibacy's history before making decisions about it.[178]

To begin with, Christ did not require celibacy, and chose married men. Neither did the scripture that followed demand celibacy of anyone, even though it was seen as apt for the expected end of the world. St Paul, while regarding celibacy as superior, left it as a free choice ('concerning celibacy I have no commandment of the Lord,' I Cor., 25, 40), insisting merely that ministers be 'the husband of one wife'.

In the three centuries that followed, there were both married and unmarried ministers. Clement of Alexandria could write: 'Really also the husband of one wife is accepted by the Church, be he priest, deacon or layman, as long as he uses marriage without blame. He will take part in salvation by raising children.'

According to Edward Schillebeeckx, in his book, *The Church with a Human Face*, celibacy has its origins in a partly pagan notion of ritual purity.[179] First, in the fourth century, came a law that forbade a married priest from having sexual intercourse the night before celebrating the Eucharist. But then the Western Church began to celebrate the Eucharist daily, so this abstinence became, in fact, a permanent condition for married priests.

'At the origin of the law of abstinence, and later the law of celibacy,' Schillebeeckx says, 'we find an antiquated anthropology and an ancient view of sexuality.' As St Jerome put it, expressing the notion of both pagans and Christians of his time: 'All sexual intercourse is impure.'

Understandably, this obligation on married priests, to live with a wife as if she were a sister, was an intolerable burden and 'led many priests into deplorable situations,' as Schillebeeckx describes. 'These ancient councils bear abundant witness to this.' So in 1139, at the Second Lateran Council, the Church resorted to drastic means: it forbade altogether the marriages of priests, and declared such marriages null and void. The law of abstinence had become a law of celibacy. And, again, ritual purity was the decisive motive. 'One does not approach the altar and the consecrated vessels with soiled hands' had been the pagan view, now enshrined by the Christians in their law of compulsory celibacy.

There were two further developments, neither of which were at the origin of the law of celibacy, but which had some influence on its consolidation.

Firstly, more and more bishops began to be appointed from the monks, who had vows of chastity, and these gradually imposed monastic notions of virginity as suitable for all priests, even those not living in monasteries.[180]

The second development was the acquiring of property by the Church. There was a real danger that legitimate children of priests could inherit, thus depriving the Church of its property. It became critical as many of the clergy were nobles, some even royalty. Hence a further (economic) motive for retaining celibacy for priests, since illegitimate children could not inherit.[181]

Incredible harshness was at times used to enforce the law of celibacy. The Council of Toledo, in 655, had decreed the enslavement of the offspring of clerics, which was incorporated into general Church law, along with the enslavement of the wives of clerics.[182] Much later, that law was put into ferocious effect, under Pope Gregory VII in the eleventh century, when the marriages of priests were savagely broken up and priests' wives and children made into slaves.[183]

The 1139 celibacy law did not end matters, but in many cases merely changed marriage into concubinage. A document prepared for the bishops in the Second Vatican Council, by eminent Church historian Hubert Jedin, and still marked SECRET, contains the following passage:

> As it is certain that there have always and everywhere been priests who lived exemplarily, so a noticeable proportion, especially among the parish clergy, kept able-bodied women in their prime, when they had no blood relations, in

order to look after the housekeeping and agriculture, on which their economic existence to a large degree depended. They lived together with them and by them had children who often grew up in the vicarage. It would be a mistake to imagine that these permanent concubines, especially in the countryside, would have aroused a lot of scandal. We know of many cases where these 'keepers of concubines' possessed the sympathies of their parishioners and were looked on as good and virtuous pastors. So they should not be judged out of hand to be simply morally unprincipled brutes. . . .

The keepers of concubines were in many dioceses punished by fines and then tolerated; what is much worse is that these fines (the 'whore-tax') formed a not inconsiderable source of income for the Bishop and Archdeacon. The Bishop of Luettich, Cardinal Erhard V. der Marck, frankly admits this bad state of affairs. There is solid evidence which comes from the account books of the ecclesiastical officialates.[184]

Then came the Reformation, and the Council of Trent, by which the Roman Catholic Church reformed itself and remodelled the priesthood to what we know today. But even then the Emperor Charles V begged the Council fathers to allow priests to marry. The following years proved him wise. Professor Jedin again:

> Even long after the Council of Trent, a part of the people of Switzerland ranged themselves on the side of those with concubines against Nounce Bonhomini who wanted to impose the law of celibacy in all strictness. 'Many keepers of concubines,' writes the Catholic historian Oskar Vasella, 'enjoyed the trust of the people. Despite all human failings, they carried on their care of souls in unconditional loyalty to their calling and devoted love towards their flock.'[185]

This is backed up by Father Michael Pfiegler, in his book *Priesterliche Existenz* [Priestly Existence]. Even after the Council of Trent, although the law of compulsory celibacy had been promulgated with urgency, St Clement Hofbauer found in Poland a large part of the clergy married. The situation in Latin American was no better, Pfiegler says. An interesting aside is that the last Catholic bishop of Iceland was given absolution along with his wife, before being hanged by Lutherans in 1550. He was hanged along with two of his sons.

But why did the Council of Trent insist on compulsory celibacy in spite of so much evidence that it could not work? Professor Jedin suggests it was an over-reaction to the Protestants, who had recommended marriage for priests, and had insisted that celibacy was God's gift only to a few. 'Therefore the Church entrenched its position and did not let itself discuss the problem, either from the viewpoint of theology or of practical circumstances.'

Note that the above quotations are not from some anti-Catholic historian, but from a secret document prepared for the information of the bishops at Vatican Two.

But what of compulsory celibacy today? Schillebeeckx says there are only two worthwhile arguments against it. Firstly, is it credible to people? Hardly: 'Now, celibate priests are constantly under the suspicion of "wanting to marry, but not being allowed to", as the common saying goes.' Secondly, Christian communities have a right to leaders and to the Eucharist, and if compulsory celibacy is depriving them of such leaders, then it must be questioned. 'In such a situation,' he says, 'Church legislation, which can in any case be changed, must give way to the more urgent right to the apostolic and Eucharistic building up of the community.'

The reason, of course that compulsory celibacy is not credible to people is that it is not seen to work today, any more than it did in the past. In fact, it seems to be unworkable. Now it is an axiom of jurisprudence that 'unworkable law is bad law'.

SUPPORT GONE

Compulsory celibacy is, in fact, less workable today than ever, because its original basis of ritual purity has been kicked away – by no less an agent than the Second Vatican Council. When the Council proclaimed the sacredness of the marriage bond, and expressly stated that 'the actions within marriage, by which the couple are united intimately and chastely, are noble and worthy ones',[186] it was rejecting the notion of unclean sex, sounding the death knell of the compulsory celibacy built upon it, and proclaiming that celibacy and marriage were of equal value.

Schillebeeckx has observed that 'when marriage is given its full value, and it is a sacrament, then vocations to religious celibate life will decrease'.[187] Likewise the numbers of those already celibate will decrease, as thousands leave. And those who remain will demand adequate arguments for compulsory celibacy. They will not, however, get them.

I myself have heard dedicated priests asking for such arguments. One was a senior priest of the Chicago Archdiocese, who asked me not to identify him. A man of mature years in a key administrative position, he described to me in 1987 how the diocese was abandoning its 'pyjama parties' – overnight gatherings of younger priests at Mundelein Seminary, held to discuss integrating sexuality and spirituality in a priest's life. 'The groups raised so many issues,' he told me, 'that we're going to have to scrap the rest of the pyjama parties. These young priests want a more credible explanation of celibacy, which can reach the heart as well as the mind, and the Church's arguments are not making any sense. A guy of twenty-five is saying, "I want to know why I'm asked to live this life style, and if you can't convince me, do you have a right to ask me to live it?"

'We have a huge job ahead of us,' this senior priest told me, 'and I don't think the Church can continue to say, be celibate, and not give guys a credible rationale for remaining so.'

Many people feel like this priest: they presume that somehow, somewhere, such a credible rationale must exist. That somewhere, in some secret recess of our Church, somebody has A Reason Why, otherwise the whole Church would not still continue with compulsory celibacy – would it? Or wouldn't it? It's the old story of the Emperor's New Clothes.

The tragedy is, no such credible rationale exists. There are powerful arguments for celibacy, but they are valid for freely chosen celibacy, and are not really applicable to enforced celibacy. And that is why, at pyjama parties or anywhere else, no one is able to come up with any. The Emperor has no clothes.

Indeed, all around the world, eyes are opening to that fact. And voices, from the bottom to the top of the Catholic Church, are calling out for married priests.

As long ago as the Synod of 1971, one-half of the bishops wanted a married priesthood. According to Father Jan Kerkhofs, the ordination of married men has been urged by the following: the national synods of Denmark, the Netherlands, Flanders, Austria and Switzerland (West Germany was in favour but the bishops would not discuss it); the representative American congress 'A Call to Action'; the Indian Congress on the Renewal of the Ministry; the colloquium of the Federation of Asian Bishops' Conferences; the combined bishops of Brazil, Bolivia and Paraguay; and the synod of Fianarantsoa in Madagascar.[188]

Likewise asking, Kerkhofs says, have been 'the National Conferences of Priests in England, the United States, Zaïre, South Africa; the Assembly of Provincials of the Oblates [missionary order] in Asia; the European Colloquium of Parochial Clergy; the Barcelona Assembly of Priests; the Catholic Aymaras in Peru with support from their bishops; the bishops of Chad, Cameroon, Central Africa, and so on.'

The same request has been made, privately to the Pope, by the Union of General Superiors of religious orders, including the heads of the Dominicans, the Franciscans, and the Jesuits.[189]

These voices have grown to a crescendo, with even cardinals asking for married priests, including Cardinals Arns and Lorscheider of Brazil, Cardinal Pellegrino of Italy, Cardinal Hume of Britain, and Cardinal Darmojuwomo of Indonesia.[190] As long ago as the 1971 Synod, Cardinal Suenens asked for married priests.[191] Archbishop Malula of Kinshasa, Zaïre, president of the African bishops, says we must ordain married couples to take over the teaching of Christian doctrine.[192]

Bishop James Malone, in his final address as president of America's National Conference of Catholic Bishops, 1986, returned to the problem: 'How are the bishops of this country going to provide for the Eucharistic worship of the Church in the United States?' he asked. 'If trends continue, by the year 2000 we will have half the number of active priests serving the Church in this country.'[193]

Archbishop William Borders of Baltimore expects changes. 'Obviously we're going to have to rethink the approach we have to ordination,' he said in August 1984, 'because you know celibacy has never been a real doctrine. It's a matter of discipline. And any discipline in the Church can be changed or it can be suspended. So doctrine is not changed. It is discipline and custom that is affected.'[194]

Bishop Jacques Gaillot, of Evreux in Normandy, called publicly for the ordination of married men in the 1988 annual gathering of the French bishops in Lourdes. He criticised attempts to secure the return of priests from Lefebvre's extreme right-wing movement, while in the Church ordinary priests were being forced to leave because they wanted to marry, and good men were being refused ordination because they were not celibate.

'Is it not extraordinary that we deploy so much effort to bring back people who are far from Vatican Two on essential points of faith,' he asked, 'while we are resigned to the departure of priests of value for the sole reason that they have rejected the undertaking of celibacy? How long are we going to deprive the ministry of married priests who remain available for service to the Church?' he asked.

Tragically, Bishop Gaillot later had to apologise for his words. This, of course, does not detract from their truth, but only testifies yet again to the level of fear and control exercised by Rome over its clergy.

In late 1988, the US Bishops' Committee on Priestly Life and Ministry published a ground-breaking report that claimed a 'serious and substantial morale problem' among the nation's priests, many of whom are overworked, lonely and sexually troubled. For the first time speaking openly of problems long hidden, the bishops said some priests are just going through the motions, and many 'have settled for a part-time presence to their priesthood.' A major reason for these problems among the priests, and for clergy leaving the priesthood, is, according to the bishops, compulsory celibacy.[195]

These views are borne out in various interviews I have had with members of the Church's hierarchy.

'I personally believe', Cardinal Lorscheider told me in 1988, 'that optional celibacy would be a stronger value – it would be a greater sign value, because many here [in Brazil] believe that a priest is only celibate because he is obliged to be . . . Maybe basic communities will arrive at the point of optional celibacy. But only if the communities want it – it should not be imposed from above. I think the last synod threw cold water on something that was boiling: they accentuated specific ministries of priest, laity, and so on, without looking at ministry in general.'

Archbishop Flores of San Antonio, Texas, spoke to me of Protestant denominations in his area: 'They have married clergy yet they are hard workers. Somehow their marriage is not an obstacle. I could see the possibility [for us] of individuals who could be married and definitely effective.'

He stressed that the laity were more willing now to accept married priests, just as they had come round to the idea of married deacons: 'At first we were afraid the laity would not accept deacons, and there were some problems at the beginning. But after almost twenty years, I don't know of many people who don't accept them. There's a parallel here.'

Bishop Angelico Sandalo of São Paulo was emphatic on the need for married priests. 'I think this is a matter of urgency,' he told me. 'The more we work to try and have celibate priests, the less we have priests to attend all our people.

'To tie the exercise of priestly ministry to the charism of celibacy is merely a matter of discipline, and not in theology or early history. The Church ought to change it. Far more important than tying celibacy to the exercise of priesthood is that priests, married or not, should be present to the people.'

Celibacy or Mass

Dom Angelico has put his finger on the nub of the issue (which is Schillebeeckx's second argument against compulsory celibacy): the whole controversy about priestly celibacy has now come down to as stark a choice as any in the history of the Church – we can have either compulsory celibacy OR the Mass. We cannot have both.

Dean R. Hoge, in his recent book, *The Future of Catholic Leadership*, states categorically that the key to vocations is that married men be ordained:

> This option needs close examination because of its important effects. As we have seen, the celibacy requirement is the single most important deterrent to new vocations to the priesthood, and if it were removed the flow of men into seminaries would increase greatly, maybe fourfold. *Therefore this option provides a solution to the shortage of priests.* [author's italics][196]

It is as simple as that. Hoge's conclusions are widely supported, and underlined by overflowing US Protestant seminaries, where enrolment rose from 42,627 in 1979 to 58,851 in 1983, which is an increase of 14.6 per cent.

A study made by Catholic University makes it even clearer that rising opposition to celibacy is the key factor in the Catholic Church's decline in ministers. 'There is no doubt', the study says, 'that the celibacy requirement is a major hindrance to vocations today. Although it was not a major hindrance in past decades, social changes have produced new attitudes about sexuality, personal freedoms and life styles.'

George Gallup Jr (of Gallup Poll) has concluded from surveys that about 5 per cent of American youth are seeking some outlet for ministerial service, although they do not seek to be ordained.[197]

Gallup's and Hoge's conclusions are mirrored in other parts of the world. A paradox in the Netherlands is that while the country's bishops and priests agonise about the future, there are over 800 young people, men and women, avidly studying theology at the country's universities. But they refuse point blank to be ordained. This is the Dutch paradox: a dwindling, ageing priesthood, and right beside them an immense pool of energy, youth, commitment and theological awareness. 'Those 800 are there,' Father Lambert van Gelder says, 'and my hope is that eventually the Church will ask them to serve, simply because of the shortage. But the Church will still have to give in on some things, if it wants to have them as priests.' In particular, on compulsory celibacy.[198]

We saw in Chapter One that in the Third World too, the number of priests is in drastic decline relative to Catholic population, and we find African bishops calling for the ordination of married catechists. The problem is reflected in Latin America. There the only possible source of native priests are the leaders to be found in local communities, who, of course, are married. They would, incidentally, be the best possible kind of priest, according to churchmen on the spot – in touch with their people, already respected, already active. Father George Protopapas writes, in another paper from my cache of 'secret' documents prepared for the Vatican Council:

> In view of the present structure existing in South America and Central America, would it not be preferable and more advantageous for the Kingdom of God to have the priesthood conferred not only to celibates but also to married men? . . . The clergy must be able to count on as co-workers a married clergy. I mean by this that we should ordain as priests married men who have given proof of solid faith, good judgement, men who have given meaning to their life. At least quantitatively speaking the Church would

be in a much better position to cope with the ever increasing
population.[199]

It was in this context that Cardinal Hume's famous 'call' for
married priests took place. 'At a meeting in Belgium we were
discussing the situation in South America,' he told me in our
interview, 'where it was alleged that Christian communities were
meeting around the word of God, and were not involving
themselves in celebrating the Eucharist, because there were no
priests. Well, my contribution was to say, "I don't think it right
and good that the Christian community should just live off
scripture without the Eucharist. In such a situation, then, one
might have to consider opening up the question of ordaining
married men, so that people would not be deprived of the
Eucharist and the Sacrament of Reconciliation." It was some
wretched reporter who turned it into headlines.'

Hoge's book states categorically that the vocation shortage is
long-term, not just temporary, and that it can be solved only
through institutional measures. In a nutshell, then – if compulsory celibacy continues in the Catholic Church, there will be
ever-increasing areas of the world that will be without priests,
and therefore without the Mass. Thus it is a choice between
celibacy and the Mass.

According to theologians, the People of God (that is, the
Church), have an absolute and inalienable right to the Eucharist.
What, then, is to be said of those who would deprive them of that
right, by maintaining, in the face of all evidence, a compulsory
celibacy that does not even work?

It becomes even less workable if some church authorities
encourage priests to seek non-sexual intimacy with women as an
antidote to loneliness or as a way to mature. If a man can
combine such intimacy with chaste celibacy, well and good.
Indeed we saw how such friendships can be deeply rewarding
and beneficial. But for many men it will inexorably drive
towards sexual fulfilment, as is the nature of things. Therefore
the option of marrying must be available as a safety valve,
otherwise the policy of encouraging intimacy will lead to
unchaste celibates and exploited women.

And even if the intimacy never becomes physically sexual, it
can lead to hurt if the woman is open to marriage while the
celibate is not. Teilhard de Chardin, in his last years, spent hours

weeping uncontrollably for the hurt done to the three women who had chastely loved him at different times in his life.

WHY?

So why is compulsory celibacy being maintained? One can only guess. The whole clerical ethos is bound up with it, and could collapse if celibacy ended. As Cardinal Pallavicini, secretary of state to Pius VI, said, around 1780, 'If priests can marry, the papal hierarchy falls, the Pope loses respect and supremacy, married clergy will be tied by their wives and be dependent on the state.'[200]

And compulsory celibacy is, or was, incredibly efficient – the ultimate management technique, giving total control and total mobility of personnel, and rendering priests independent of this-worldly interests and free of lay control. Peter McCaffrey of Aberdeen University suggests that the celibacy rule has endured so that people would be dependent on a priesthood with a purified knowledge (a knowledge more readily available to the celibate).[201]

Close to the kernel is the confusion between voluntary and compulsory celibacy, where arguments eminently valid for freely chosen celibacy are being misapplied to support a celibacy imposed by law on everyone.

Also today there is certainly an economic motive for retaining compulsory celibacy: if married priests and families enter the picture, Church authorities fear it would entail a drastic restructuring of Church finances. The fear has less basis than it would first appear. Restructuring might be needed, but it would not necessarily cost more. Married priest Don Conroy, now a psychologist in Minneapolis, put that case in a letter he wrote to me. He writes, of course, in a North American context:

> You mentioned finances, viz., whether a married clergy would cost more. I doubt it. I think the opposite. It costs a lot of money to keep Father celibate. When I was a celibate priest, I would have gladly divided our living expenses by the number of priests in our house and taken that, plus my $]150 a month, as my salary. Those of us who lived the life know that it cost a lot – the parish purchased everything, food, bed, chairs, all living needs including sheets and towels, plus booze, housekeeper, parties, etc.

This is an important point – the priest caste is 'kept' – he does not experience money moving from his pocket to the grocer, and so on. What does he own? Clothes, car, recreational equipment. Here in Minnesota, most have a year-round home on a lake within driving distance. I am not making this up. A relative of mine is a priest and there are two or three others who have cabins [homes] close to his.

There is a problem of dignity here. While the priest's brothers and sisters are struggling to provide for family – and that includes education – the [secular] priest, who has no vow of poverty, is exempt from the basic financial experience, and lives with surplus money, with which he owns a second home with bed, chairs, food, etc. The first home simply comes as a perk.

My point: Do not continue to promote the crazy idea that the celibate priest costs less than a man with a set salary – like the rest of us.

Inertia probably also has a great deal to do with Church reluctance to look again at celibacy: the Barque of Peter is rather like a supertanker, and takes a long time to slow down and set a new course.

Richard Schoenherr sees the Vatican's attitude as a last-ditch stand before radical change. As he put it to me in an interview: 'It was Marx who said that no new form arises before a group is totally convinced that all the life is gone from the old. How are we to know that life is gone from the compulsorily celibate male ministry, unless we extol it?'

He says it is a sort of Last Hurrah: 'That explains the bizarre behaviour, like not allowing girls to serve at the altar, yet allowing women to read the lessons. And like saying celibacy is a closed issue, and that there's no problem here, and that it's the result of materialism.

'These are bizarre statements, flying in the face of reality. To me it makes no sense, except sociologically: before you bury something, you want to make sure it is dead. Rome is just beating a dead horse, because they're not quite sure it's dead yet.'

Gianni Gennari, in his *Paese Sera* column, lays much at the door of Pope John Paul II: 'Almost always the same problems, which he continues to confront with his total refusal. The only reason for his NO is the fact that he says NO, as if only he counted in the Catholic Church . . . And that NO counts against every possible YES, against all the requests of everyone else, against all the recognised pastoral needs, against all the positive findings of the worldwide episcopate.'[202]

NO PANACEA

While little can be uttered in favour of enforcing celibacy on all priests, in fairness it should be said that arguments are advanced against married priests which deserve to be looked at. Such arguments can be summarised in three propositions: (I) a married priest would be less available to God's people, less free for risks or heroic actions; (II) he would be more tempted to a bourgeois life style; and (III) an uncommitted wife could impede his priestly work.

Protestant pastor families could help us greatly in our study of these questions. But let us not forget that in the Catholic Church we have a unique laboratory waiting to be used – namely, the priests who have already left and married, many of whom are engaged in some kind of ministry.

In my encounters with these priest families around the world, I kept such questions in mind. And, without wishing to make Aunt Sallies out of the questions (setting them up only to knock them down), I am persuaded by what I have seen that they can all be answered in favour of married priests. I can only touch briefly on each here.

I. Availability?

Undoubtedly, a married priest will need time for his family. One such married priest, now back working full-time in a US West Coast parish (as a non-sacramental minister), asked his pastor if he could come in late the following morning, as his wife works and they had no babysitter.

'You have to be here,' the pastor said.

'I can't tomorrow. You've got to understand I'm a married person.'

'That's your problem.'

'Yes it is. And I'm taking the time my family needs,' replied the married priest.

There are going to be many more such interchanges, if changes come to the celibacy law.

A married priest in Minnesota has been jailed a number of

times for demonstrating against a corporation engaged in weapons research. This has been most difficult for his wife: 'Sometimes,' she told me, 'I felt the kids and I get on the back burner.'

These are very real problems, but it does seem to be a matter of balance. It turned out that the priest was being required to work at the church from 7 a.m. until 10.30. every night. Of course, there was a conflict. And the demonstrating priest now takes a lower profile, and stays out of jail. Though he is less outwardly active, he told me, he is far more intensely involved in ecological and peace issues now, because he has children and their future to care about.

In Auschwitz, celibate priest Maximilian Kolbe offered to take the place of the father of a family who was to be put to death. Today he is a saint. The Church will always have need for such heroes, but we have a far more immediate need for thousands more vocations, which compulsory celibacy is preventing.

And heroism has never been confined to celibates. Nor has dedication. It was young Jennifer Zwick, whose priest-father runs the Casa Juan Diego in Houston, who said to me: 'They say celibacy gives you more time free. But look at my father – it's incredible what's going on here. He is available most of the time, and he's a married man. Yet I know a lot of celibate priests who have answering machines. There's some kind of contradiction there.'

Don Conroy sees the question of availability as a red herring: 'I was on call as a priest for the only emergency hospital in Minneapolis, and I have been on call as a psychologist working in a medical clinic with ten doctors,' he told me. 'Availability is not an issue. I have done both. I have been available in both professions. This is a personality-energy issue, not one related to the profession of priest or doctor or psychologist.'

According to Vilma Gozzini, Italian theologian from Florence, Italy, the argument of greater availability, as a justification for obligatory celibacy, is not convincing. It is not availability, but the attitude in the heart of the minister, which makes the difference, she says. And this attitude can be made positive and enriched by marital love and family.[203]

Father George Protopapas, in his paper written for the bishops of Vatican Two, put the matter in a Third World context:

It is commonly said that celibacy permits a priest to belong to no one and to all. We are speaking here of the total [availability] which celibacy is supposed to guarantee. In an abstract setting this is true . . . but, according to the testimony of zealous and spiritual priests who work in these sectors, celibacy does not make them free, more at liberty to work, but, on the contrary, celibacy actually hinders their pastoral activities.

This is paradoxical, but nonetheless true. In certain countries the way of life of the celibate priest categorically prevents him from personally mingling with the people and adjusting to the concrete reality, and consequently prevents him from assuming it and presenting it to God. His celibacy confines him to the exercise of his priesthood for himself and not for others. He lives separated from the stream of life, he becomes a priest for himself and not for others . . . The celibate priest cannot take root among his people.[204]

II. Bourgeois lifestyle?

In his book, *Theology of Liberation*, Gustavo Gutierrez quotes in a footnote an open letter to Dutch married priests from a group of Argentinian priests:

> While you were celibate, you did not know how . . . to be the voice of the exploited countries, those suffering the consequences of the unjust economic policy of the leaders of your countries. We hope that once you are married you can do this better. Indeed, if marriage does not help you to be more open to the world in general . . . you will have accomplished nothing more than becoming more bourgeois. Remember that while you seek the right to establish a home, many poor people in the Third World are renouncing theirs to give themselves completely to the liberation of their brother.[205]

A fair warning. I have met priests who married and who seem to have sold out for a mess of pottage. Mercifully, I have not met many, but they are a sad spectacle. However, the hundreds of other married priests I have met convince me it does not have to be so.

I believe the key is continued dedication to the Works of Mercy – 'I was sick and you visited me; I was hungry and you gave me to eat' – within the limits of one's situation. Members of a married priest group whom I met in Colombia suggested it is all about renouncing materialism: 'The priests you meet, theoretically celibate, are they less bourgeois, and more courageous? The situation of being bourgeois, whether married or not, depends on a person's involvement with the consumer society, rather than on being married or not. Materialism, not marriage, is what matters.'

I found my ideal in those married priests who have continued to work for the truly poor in Latin America. They and their families live by the *barrios* and *favelas*, and their families seem imbued with purpose.

Curiously enough, even for them, the children are the danger. A married priest in Lima, Peru, explained it to me: 'You get married – it doesn't change a thing. But having kids does. Do you really want to send your kids to that school up there? You know what it's like. What about a car to take them there? And what about a telephone? What about hygiene?' Or what about growing up with the wrong accent?

Joe and Jacqui McCarthy have made their decision: they are bringing up their two-year-old boy right there on the edge of a Recife slum. I asked Joe if he wasn't being unfair to the child.

'We've thought about that,' Joe said. 'But no matter what you do, you are imposing on the child. Either way, the child doesn't get a chance to choose.

'Besides, the type of neighbourhood we are mixing in, we feel we are doing the child a big service, by letting him grow up in this environment. The values here – he has a lot more to gain here than anywhere else.'

But what about his future?

'The biggest service we can give to him, is the example of our dedication, and the ideals we are trying to put into practice. In Christian terms, in faith terms, what we can pass on to him is the type of life we are living, which we are trying to make relevant, significant and important. We don't feel we can give him anything more valuable than that. He'll grow up in that atmosphere, and he'll reach the point of choosing anyway.

'The other option? We'd live a life centred on getting on in life, being important, climbing ladders. Then he'd grow up with those values if that is the case. It's one or the other.'

Will Joe and Jacqui be able to put enough money by for the youngster's education?

'The whole thing in our life is our insecurity. We can't plan for very long. We can't afford to worry. Jacqui comes from a wealthy family, but my father was a factory worker who never earned a lot and never worried about it. He passed on his values to me.' They were giving themselves to God's service, Joe said. And they were trusting that God would provide.

I believe that people like Joe and Jacqui are truly prophetic: pioneers, testing our paths for the very first time, paths which will be trodden by countless priest families in the centuries to come.

The ideal must be a consummate balancing act: to live and bring up your children among the wretched of the earth, yet, rather than sink to becoming wretched too, to bring the wretched up to the standards, spiritual and material, you try to hold on to. And learning from those wretched, and trying to acquire their courage, their endurance, their sheer downright goodness. May God give you strength, Jacqui and Joe McCarthy. And your little boy too.

III. Uncommitted wives?

Yes, it is a reality. Just as there are uncommitted husbands. Protestant denominations have long experience of varying levels of commitment on the part of a spouse – the spouse dedicated to ministry, verily the pastor's other half; the spouse who manages to balance being a minister's wife with a full life of her own; and the unconcerned spouse who resolutely goes her own way. Protestants manage to accommodate them all. And it's not confined to ministers: Tom Wolfe, in his book, *The Right Stuff*, highlights the problems of being wife to a dedicated aviator or astronaut.[206] Their problems appear tougher than those of any pastor's wife. Yet no one so far suggests celibacy for astronauts.

Just two observations.

Marriages between nuns and priests appear to be more than usually successful. The reason often given is that a nun already shares much of the Church background and interests of her husband, as well as his pastoral drive. A great deal can be taken as understood, and she can relate easily to his anguish and his fulfilment, as he can to hers. I suggest that such marriages would be ideally suited to ministry. Either both partners could be involved in ministry, or at least the spouse would have an understanding and tolerance of the stresses of such work. I have seen examples of such couples happily engaged in ministry, like

Matt and Sandra Purcell. It is worth noting that 60 per cent of
the priests who marry in the United States take nuns as wives.

Also, one must distinguish between ordaining married men,
and inviting back to ministry those priests who had left to marry.
The wives in each category are in quite different situations. If a
married man were to be ordained, his wife presumably would be
a party to the decision, and would be aware of the problems to be
encountered. Whereas a woman who married a priest might not
be at all agreeable to his returning to the ministry, and would
have every right to say so. As Teresa, wife of married priest
Lauro Motta, told me in Fortaleza, Brazil: 'To leave was his own
decision. But to return to ministry would be OUR decision.'

What it all amounts to is that making celibacy optional is no
panacea. Of course, it will bring new problems which we will
have to face. But that's what life and growth are all about. The
cause of most problems are solutions. And yet we must try those
solutions, otherwise we would never have ended the Second
World War for fear of the problems peace might bring.

In the matter of celibacy, as in anything else, it comes down to
the scriptural bottom line, 'By their fruits you shall know them'.

There is an assumption that when the Church establishes a
requirement, it be seen to have a beneficial result for people. The
requirement is good for those who take it on, and it is also good
for those whom they influence. An excellent example is the
requirement laid down for living in a monastery or in a religious
order – namely the vows of poverty, chastity and obedience.

Can we say the same about the blanket celibacy requirement
which is demanded of all secular priests living among us? Is it
beneficial? In other words, does it promote growth and maturity,
responsibility and spiritual development in all or most of those
priests? And is it beneficial to the community? It does neither. A
psychologist wrote to me on this point:

> One thing I have noticed as I have studied and practised as a
> psychologist – if a person is expected or required to adopt a
> behaviour or set of behaviours, we must have assurance
> that such behaviours are in the long run truly beneficial,
> truly fit that person's nature . . . Compulsory celibacy does
> not meet this litmus test.

Indeed it does not. This book surely bears witness to the havoc it
causes to the souls and bodies of the individual priests who must

endure compulsory celibacy, as well as to those who become associated with them.

And it also bears witness to the havoc it causes in the community, deprived of leaders and the Mass.

We, the Church, the People of God, must come to a decision on compulsory celibacy, or lose the Eucharist that Jesus gave us. And if we make no decision? That, Dean Hoge points out, is a decision in itself. It is tantamount to opting for congregationalism — a Church without ordained ministers and without the Mass.[207]

12

UNLESS THE SEED DIE

All true working is rooted in deepest doubt, all genuine creation rests in the most radical negation, all pure world-
affirmation proceeds from the most ultimate despair.

Martin Buber

'I TELL YOU THE truth: unless the seed falls to the ground and
dies, it remains only a single seed. But if it dies, it produces
many seeds' (John 12, 24).

An earlier chapter showed how the experience of leaving the
ministry is redolent of death. It is a kind of dying for the man
who leaves; it is a bereavement for his relatives, and for the
priests who remain behind. But I believe the whole Church feels
itself bereaved, and is in mourning for its 100,000 sons whom
it considers dead. And the institution seems to be going through
the same stages of mourning that some of its remaining priests
went through — first, shock and then denial. Then the 'forbidden topic': those 100,000 have ceased to exist.

Yet it need not remain at that point. Bereavement is a process,
not a static condition, and the Church can go on to develop a

new relationship with its sons whom it currently mourns. Those 100,000 are now seeds, sown among the People of God. For the first time, thousands upon thousands of priests are there in the workplace, side by side with everyone else. Attitudes and ideals remain, and these attitudes can transform a workplace. At the very least, people perceive that these men are not renegades or apostates, and begin to accept the possibility of having a married priesthood. Polls of the laity are reflecting this more and more.

This final chapter, then, deals with the unfinished business of the bereavement, and the joyous new life that is sprouting from that tearful sowing.

RECONCILIATION

Leave your gift at the altar, and go first and be reconciled, says Jesus. It is so obvious, yet there are thousands of priests, celibate and married, who are not yet reconciled. All are inexorably growing older. Some are dying alienated from others. The laity and the new young priests are being handed this legacy of alienation of brother from brother. And the wives and the children of priests are burdened with the same legacy: one hears wives sadly joking about children who come into this world 'with more than original sin'.

Yet how can a Church reconcile man to God, and preach reconciliation of man to man, when its own priests are still angry at each other? And what stops so many priests on either side from reaching out?

Rome psychologist Fernando Iachini, himself a married priest who has known great anger, says we must first admit our anger, even our hatred. The priests who stayed must acknowledge their feelings against those they see as having betrayed them. Those who left must acknowledge their own sense of Church injustice: 'At the bottom of our experience as priests who left,' Iachini explained to me, 'is the consciousness that our Mother the Church did great violence to us as persons, depriving us of liberty, identity, maturity, individuality. That she was a *matrigna* – a stepmother – rather than a mother. This provoked our hatred towards the Church.

'But we had been taught in seminary never to hate, and this is impossible for man. We must first allow ourselves to hate what is human in the Church. God meets man where he is, on the sinful road. And hate is part of that.

'But then, we must overcome this hate with forgiveness. After hating, we must go one step further, and forgive. That is human maturity, and also Christian perfection.'

Iachini says if we do not go beyond hate, if we do not get the courage to pardon the Church, we can never grow, never be at peace. And the same is true of priests who cannot pardon those who left. 'We'll always be nailed to the cross of the past,' he says.

This forgiving, according to Iachini, is what Freud-disciple Melanie Klein calls reparation. 'Both Freud and Klein were concerned with the Jews' need to forgive, and in this point of reparation, Klein came very close to Christian redemption.'

Both resigned and active priests frequently expressed to me a longing for reconciliation. 'The Church has undergone a terrible fragmentation,' one resigned priest said to me. 'I am one of those fragmented bits. I have a different community now – my family – but I am still very much aware of the religious community I left. Is there anyone who could take the leadership, to see what connections can be made between us all?

'The cross is in all our lives: I have the pain of departure; those who stayed have the pain of losing us, of reduced numbers, of reduced vocations. Could someone bring it all together – the love, the anger, the uncertainty, the fragementation?

'I see myself still as a part of the Dominican Order that formed me. I still think like them. I see myself almost as working out on a mission, trying to get by with whatever bit of spirituality I retain from my days in community.

'The founder of that order, early on, scattered his men all across the world. They refer to it as "The Scattering of the Seed". Somehow I still feel as one of that scattered seed.'

Psychologist and married priest John Dubay, following family therapy, suggests, in a letter, a three-part approach to reconciliation between priests:

First is to **return,** to go back to the source of the injury. As I move toward the person, I gain strength to overcome feelings of guilt, shame and resentment. It restores some trust . . . and opens the door to possible dialogue.

Second is **dialogue.** Here each side has to state needs and expectations of the other. As I ask something of you, I continue to care enough about the relationship to risk your rejection, and trust you to be able to give to me.

Third is **creating trust**. We ask for consideration and try to give it, making clear it is not an attempt to wipe the slate clean. It is to be hoped that as we share the pains of our experience, new ways and options to care for one another will be found.

Dubay points out that just as marriage is not static, likewise priesthood is something evolving and unfolding for each person. Yves Congar had stressed that 'the priesthood is essentially a prophetic rather than simply a ritual priesthood'. If married priests could be seen to have moved to new expressions of priesthood, then there is really room for all. Dubay:

> Celibate priests would be able to view married priests as resources and vice versa. Men who once were brothers in grace could return to that state . . . [It could be a] resource to many celibates who are fighting great obstacles in efforts to remain loyal to the Church. The journey of grace of the married priest and his efforts to be loyal to his priesthood could be the other side of the dialogue. A dialogue that could liberate both sides in their priestly existence and deepen their convictions.
>
> [The dialogue would reveal] a continuum of priestly existence. A sense of this continuum will make it possible in time to set up rites of passage from one stage of priesthood to another. In time, people will perhaps be called to ordination at various points on the continuum. Rites of passage would also eliminate the pain that is experienced now as one passes from the celibate to the married priesthood . . . a transition which in the past has been seen as a death would be seen in terms of life and growth.

There are, of course, many priests, both those who stayed and those who left, who are already attaining personal reconciliation. When Father Joe Kramis receives a telephone call from another Seattle priest saying, 'I've got three married priests in my parish. Will you tell me how I can use them?' it is a sign of redemption. When married priest Ron Titus can say, 'I realise I had more or less excommunicated the Pope. Well, now I accept him,' it is redemption. As it is when Mark Zwick can say, 'Somewhere along the line, Louise and I decided not to see the Church as an enemy. After the faith crisis of the 1960s, the more we looked round, the more we came home again. We found we could live with the Church.'

Reconciliation seems to come hardest to the institution itself. And the closer to the top of the pyramid, the less reconciliation there seems to be. So that we find the Vatican forbidding employment of married priests, withholding dispensations from men long married, sometimes until their deathbed, and failing in the simple courtesy of even acknowledging receipt of the petitions for dispensation. And we hear of the Pope saying, 'I'm in no hurry. We didn't leave them: they left us.' I suppose it is understandable: the institution perceives the married priest as a threat to its structures. But it is sad, and so different from the father of the Prodigal Son, who came running to meet him.

Yet further down the pyramid there are some splendid attempts at institutional reconciliation. The institution is only an abstraction, and these are men of flesh and blood who are reaching out. So we find Cardinal Bernardin of Chicago arranging pensions for all resigned priests who have given twenty years' service[208] ('our brother, Joseph', some of the resigned priests call him). There is a similar pension scheme in the diocese of Duluth, and a particularly generous one in Lafayette, Louisiana.[209]

Some of the religious orders, especially the missionaries, have evolved and matured considerably in their relationship to their married priests and families. Outstanding are Maryknoll, the Kiltegan Missionaries, and the Oblates. The Oblates, at their 1986 general chapter in Rome, formally declared their intentions towards their married priests: 'In our apostolic ministry, we should willingly involve those former Oblates and laicised priests who might be disposed to serve the Church in collaboration with us – to the extent that Church law permits.'[210]

My favourite story is from the Netherlands. Every morning when the brethren of a famous monastery file to the chapel for Mass and prayer, with them are a husband and wife in their sixties. Father Maarten had once been a priest of that community, until he left twenty years ago and eventually married. He is now retired, and has rejoined the community, this time with his wife. They have a small apartment on one of the floors of the monastery.

'He and his wife are well accepted there,' a Dutch priest tells me. 'She is a former religious sister. Both she and her husband perform a big role in the life of that community. They also organise series of lectures, and both of them preach at public Masses.'

LEAVEN

It has been usual to think of the 100,000 priests who resigned formal ministry as 'lost to the Church'. However, one could see them as having moved to another part of the Church – moved from out of the clerical enclosure and in among the People of God. This is the first time that thousands of priests are meeting people without any barriers, sharing their joys and sorrows, hopes and fears, working with them, living family life among them, identifying with them. And, above all, giving witness.

People watch. Once a man is known to be a resigned priest (and I believe it is both healthy and exhilarating to identify one's background), he is in a unique position to preach by example what he used to put in words. And to reach where a cleric could never go. With the added witness that he no longer 'has to' live a life of dedication.

People do watch. If they can say, about married priests and their families, 'See how these Christians love one another', then the priest and his family become a leaven, transforming society from within, rather than preaching at it from outside. I have seen enough examples of this around the world that I find myself wondering if the Holy Spirit did not call priests out from their rectories just to become such a leaven. 'A spiritual vortex' is what Father F. X. Murphy calls these priest families – all told, a quarter of a million people, some of whom are quietly transforming both the world and the Church, just by the manner of their lives.

How do such lives affect the world around them? Let me count the ways. In Latin America, indeed everywhere, there is the option for the poor, and there are base communities through which that option is being exercised by many priest families. And they are bringing Christ into the workplace, simply by retaining Christian attitudes, and 'doing the ordinary things extraordinarily well', as St Thérèse said.

Archbishop Weakland of Milwaukee, Wisconsin, observed in 1986 how American Catholics have never really made the leap from personal spirituality to social action.[211] Granted that priests are no more trained than lay-people to make that leap ('they are trained in ritual, not in social action; they are trained to "say the words", not to perform the deeds,' as Don Conroy put it in a letter to me). Yet a priest at least has an education that could be the basis of awareness, and one who has already made that most drastic leap into lay life and marriage, might make other leaps as well. If he can grow to hunger and thirst after justice (for others, not just for himself), and to act on it where possible, then he brings Christian values where there may have been few.

And there is no doubt whatsoever that the lives of good married priests and their families must, in the long run, transform the Church itself. For the Church, too, is watching. As Robert O'Brien has written:

> The Church is looking for signs of progress or regression in the spiritual vitality of married priests and of those influenced by this new state of Christian life. The process of discernment seeks to discover the 'will of God', to look at evidence which is consistent with all that Christians believe about God. . . .
>
> The pioneers in living the priestly vocation and the calling to marriage are presenting God with evidence of a relative success or failure to grow in marital, parental and community love. To the extent the married priests are patient, affectionate, caring and daring Christians, they are persuading God to foster their experiment. They are giving God evidence that strong love for God comes from married priests and their wives.
>
> The results will be a change in Church policy. The change will be attributed to a synod, or to the Bishop of Rome, or to a papal congregation. But the discerning Catholic will know that the change is the will of God, consequent to the actions of the first generation of married Latin Rite priests and their spouses.[212]

It may take a long time. As the Chinese proverb goes, 'The seed does not see the flower.' But the Catholics of the next century must surely benefit from the lives of that first prophetic generation of married priests.

PROGNOSIS

What in fact does the future hold for us, the Church? Here angels fear to tread. But certainly there are two distinct currents within the Church. I am reminded of the line from a poem, 'Those behind cried forward, and those in front cried back.'

First, there is what can only be called a reactionary backlash, right at the very top of the pyramid. It is particularly obvious in a macabre race against death, whereby the present Pope is appointing as many ultra-conservative bishops as possible before his time runs out. It is a bit like a US president packing the Supreme Court to ensure a continuation of his views for decades to come.

Brazil, great crucible of the Church, is cooling and darkening. 'A shadow,' says Penny Lernoux, 'has begun to envelop Latin America's Church of the poor. Slowly but inexorably, the institutional Church is shifting away from a prophetic stance, to . . . political conservatism, through the continuing appointment of Vatican yes-men as bishops.'[213] Whereas a champion of the poor, like Bishop Pedro Casaldaliga, is summoned to Rome for secret interrogation, and told to sign a document admitting wrongdoing.[214]

Peru, mother of liberation theology, has shifted emphatically to the right. Its hierarchy, once the most progressive in Latin America, is now full of new bishops, described by Jesuit Jeffrey Klaiber as 'timid, closed, and very dependent on the Pope. They show little creativity or pastoral vision: they can only foster a weak and mediocre Church.'[215] In Chile, between 1977 and 1987, the Vatican replaced twelve of the country's thirty-one bishops with right-wing churchmen.[216] The Pope is fashioning the United States, too, in his own image, having appointed almost 140 of the nation's bishops, almost half of those active. Similar things are happening in the Netherlands, Austria, Germany, Italy – the lights are going out all over Europe.[217]

All but one of the Netherlands' former church leaders are gone, with ultra right-wingers now in six out of the seven dioceses. The country, once a ferment of experimentation and hope, is sullenly turned off. 'The Roman army of occupation,' some Dutch priests are calling their new hierarchy.[218]

In 1988 the church in Cologne, Germany, saw over 3,000 people quit, when ultra-conservative Cardinal Joachim Meisner

was forced on the diocese, against the will of the diocese and of
the civil government, and in violation of the spirit of the
Concordat.[219]

Yet while these ultra-conservative waves thunder on the
beach, there is an undertow, pulling powerfully towards change.
It is a change more drastic than anything up to now. A radically
altered world and Church have upped the ante, and the marriage
of priests is only one among many issues.

According to Rosemary Reuther, writing in the journal
America, the Church is facing challenges, both within and
without, in three separate areas. How it responds to these will
determine whether it can renew itself effectively and give witness
and leadership in the world. There is the challenge from
liberalism, democratic values and human rights in the Church;
the challenge from feminism and sexual morality; and the
challenge from Third World liberation. The future of priesthood
and ministry is woven through all three.

Firstly, the challenge from liberalism. In the Syllabus of Errors
in 1864, Pope Pius IX had declared it was an error to say that the
'Roman Pontiff can and should reconcile himself to progress,
liberalism and modern civilisation'. The official Church rejected
religious liberty, freedom of conscience, women's suffrage and
democratic government. However, in our day the Church has
come round to speaking up for most of these things and for
human rights – not only in places like Latin America, but even in
Rome.

And the world is willing to listen to Rome: as Rosemary
Reuther points out, the Pope is probably the only global leader
who would be listened to in all three worlds: the capitalist,
socialist and Third Worlds.

But the challenge is for Rome to practise what it preaches. As
yet, it fails to do so. Reuther: 'The partial rapprochement of the
Catholic Church with liberal values is contradicted most blan-
tantly by the inability of the Catholic hierarchy to apply these
principles to itself as an institution. . . . In many . . . areas, such
as fair wages, just contracts, the right of Church employees to
unionise, the right of assembly and free press, the Catholic
Church fails to apply to itself the civil rights it has defended in
society.'

The second challenge comes from feminism. The institutional
Church is steeped in fear of sexuality and women. That is why it

is kinder to clerics who use women than to clerics who marry them. This book has dealt with the institution's fight to retain an unworkable celibacy, but the problem is now vastly broader, and has to do with the institution's attempt to marginalise women completely. The question of whether priests can marry women is only a small part of the challenge: it has moved far beyond that to questions of whether women can adequately represent Christ and thus be ordained; of whether this male-run institution can continue to prohibit contraception, a prohibition that can promote abortion, and which was maintained only so that the institution might not lose credibility by being seen to change.

And the third challenge, perhaps the greatest of all, comes from the fact that Catholicism is becoming more and more a Third World Church. The challenge, then, is to move away from the rich and powerful and to identify truly with the poor as they struggle to liberate themselves from unjust social structures that are contrary to the Gospel. It is the most daunting challenge of all because, says Reuther, 'to defend the rights of the poor is to make oneself the marked target of those in power . . . To opt for the poor is to lose one's place among the powerful, to choose vulnerability, perhaps torture and death. It is to choose to be a martyr Church.' It is the challenge of liberation theology.[220]

Questions of why priests leave, and whether celibacy should be optional, seem to grow pale and even self-indulgent when placed beside such massive challenges. Yet that is an illusion. Such questions are tightly interwoven in all three of those challenges. They are, in fact, a part of them. They are part of the struggle within the Church for human rights – the right to honourable dispensation, the right to marry, the right to found a family, the right to liberty under God. They are part of the feminist struggle, to which the institution is saying, you cannot be a priest if you are a woman or if you are married to one. And those questions are deeply a part of the option for the poor, because in the Third World the only way those poor will have leadership or the Eucharist is if respected married family men can be drawn from within the community, and ordained to provide them with those two necessities.

The crisis in the priesthood is far from being a side issue. It is close to the centre, jostled, of course, and sharing place with all these other issues: the full integration of women in the Church, including their ordination to the priesthood; the question of whether ministers should be drawn from their local community, and called by that community to serve, instead of being sent in from outside; even whether such ministers would derive their power from that community; the question of whether the ministry should be less sacral (Father Leonardo Boff describes it now as 'a spiritual supermarket to which the priest holds the key'), and more given to preaching the Word of God; whether priestly ministry could be for a limited number of years; whether bishops and other leaders should hold office for a set period, as leaders of religious orders do.

The Rock of Peter is rocking, and already the stone floor of the Catholic Church has shifted under our feet. Jesuit Father John A. Coleman explains there are several major ways in which this shift has occurred, none of which is likely to be reversed.[221]

The first is the crisis of identity in male celibate priests, reflected in the vast exodus described in this book, but even more in the worldwide refusal of sufficient Catholic men to become priests.

Consequently, there is an ever dwindling number of priests relative to population throughout the world, and that is the second aspect of the shift.

The third follows from it: the laity are moving in to take over. In answer to the worldwide scarcity of priests, there has been an explosion of non-ordained ministries. It may surprise some readers to know that in parts of the Third World, lay-people are appointed to do baptisms, marriages, Eucharistic services, visitation and communion of the sick, burial services, preaching, counselling, parish administration, practically everything a priest used to do except the words of consecration and of absolution.

The laity, of course, are just taking back all the functions that were stolen from them by the clerics, functions only being yielded up because there are no longer enough clerics to do them. As Coleman points out, 'it is in the interest of the Church, worldwide, to conceive of ministry in ways that undercut clerical caste, a sacred all-embracing order of ministry and mandates, by substituting instead the designations of natural leaders of a community for ministerial functions in the community.'

So already, whether we like it or not, we are at the point where communities are selecting and putting forward their own ministers. And the laity are never going to give back what they have won. We are talking about the death-knell of clericalism.

Also, like it or not, we have married priests. Granted that so far only married convert Protestant clergy are being ordained, and granted that Rome may have done it for political reasons only (it has been alleged that these clergy are welcomed precisely because they are generally opposed to women's ordination). However, the principle of an all-celibate clergy has been breached. (It would be more accurate to say there never really was the principle of an all-celibate clergy, since, in the vast eastern part of the Catholic Church, priests have always been free to marry. Compulsory celibacy would be better viewed as a peculiarity of the western Latin rite of the Catholic Church, at odds with the more general principle of a married clergy throughout the Church.)

And we already have women pastors in the Catholic Church. Even in the United States, parishes are being handed over to nuns to run them. One of a dwindling number of circuit-rider priests gallops in from time to time to preside at Mass, and consecrate some Hosts, and that's about it. Apart from that, Sister is pastor, whether or not they give her that title. Is it any wonder, then, people are asking why she is not ordained, especially when there is hardly a theologian of distinction today who objects on theological grounds to women's ordination?

'Make no misjudgement,' Eugene Kennedy says. 'Working out the conflict over an expanding role for women is the main business and moral obligation of the American Church in the next decade.'[222] And not just the American Church: women form half the People of God wherever they are found.

All these things are coming to pass, quietly, not in the administrative central bunker of the Catholic Church, but on the outer edges, and seeping inwards towards the middle. There is nothing that can stop it.

What is really happening, is that European Christianity is mutating into World Christianity, as Karl Rahner pointed out before his death.[223] This book is about a shattering, but it is the Shattering of the old, European, Roman, clerical mould, which can no longer contain a Christianity of the World. And all the Roman appointments of reactionary bishops in the world can do no more for that mould than all the King's men were able to do for Humpty Dumpty.

The Roman Catholic Church deals in centuries, but these seismic shifts have come faster than we ever imagined. Perhaps all Church change in speeding up, as world change is. Perhaps the people in Rome will ordain married men soon. Perhaps not. It will certainly have happened before they allow ordained priests to marry. And both may happen before they let resigned priests return.

But does it matter? There is ministry, full measure and overflowing, waiting to be done – enough for all the resigned priests in the world, and for all the lay ministers, and for all the women of the People of God.

And many of the priests who have left are no longer waiting for a nod from anyone: there is ministry to be done, and they are glad to take it upon themselves. They have never wanted to abandon ministry, except the formal clerical kind, just as they never wanted to abandon the Church. These are the men of whom Peter Hebblethwaite speaks: 'They not only remain in the Church out of conviction, but they cannot conceive of leaving it, and for a very simple reason: they think of the Church simply as humanity, in so far as it has recognised, however falteringly, its vocation in Christ. They can no more leave the Church than they can take leave of humanity. To do so would be a form of spiritual suicide.'

Priests who resign or who marry have not left anything except the clerical condition. And there remains to all of them that most fundamental of all ministries, to do the ordinary things extraordinarily well.

In November 1987, Cardinal Bernardin joined a group of married and resigned priests and their wives in Chicago, to make a retreat together. In his homily at the close of the retreat, the Cardinal said that an unremitting search for God's will is a key part of the role of resigned priests today:

> Sometimes the call to priesthood or religious life and the charism of celibacy no longer seem as simultaneous and inevitable as once they did, and you find yourself a resigned priest or a former religious trying to fit into a Church in desperate need of ministers. . . .
>
> As I listen prayerfully to today's Scripture readings, this is what I hear: that the Kingdom comes when people struggle to be faithful to Wisdom in the midst of sometimes unforeseen circumstances . . . We can never give up, aban-

don the vigil, or assume that – for whatever reason – the issues we struggle with cannot somehow, someday, be worked out. To do so would be a breach of faith. For nothing happens without God's knowledge; nothing happens without some purpose.

I am deeply touched by your organisation WOERC. As a group, you remain faithful to wisdom in the heart of the ambiguity of experience. You are people who continue to search for ways to serve the Lord in the Church of Chicago, in your present forms of life as resigned priests and former religious. I can only guess what the personal cost must be. I bless your sacrifice and struggle.

And this is the heart of what I want to say to you: let's not give up on one another, the Church, or the belief that – within this struggle, within this vigil for Wisdom – we shall find Wisdom sitting by our gate. . . .

I will promise that I will struggle with you to discern where the Spirit is leading us. As with so many other complex, sensitive issues, I do not know the answers. But I do know that if we do not work together, if we do not keep watch together, our answers will be stillborn. . . .

When people struggle to be faithful to Wisdom in the vagaries of life, the Kingdom of God is made manifest. I have no facile solutions today, my sisters and brothers – only the deep belief and trust that our vigil in the night of this ambiguity will meet God's transforming Wisdom.

I promise to watch and struggle with you.

That indeed is the prognosis for resigned and married priests – a future of struggle. It is, however, a struggle not against the Church, but hand in hand with all its priests and people, a struggle to find God's will, and waged in love. In the evening of your life, as Paul Claudel said, you will be judged on your love.

When I knelt all those many years ago to make my vows, my Dominican superior held my hand and heard my heartfelt words. Then he solemnly said, '*Deus qui incepit, ipse perficiet* [God, who began this, will also bring it to perfection].' I believe those words will be fulfilled in the Holy Roman Catholic and Apostolic Church. I believe they will be fulfilled, too, in the struggle of every one of her priests – both those who remain clerics, and those who do not. For thou are a priest for ever.

EPILOGUE

As I WAS WRITING this final chapter, I received a telephone call from the United States, which brought me up to date on Maggie and Father Jack, who were described in Chapter Seven. Father Jack is the priest who had loved Maggie, but had never left, and had remained celibate. He developed cancer of the throat, and went to Maggie's home a couple of times a week for a meal.

The update. Father Jack did not come to Maggie's for a few days. Finally, she went to look for him. She met the pastor, who told her Father Jack was probably in his room. No, he hadn't seen him for a couple of days.

'There are times a priest needs to be alone with God,' the pastor told Maggie.

She brushed past him, and went to Father Jack's room. There she found him lying on the bed, covered in blood. 'Pack my bags, Maggie,' he whispered. 'I'm coming with you.'

She took him to hospital, and then to live at her home. He lived with her until he died.

APPENDIX

Some useful addresses

USA

Corpus
4124 Harriet
MINNEAPOLIS
Mn 55409
Tel. (612) 827–1818.

Woerc
East Point Tower 11B
6101 N Sheridan Rd
CHICAGO
Il. 60660–2098
Tel. (812) 274–4559

Good Tidings
Box 283
CANADENSIS
Pa 18325
Tel. (717) 595–2705

Connections
16014 Eagle
SAN ANTONIO
Tex. 78247
Tel. (512) 822–0886

EUROPE

International Federation of
Married Priests' Associations

c/o Pierre Lautrey
2 sq du Dr Courcoux
93260 LES LILAS
France
Tel. (1) 253.74170

Advent
58 Grassmere Avenue
Merton Park
London SW19
Tel. (01) 540–0789

Movement for Ordination of
Married Men (MOMM)
c/o Rev Michael Gaine
St. Mary's
45 Highfield Street
LIVERPOOL L3 6AA
England
Tel. (051) 236–7801

Leaven
52 Castlepark Road
Sandycove
Co Dublin
Ireland
Tel. (01) 857459

New Bearings
(Address unlisted)
Tel. (01) 340–4791

NOTES

(Unofficial translations by this author from non-English originals are indicated by the word 'translated'. The word 'author' below means the author of this book.)

Prologue
1. *Il Resto del Carlino*, 20 February 1985, Translated.
2. *Corpus Reports*, July 1987, Vol. 13, No. 4. Also Corpus: Fact Sheet on Crisis caused by Priest Shortage. Minneapolis, 1987.
3. *Le Soir*. Brussels: 31 August 1987. Translated.
4. *Houston Catholic Worker*. August 1988. Page 1.
5. MOMM (Movement for the Ordination of Married Men) *Information Bulletin*, No. 5. December 1984. Page 26.
6. Corpus: Fact Sheet on Crisis caused by Priest Shortage. Minneapolis, 1987.
7. Pope John Paul II: Address delivered in Philadelphia, October 1979.

Chapter 1
8. Information from Dr Terry Dosh, national co-ordinator of Corpus.
9. Photocopy in author's files.
10. McKenzie S. J., John L. *Authority in the Church*. London: Chapman, 1966. Page 183.
11. Jim Brandes did, in fact, briefly accept his assignment to Victoria, Texas, but left the ministry from there.
12. Joe Till did not, in fact, leave, and is still a priest in San Antonio Archdiocese.
13. Letter, 16 September 1968, addressed to: Pope Paul VI; Carlo Cardinal Confelonieri, prefect of Sacred Congregation of Bishops; Archbishop John F. Dearden, president, National Conference of Catholic Bishops; Archbishop Luigi Raimondi, Apostolic Delegate to the United States: Archbishop Robert E. Lucey, of San Antonio, Texas. Addressed from PO Box 7238 Station A, San Antonio Texas, 78207. Photocopy in author's files.

14. *Diocesan Directory*, San Antonio, Texas. Editions of 1967 and 1988.

15. Schoenherr, Professor Richard. 'Trends in Ministry: Patterns in decline and Growth.' Lecture.

16. Corpus Fact Sheet. 1987.

17. Information from Professor Richard Schoenherr, Sociology Department, University of Wisconsin at Madison.

18. Corpus Fact Sheet. 1987.

19. *Corpus Reports*. November 1985. Vol. 11, No. 6.

20. *US News & World Report*. 18 June, 1984. Page 43.

21. Corpus Fact Sheet. 1987.

22. Information from Professor Richard Schoenherr, University of Wisconsins at Madison.

23. *Le Figaro*. Paris: 3 November, 1987. '*Notre Vie*' section. Translated.

24. Ibid.

25. Information from Gianni Gennari, Rome.

26. KASKI report. Den Haag, Holland. Updated by Father Lambert van Gelder.

27. Irish Catholic Bishops' Council for Research & Development. Figures up to 1985 only. Supplied to author by council office in Maynooth, Ireland.

28. Information from Rumos, Brasilia.

29. Information from Father Michael Gaine, Professor of Sociology at Christ's and Notre Dame College, Liverpool.

30. *Annuarium Statisticum Ecclesiae*. Vatican City. Quoted in *Corpus Reports*. vol. 12, No 5. September–October 1986.

31. Corpus Fact Sheet, 1987.

32. Grollenberg, Kerkhofs, Houtepen, Vollebergh & Schillebeeckx. *Minister? Pastor? Prophet?* London: SCM Press, 1980. Page 10.

33. *America*. Vol. 144, No. 12. 28 March, 1981. Pages 243–9. Article by John A. Coleman SJ: 'The Future of Ministry'.

34. Ibid. Also *Clergy Review, 62*. London: 1977. Pages 26–32.

35. *Le Soir*. Brussels: 31 Aug., 1987. Translated.

36. *America*. Vol. 144, No. 12. 28 March, 1981. Page 247.

Chapter 2

37. Lernoux, Penny: Paper delivered at 2nd Inter-American Meeting of Catholic Religious at Bogota, Colombia. August 1974. Quoted in: Lernoux, Penny: *Cry of the People*. London: Penguin, 1982. Page 454.

38. Pancera, Mario. *I Novi Preti*. Milan: Sperlinge-Kupfer, 1977. Pages 145–69. Translated.

39. Canon 284 of the 1983 Code of Canon Law requires clerics to wear 'suitable ecclesiastical dress' in accordance with the norms established by the episcopal conference or by legitimate local custom.
40. *Commonweal.* 13 October, 1978. Pages 655–8.

Chapter 3
41. Kubler-Ross, Elisabeth. *On Death and Dying.* New York: Macmillan, 1977. Page 110 et al.
42. *Time.* 23 February, 1970.
43. Corsello, Antonio. *È Tempo di Parlare.* Rome: Seristampa Comiso, 1986. Page 69. Translated.
44. Ibid., page 61.
45. Ibid., page 58.
46. Ibid., page 62.
47. Letter from T. A. D. Godwin Pieris. Photocopy in author's files.
48. *Wall Street Journal.* New York: 24 April 1979. Page 1.
49. *National Catholic Reporter.* 29 January, 1982.

Chapter 4
50. MOMM (Movement for the Ordination of Married Men) Information Bulletin, No. 9. Liverpool: 1 October, 1988. Page 33. Text of lecture by Bishop P. Kalilombe at the AGM of MOMM, 10 March, 1988, in London.
51. *Western People.* Ireland: 16 December, 1981. Page 15. Article by Father Brendan Hoban.
52. *Paese Sera.* Rome: 20 January, 1983. Translated.
53. Ibid.
54. Williamson, Benedict. *The Treaty of the Lateran.* London: Burns, Oates & Washbourne, 1929. Page 54.
55. Pancera, Mario. *I Novi Preti.* Milan: Sperlinge-Kupfer, 1977. Pages 11–36. Translated.
56. Williamson, Benedict. *The Treaty of the Lateran.* London: Burns, Oates & Washbourne, 1929. Page 62.
57. Letter in author's file.
58. Information from Father Lambert van Gelder, Nijmegen, Holland, who reports that the matter was widely featured in the Dutch Press.
59. Information from Professor Eduardo Hoornaert, Fortaleza, Brazil.
60. *Charisma.* November 1983. Page 22.
61. Photocopy of letter, in author's files.
62. Letter in author's files.

63. Winninger, Father Paul. 'Powers & Duties of Holy Orders'. An unpublished document prepared in advance for those taking part in the Second Vatican Council, and marked SECRET. Copy in author's files.

64. Letter to author.

65. Information confirmed in writing by Vivian Linahen. She has also given this author a full file of correspondence with the diocese on the matter.

66. Copy of letter, in author's files. Recipient has written it from memory, but recalls its exact words.

67. Photocopy of letter, in author's files. Translated.

68. Photocopy of letter, in author's files.

69. *Paese Sera*. Rome: 22 December, 1984. Translated.

70. *Rumos*. Brasilia: May–June 1987. Page 4.

71. Telephone interview with author.

72. Reported to author by three different US priests, none of whom wished to be identified.

73. Reported to author, August 1987, by Luciano Paglialunga, Italian married priest to whom it happened.

74. Photocopy in author's files.

75. Questionnaire for Petitioners for Laicisation with a Dispensation from all Obligations arising from Solemn Profession and Sacred Ordination. Copy in author's files.

76. *Concilium No 73*. Herder. 1972. Page 107, ff.

77. Congregation for the Doctrine of the Faith: Private Instruction to Ordinary. Vatican City: 7 March, 1975. Copy in author's files.

78. Coriden, Green & Heintschel. *The Code of Canon Law: A Text and Commentary*. London: Geoffrey Chapman, 1985. Pages 236–7.

79. Letter to author.

80. Van Dijk, B. & Salemink, Th. *Van Beroep: Pastor*. Hilversum: Gooi & Sticht, 1986.

81. Letter from the Sacred Congregation for the Doctrine of the Faith. Photocopy in author's files. Translated from Italian original.

82. Photocopy of letter, in author's files. Translated.

83. Universal Declaration of Human Rights. Full text appears in Unesco. *Human Rights: Comments and Interpretations*. London: Allen Wingate, 1950. Pages 273–80.

84. Padovano, Anthony: Address delivered 18 June, 1988, to the First US National Conference on a Married Priesthood, American University, Washington DC. 17–19 June, 1988.

85. *America*. 1 March, 1986. Page 154. Reprint of keynote address to

annual Call to Action assembly, Chicago, Illinois, November 1985.
86. Letter in author's files.

Chapter 5
87. Kennedy, E. C., & Heckler, V. J. *The Catholic Priest in the United States: Psychological Investigations.* United States Catholic Conference. Washington, DC, 1972. Page 51.
88. Ibid., Page 12.
89. *Journal of Clinical Psychology.* Vol. 33, No. 1. January 1977. Kennedy, Heckler, Kobler & Walker. 'Clinical Assessment of a Profession: Roman Catholic Clergymen.'
90. Ibid.
91. Rollo May. *Love & Will.* New York: Norton & Co., 1969. Page 311. Quoted in Goergen, Donald: *The Sexual Celibate.* London: SPCK, 1979. Page 63.
92. Homily by Cardinal Bernadin, Chicago, May 1987. Words addressed to married priests from Mundelein Ordination Class of 1962.
93. Report by Dr Terence Dosh on Corpus survey.
94. *Texas Historian.* Vol. 47, No. 3. January 1987. Pages 16–17. Kelly Derden. 'Conflict and Compromise: Legislated Celibacy and its Impact on the Roman Catholic Priesthood.'
95. Bellah, Robert, et al. *Habits of the Heart.* New York: Harper & Row, 1985.
96. Beaver, W. Robert: *Successful Marriage.* Quoted in Dubay letter (below).
97. Letter in author's files.
98. Address delivered 18 June, 1988, to the First US National Conference on a Married Priesthood, American University, Washington DC. 17–19 June, 1988.

Chapter 6
99. Report by Dr Terence Dosh on Corpus survey.
100. Information from Corpus.
101. Kelly, Edward. *Cry Out to the Church.* Quezon City, Philippines: Phoenix Publishing House, Inc., 1984. Pages 175–6.
102. Letter to author.
103. *The Guardian.* 7 October, 1986.
104. Schillebeeckx, Edward. *Ministry.* London: SCM Press, 1981. Page 77.
105. *The Irish Times.* Dublin: 3, 5, 6, 7, 8 May, 1986.
106. Coriden, Green & Heintschel. *The Code of Canon Law: A Text*

and Commentary. London: Geoffrey Chapman, 1985. Canon 1752.
107. Listing compiled by Corpus, 1987.

Chapter 7

108. *Sojourners.* 12 December, 1987. Pages 12–15. This very beautiful and moving article by Vicki Kemper and Larry Engel is the basis of the story.
109. *Seattle Times.* Seattle: 15 March, 1987.
110. *New York Times.* New York: 11 September, 1987. Report of New York Times–CBS News poll, conducted 24 August to 1 September, 1987.
111. *Los Angeles Times.* Los Angeles: 20 August, 1986.
112. *Upturn.* Bulletin of Association of Chicago Priests. Tim O'Connell: 'The Look of a Happy Priest.' Photocopy of undated article.
113. Greeley, Andrew M., *The Cardinal Sins.* W. H. Allen, 1981.
114. *Breviary of the Order of Preachers.* English language edition. 1967. Part I. Page 1109.
115. Murphy, Paul I. *La Popessa.* New York: Warner, 1983.
116. Van Hemert, Guus. *Some Remarks on Teilhard de Chardin's L'Evolution de la Chastété.* (Offprint from *Fides Sacramenti: Sacramentum Fidei*). Netherlands: Van Gorcum, 1981.

Chapter 8

117. Lueg, Anne (ed). *Ein Sprung in der Kette.* Solingen: Initiativgruppe der vom Zölibat betroffenen Frauen, 1985.
118. Goldmann-Posch, Ursula. *Unheilige Ehen.* Munich: Kindler Verlag, GmbH 1985.
119. Good Tidings brochure. Canadensis, Pa. 1987.
120. Letter to author from Father Lambert van Gelder, Nijmegen, Netherlands.
121. Letter to author.
122. Katholische Nachrichten Agentur. News bulletin, dateline Cologne: 29 January, 1985. Translated.
123. *Concilium No 73.* Herder. 1972. Page 28.
124. *St Anthony Messenger.* August 1986. Note: 'Father William Wells' is a pseudonym.
125. *Chicago Tribune.* 8 August, 1986. Page A–16.
126. *Catholic Herald.* London: 8 May, 1987. Page 4.
127. Photocopy of letter, in author's files.
128. *De Tijd.* 7 August, 1981. Pages 36–41.
129. *Now is the Time.* Bulletin of the Advent Group. London: August 1986. Page 11. Advent translation of letter that originally appeared in *Batir,* bulletin of Marseilles married-priest group.

130. Ibid., September 1987. Page 11.
131. Document written by interviewee for this book, and reproduced here with her written permission. Original in author's file.
132. Sipe, Richard: Address delivered 17 June, 1988 to the First US National Conference on a Married Priesthood, American University, Washington DC, 17–19 June, 1988.
133. *Commonweal.* 19 June, 1987. Page 382.
134. Vogels, Heinz-Jürgen. *Sieb des Satans.* Bornheim: Franz Paffenholz, 1966.
135. *Clerical Celibacy: An Asset or a Liability?* Page 2. An unpublished document prepared in advance for those taking part in the Second Vatican Council, and marked SECRET. No author's name. Copy in this author's files.
136. Napier, Augustus Y., & Whitaker, Carl A. *The Family Crucible.* New York: Harper & Row, 1978. Page 20 ff.
137. O'Brien, John A. (ed). *Why Priests Leave.* New York: Award Books, 1970. Page 182.

Chapter 9
138. National Opinion Research Centre: *The Catholic Priest in the United States: Sociological Investigations.* Washington DC: United States Catholic Conference. 1972. Pages 281–2.
139. MOMM Information Bulletin, No. 4. Liverpool: April 1984. Page 49.
140. Congar OP, Yves: *Communidades Ecclesiais de Base.* Petropolis: Brazil: Vozes. 1973. Pages 144–145.
141. *Vozes.* Petropolis, Brazil: July 1967. Merton's 'Statement on Celibacy' first appeared here in Portuguese, entitled, '*Thomas Merton e Celibato*'.
142. *The Irish Times.* Dublin: 29 December, 1988. Page 10.
143. Quoted by Richard Sipe, in address to National Guild of Catholic Psychiatrists, Montreal, Canada. 8 May, 1988.
144. *Social Forces.* Vol. 33. No 4. May 1955. Pages 316–21. Article by S. Dornbusch: 'The Military Academy as an Assimilating Institution.' Abridged in – Broom & Selznick: *Sociology.* New York: Harper & Row, 1969. Pages 110–13.
145. Sipe, Richard: Address to National Guild of Catholic Psychiatrists, Montreal, Canada. 8 May, 1988.
146. Weber, Max. *The Sociology of Religion.* Translated by Ephraim Fischoff. Boston: Beacon Press, 1963. Page 29.
147. *Sociological Analysis.* 1987. No. 47. Article by Richard A. Schoenherr: 'Power and Authority in Organised Religion: Disaggregating the Phenomenological Core.' Page 54.

148. Merton, Robert K. *Social Theory & Social Structure*. New York: Free Press, 1968. Pages 251–6.

149. Fisher, H. A. L. *A History of Europe*. London: Fontana, 1968. Vol. 1, Page 418.

150. Dolan, John P. *History of the Reformation*. New York: Desclee Co., 1965. Page 231.

151. *The Tablet*. London: 18 August 1984. Pages 788–9.

152. *New York Times*. New York: 22 October, 1986.

153. Information from Father Brian Holmes CSSR, Fortaleza, Brazil.

154. *National Catholic Reporter*. 13 November, 1987.

155. Kenny, Anthony. *A Path from Rome*. Oxford: Oxford University Press, 1986. Page 149.

156. Dolan, John P. *History of the Reformation*. New York: Desclee Co., 1965. Page 227.

157. Jedin, H. 'The Celibacy of Priests in the 16th Century'. Pages 1–2. An unpublished document prepared in advance of the Second Vatican Council, and marked "SECRET". Copy in author's files. A quotation from the document, on the 'whore-tax', appears in Chapter Eleven.

158. *Origins*. 6 November, 1981, Vol. 11, Page 333. Reprinted in Priests for Equality pastoral, *Toward a Full and Equal Sharing*. West Hyattsville, Md.: 8 December, 1985. Article 2, page 1.

159. Priests for Equality pastoral, *Toward a Full and Equal Sharing*. West Hyattsville, Md.: 8 December, 1985. Article 33, page 20.

160. *America*. 18 October, 1986. Page 205.

161. *AGEN* Bulletin. São Paulo, Brazil: 16 January, 1988. Pages 2–3.

162. *The Tablet*. London: 12 December, 1987. Page 1346. Article on – Kaiser, Robert Blair. *The Encyclical that Never Was: The Story of the Pontifical Commission on Population, Family and Birth, 1964–66*. Sheed & Ward, 1987.

163. Boff, Leonardo. *Ecclesiogenesis*. New York: Orbis Books, 1986. Page 2.

164. Congar OP, Yves. *Communidades Ecclesiais de Base*. Petropolis, Brazil: Vozes, 1973. Pages 144–5.

165. *MOMM Information Bulletin*, No. 9. Liverpool: 1 October, 1988. Page 32. Text of lecture by Bishop P. Kalilombe at the AGM of MOMM, 10 March, 1988, in London.

166. 'The Conflict Situation of the Priest in the Modern World'. An unpublished document prepared in advance of the Second Vatican Council. Unsigned.

Chapter 10
167. *MPC Catalogo Geral*. Brasilia: Informativo Rumos, 1984. Page 3.

168. Bulletin of CO.SA.RE.SE. Barcelona–Madrid: March 1987.
169. *Dichiarazione d'identità del Movimento 'Vocatio'*. Rome, Italy. Translated.
170. *Paese Sera*. Rome: 14 April, 1981. Translated.
171. Ibid., 3 March, 1982. Translated.
172. Ibid., 23 June, 1986. Translated.
173. Universal Synod of Married Catholic Priests and Wives: Report to the Synod of the Conversation of the Secretary, Paolo Camellini, and the Co-ordinators L. van Gelder and H.-J. Vogels, with Msgr. Canciani, pastor in Rome and Consultor of the Congregation of Clergy. Rome: 25 February, 1985.
174. Padovano, Anthony. 'Send Us'. A proposed Pastoral Statement from the 1985 International Synod of Married Priests & Spouses. Ariccia. August 1985.
175. Both documents unpublished. Circulated as photocopied typescripts in advance of the International Congress of Married Priests & Wives at Ariccia, Italy, 23–28 August, 1987.

Chapter 11

176. Easwaran, Eknath. *Gandhi the Man*. Petaluma, California: Nilgiri Press, 1983.
177. Gallagher, Charles A., & Vandenberg, Thomas L. *The Celibacy Myth: Loving for Life*. Crossroads Publishing Co., 1987.
178. *Corpus Reports*. Vol. 12, No. 1. January–February 1986. Page 2.
179. Schillebeeckx, Edward: *The Church with a Human Face: A New & Expanded Theology of Ministry*. London: SCM Press, 1985. Pages 240–9.
180. O'Hanneson, Joan. *And They Felt No Shame*. Winston Press, 1983. Page 93.
181. Dolan, John P. *History of the Reformation*. New York: Desclee Co., 1965. Page 226.
182. O'Hanneson, Joan. *And They Felt No Shame*. Winston Press, 1983. Page 93.
183. Gage, Matilda Joselyn. *Woman, Church & State*. Salem NH: Ayer Co., 1985 (reprint of 1893 edition). Pages 72–84.
184. Jedin, H. 'The Celibacy of Priests in the 16th Century.' Pages 1–2. An unpublished document prepared in advance of the Second Vatican Council. Marked 'sub secreto'.
185. Ibid., Page 1.
186. *Gaudium et Spes: Pastoral Constitution on the Church in the Modern World*. Par. 49.
187. Schillebeeckx, Edward. *The Church with a Human Face: A New & Expanded Theology of Ministry*. London: SCM Press, 1985. Page 249.

188. Grollenberg, Kerkhofs, Houtepen, Vollebergh & Schillebeeckx. *Minister? Pastor? Prophet?* London: SCM Press, 1980. Page 13.
189. Ibid.
190. Corpus fact sheet, 1987.
191. *MOMM Information Bulletin.* No. 6. April 1985. Page 4.
192. *Now is the Time.* Bulletin of the Advent Group. London: May 1988. Page 4.
193. *Corpus Reports.* Vol. 13, No. 1 January–February 1987. Page 3.
194. *Corpus Reports.* Vol. 11, No. 3. May–June 1985. Page 2.
195. Associated Press report by David Briggs. Published 26 December, 1988.
196. Hoge, Dean. *The Future of Catholic Leadership.* Kansas City: Sheed & Ward, 1987. Pages 144–5.
197. Ibid., page 190.
198. Information from Father Lambert van Gelder, Nijmegen, Netherlands.
199. Protopapas, George. 'The Priesthood & Celibacy in the Modern World.' Page 2. An unpublished document prepared in advance of the Second Vatican Council. Marked 'sub secreto'.
200. *MOMM Information Bulletin,* No. 8. Liverpool: February 1987. Page 16.
201. *MOMM Information Bulletin,* No. 5. Liverpool: December 1984. Page 25.
202. *Paese Sera.* Rome: 14 July, 1984.
203. Address delivered by Vilma Gozzini, to International Congress of Married Priests and Wives, Ariccia, Italy, 23–28 August, 1987.
204. Protopapas, George. 'The Priesthood & Celibacy in the Modern World.' Page 2. An unpublished document prepared in advance of the Second Vatican Council. Marked 'sub secreto'.
205. Gutierrez, Gustavo. *A Theology of Liberation.* London: SCM Press, 1974. Pages 122–3.
206. Wolfe, Tom. *The Right Stuff.* New York: Bantam, 1980. Pages 1–5, 13, 338–9.
207. Hoge, Dean. *Future of Catholic Leadership.* Kansas City: Sheed & Ward, 1987. Page 214.

Chapter 12
208. Letter of Joseph Cardinal Bernardin, mailed to the resigned priests of Chicago Archdiocese. 22 June, 1987. Photocopy in author's files.
209. Information from Dr Terry Dosh.
210. Oblates of Mary Immaculate. Acts of General Chapter, 1986.
211. *America.* 18 October, 1986. Page 202.
212. *Corpus Reports.* Vol. 11, No. 4. Page 3.

213. *National Catholic Reporter.* 17 June, 1988. Page 7.
214. Ibid., 7 October, 1988. Page 1.
215. Ibid., 17 June, 1988. Page 9.
216. Ibid., 17 June, 1988. Page 9.
217. Ibid., 17 June, 1988. Pages 16–17.
218. Information from Evert Verheijden, President of GOP, Netherlands.
219. *The Irish Times.* Dublin: 11 January, 1989. Page 6.
220. *America.* 1 March, 1986. Pages 152–8.
221. *America.* No. 144. 28 March, 1981. Pages 243–9. Article by John A. Coleman SJ: 'The Future of Ministry'.
222. Kennedy, Eugene: *The Now and Future Church: The Psychology of being an American Catholic.* New York: Doubleday, 1984. Page 177. As quoted in: Hoge, Dean. *Future of Catholic Leadership.* Kansas City: Sheed & Ward, 1987. Page 211.
223. *Theological Studies.* December 1979. Cited in *Commonweal*, No. 44. 28 January, 1983.

SELECTED BIBLIOGRAPHY

The following are the principal books and documents consulted. There were also 1,123 other smaller documents, such as letters, news reports and articles.

'A Shepherd's Care: Reflections on the Changing Role of Pastor.' Washington DC: US Catholic Conference, 1987.

Abbott, Walter M. *Documents of Vatican II.* London: Geoffrey Chapman, 1966.

Aceros Caceres, Hugo. *Vamos P'Alante.* Bogota: Barreto Gama, 1982.

Archdiocese of San Antonio. *Diocesan Directory.* Texas: 1967 and 1988 editions.

Baligand, Cantier, Davezies, Lajonchère, Trillard. *Echanges et Dialogue: La Mort du Clerc.* Paris: IDOC, 1975.

Barfield, Charles G. 'Of Murphy's Law and Woman.' Private circulation, 1987.

Barrett, E. Boyd. *Shepherds in the Mist.* London: Burns Oates, 1951.

Bellah, Robert, et al. *Habits of the Heart.* New York: Harper & Row, 1985.

Billanovich, Augusto. *Sacerdozio e Celibato.* Treviso: Longo & Zoppelli, 1925.

Boff, Leonardo. *Church: Charism & Power.* New York: Crossroads, 1985.

Boff, Leonardo. *Ecclesiogenesis.* New York: Orbis Books, 1986.

Bohan, Murray, et al. *Being a Priest in Ireland Today.* Dublin: Dominican Publications, 1988.

Bossa, Benjamin. *O Direito de Amar: A Queda de um Tabu.* São Paulo: Bossa, 1984.

Breviary of the Order of Preachers. English language edition, 1967.

Bronder, Saul. *Social Justice and Church Authority: The Public Life of Archbishop Robert E. Lucey.* San Francisco: Temple University Press, 1982.

Broom & Selznick. *Sociology.* New York: Harper & Row, 1969.

De Broucker, Jose. *Dom Helder Camara.* London: Collins, 1977.

Carney, J. Guadalupe. *To be a Revolutionary.* San Francisco: Harper & Row, 1985.

Carroll, Denis. *What is Liberation Theology?* Cork: Mercier Press, no date.

CEF Secretariat. *Fidelité, Celibat et Ministère.* Paris: Conference Episcopale Française, 1976.

'Clerical Celibacy: An Asset or a Liability?' An unpublished document prepared for those taking part in the Second Vatican Council, 1963.

Communità di San Paolo. *Il Cristiano e la Sessualità.* Rome: Com-Nuovi Tempi, 1980.

Congar, Yves. *Power & Poverty in the Church.* London: Chapman, 1964.

Congregation for the Doctrine of the Faith. Vatican City: Private Instruction to Ordinary, 1975.

Connetable, Joubert, Lautrey & Schwartz. *Mariés, mais Toujours Prêtres?* Brussels: CEFA, c. 1980.

Cooney, John. *No News is Bad News: Communications Policy in the Catholic Church.* Dublin: Veritas, 1974.

Coriden, Green & Heintschel. *The Code of Canon Law: A Text and Commentary.* London: Geoffrey Chapman, 1985.

Corsello, Antonio. *È Tempo di Parlare.* Rome: Seristampo Comiso, 1986.

Corsello, Antonio. *Una Chiesa e un Ambiente che Opprimono.* Rome: Privitera, 1970.

Crow, Richard. 'Second Journeys: A Study of Married Priests and Their Wives.' Master's thesis. Lakewood, Ohio: Fielding Institute, 1978.

Dichiarazione d'identità del Movimento 'Vocatio'. Rome.

Dolan, John P. *History of the Reformation.* New York: Desclée & Co., 1965.

Donahue, John M. & Oliver, David B. *Attrition & the Future of the Catholic Foreign Mission Society of America.* San Antonio: Trinity University, 1976.

Easwaran, Eknath. *Gandhi the Man.* Petaluma, California: Nilgiri Press, 1983.

Ebaugh, Helen. *Out of the Cloister.* Austin: University of Texas Press, 1977.

Egan, John P. & Colford, Paul D. *Baptism of Resistance, Blood and Celebration.* Mystic, Connecticut: Twenty-Third Publications, 1983.

Fisher, H. A. L. *A History of Europe*. London: Fontana, 1968.
Franzoni, Giovanni. *Tra la Gente*. Rome: Com-Nuovi Tempi, 1976.

Gage, Matilda Joslyn. *Woman, Church and State*. Salem NH: Ayer Co., 1985 (reprint of 1893 edition).
Gallagher, Charles A., & Vandenburg, Thomas L. *The Celibacy Myth: Loving for Life*. New York: Crossroads 1987.
Goergen, Donald. *The Sexual Celibate*. London: SPCK, 1979.
Goldman-Posch, Ursula. *Unheilige Ehen*. Munich: Kindler Verlag GmbH, 1985.
Graham, William L. 'The Psychological Experiences of Resigned Roman Catholic Priests.' Doctoral dissertation. Houston: Union Graduate School, 1985.
Greeley, Andrew M. *The Cardinal Sins*. W. H. Allen, 1981.
Greeley, Andrew M. & Durkin, Mary Greeley. *How to Save the Catholic Church*. New York: Viking, 1984.
Grollenberg, Kerkhofs, Houtepen, Vollebergh & Schillebeeckx. *Minister? Pastor? Prophet?* London: SCM Press, 1980.
Gutierrez, Gustavo. *A Theology of Liberation*. London: SCM Press, 1974.

Haag, John E. 'A Study of the Seminary and Priesthood Experience of Thirteen Resigned Roman Catholic Priests.' Doctoral dissertation. Pittsburgh: Pittsburgh Theological Seminary, 1984.
Hamburger, Gerd. *La Fine di un Tabù: Il Matrimoni dei Preti*. Turin: Piero Gribaudi, 1969 (from German original).
Hebblethwaite, Peter. *In the Vatican*. Oxford: Oxford University Press, 1987.
Hegarty, Martin J. *Woerc Directory*. Chicago: Woerc, 1986.
Hendricks-Rauch, Maureen. 'A Study of the Marriages and Marital Adjustment of Resigned Roman Catholic Priests and their Wives.' Doctoral dissertation. Greeley: University of Colorado, 1979.
Hoge, Dean. *Future of Catholic Leadership*. Kansas City: Sheed & Ward, 1987.

Jacobelli, M. Caterina. *Sacerdozio, Donna, Celibato*. Rome: Borla, 1981.
Jedin, H. 'The Celibacy of Priests in the 16th Century.' An unpublished document prepared for those taking part in the Second Vatican Council, 1963.
Joannes, Fernando. *Padres Amanhã?* Petrópolis, Brazil: Vozes, 1970.

Kavanaugh, James. *The Celibates*. New York: Avon, 1985.
Kelly, Edward. *Cry Out to the Church*. Quezon City, Philippines: Phoenix Publishing House, Inc., 1984.

Kennedy, E. C., & Heckler, V. J. *The Catholic Priest in the United States: Psychological Investigations*. United States Catholic Conference. Washington DC, 1972.

Kenny, Anthony. *A Path from Rome*. Oxford: Oxford University Press, 1986.

Kubler-Ross, Elisabeth. *On Death and Dying*. New York: Macmillan, 1977.

Küng, Hans. *Why Priests?* London: Collins, 1972.

Lernoux, Penny, *Cry of the People*. London: Penguin, 1982.

Lueg, Anne (ed.). *Ein Sprung in der Kette*. Solingen: Initiativgruppe der vom Zölibat betroffenen Frauen, 1985.

Lukas, Mary and Ellen. *Teilhard*. New York: McGraw-Hill, 1981.

McKenzie SJ, John L. *Authority in the Church*. London, Chapman, 1966.

McMurtrey, Martin. *The Mariachi Bishop: The Life Story of Patrick Flores*. San Antonio: Corona, 1987.

Merriman, Brian. *The Midnight Court*. Translated by Cosslett O Cuinn. Cork: Mercier, 1987.

Merton, Robert K. *Social Theory & Social Structure*. New York: Free Press, 1968.

Miles, Michael. *Love is Always*. New York: William Morrow, 1986.

Mocciaro & Bettazzi. *La Communità dell'Abate Franzoni*. Rome: Napoleone, 1973.

MPC Catalogo Geral. Brasilia: Informativo Rumos. 1984.

Murphy, Paul I. *La Popessa*. New York: Warner, 1983.

Napier, Augustus Y., & Whitaker, Carl A. *The Family Crucible*. New York: Harper & Row, 1978.

National Opinion Research Centre. *The Catholic Priest in the United States: Sociological Investigations*. Washington DC: United States Catholic Conference, 1972.

North Country Curate. *Via Dolorosa*. London: Sands. No date.

O'Brien, John A. (ed). *Why Priests Leave*. New York: Award Books, 1970.

O'Hanneson, Joan. *And They Felt No Shame*: Winston Press, 1983.

Occhiogrosso, Peter. *Once a Catholic*. Boston: Houghton Mifflin, 1987.

Padovano, Anthony. *Pastoral Ministry and the Non-Clerical Priesthood*. Minneapolis: Corpus Research, 1989.

Pancera, Mario. *I Novi Preti*. Milan: Sperlinge-Kupfer, 1977.

Podestà, Jeronimo & Clelia. *Caminos de Libertad*. Buenos Aires: Planeta Argentina, 1985.

Potel, Julien. *Ils se sont Mariés . . . et Après?* Paris: L'Harmattan, 1986.

Potter-Seasons. *No Weapon Save Love*. Hantsport, Novia Scotia: Lancelot, 1983.

Prefontaine, Marjorie. 'Transition: A Study of the Process Experienced by Roman Catholic Ex-clerics.' Doctoral dissertation. Denton: Texas Woman's University, 1987.

Priests for Equality pastoral, 'Toward a Full and Equal Sharing'. West Hyattsville, Md., 1985.

Protopapas, George. 'The Priesthood & Celibacy in the Modern World.' An unpublished document prepared for those taking part in the Second Vatican Council, 1963.

St Anthony, Neal. *Until All are Housed in Dignity*. Minneapolis: Project for Pride in Living, 1987.

Schillebeeckx, Edward. *The Church with a Human Face: A New & Expanded Theology of Ministry*. London: SCM Press, 1985.

Schillebeeckx, Edward, *Ministry*. London: SCM Press, 1981.

Sheppard, David & Worlock, Derek. *Better Together*. London: Hodder & Stoughton, 1987.

Sweeney, Terrance. 'Survey on Priestly Ministers'. Los Angeles: 1986.

'The Conflict Situation of the Priest in the Modern World.' An unpublished document prepared for those taking part in the Second Vatican Council. Unsigned, 1963.

Unesco. *Human Rights: Comments and Interpretations*. London: Allen Wingate, 1950.

Van Dijk, B. & Salemink, Th. *Van Beroep: Pastor*. Hilversum: Gooi & Sticht, 1986.

Van Hemert, Guus. *Some Remarks on Teilhard de Chardin's L'Evolution de la Chastété*. (Offprint from *Fides Sacramenti: Sacramentum Fidei*.) Netherlands: Van Gorcum, 1981.

Vogels, Heinz-Jürgen. *Pflicht-Zölibat*. Munich: Kosel-Verlag, 1978.

Vogels, Heinz-Jürgen. *Sieb des Satans*. Bornheim: Franz Paffenholz, 1966.

Weber, Elizabeth & Wheaton, Barry. 'The Career Change of Atlantic Area Roman Catholic Diocesan Priests after Vatican II.' Dissertation. Halifax, Novia Scotia: Mount St Vincent University, 1985.

Weber, Max. *The Sociology of Religion.* Translated by Ephraim Fischoff. Boston: Beacon Press, 1963.

Williamson, Benedict. *The Treaty of the Lateran.* London: Burns, Oates & Washbourne, 1929.

Winninger, Fr Paul. 'Powers and Duties of Holy Orders.' An unpublished document prepared for those taking part in the Second Vatican Council, 1963.

Winter, Michael. *Whatever Happened to Vatican II?* London: Sheed & Ward, 1985.

Wolfe, Tom. *The Right Stuff.* New York: Bantam, 1980.

ACKNOWLEDGEMENTS

Or rather, the reason why I cannot make acknowledgements. Many hundreds of people have helped me in my travels around the world to gather the material for this book. After having read the book, however, the reader will understand that there are many dioceses I must not identify, and many priests, both inside and outside the clerical state, who have begged to remain anonymous. By thanking people by name I risk giving clues for identifying dioceses and individuals.

So to those who received me into their homes with such love, to those who opened their hearts to me, and let me see their tears and their laughter, you have my deepest gratitude, and the gratitude of anyone whom this book may help. May God reward you. He knows who you are.

GLOSSARY

Certain words used in the text could be puzzling to the general reader. They are briefly explained here.

abbey: a monastery governed by an abbot.

abbot: the head of an abbey, or 'father' to a community of monks.

absolution: forgiveness of sin in the Sacrament of Reconciliation.

annulment: a declaration that a marriage never was valid.

apostolic delegate: a representative of the Vatican in a foreign country with which it has no diplomatic ties.

archbishop: the bishop of an Archdiocese.

base community: a small local community of Christians, who meet to reflect and act together in the light of the Gospel for the spiritual and social betterment of everyone.

basilica: an important church on which certain privileges have been conferred.

canon law: the laws of the Roman Catholic Church, collected in one book (called the *Code*). Individual laws are numbered, for example, Canon 205.

cardinal: a very high-ranking cleric in the Catholic Church, with the privilege of electing the Pope.

cassock: a long robe worn by clerics.

celibacy: the state of being permanently unmarried. Also, the western Church law forbidding ordained priests to marry, and married men to be ordained.

chaplain: a person who tends to the spiritual welfare of a specific group of persons (soldiers, prisoners, hospital patients, police, youth, etc).

chapter: the group of priests attached to a cathedral. The word is also used for the general assembly of certain religious orders.

charism: an unusual spiritual gift from God to an individual, usually for the benefit of others.

chastity: refraining from genital sexual activity when unmarried (or confining it to one's spouse when married).

clergy: a general word for officials and ministers of the Church. Usually ordained priest or deacon. Term used in contradistinction to 'laity'.

cleric: an official functionary in the Roman Catholic Church. Usually ordained priest or deacon. Term used in contradistinction to 'layperson'.

code: see 'Canon Law'.

communion: receiving the Host during Mass.

concordat: a treaty or formal agreement between the Vatican and a secular government, usually relating to the status of the Catholic Church in that particular country.

confession: telling one's sins in the Sacrament of Reconciliation.

congregation: the Vatican's equivalent of a department or ministry in civil government. Example: the Congregation for the Missions. Also called a 'Dicaster'.

consecration: the central point in the celebration of the Mass.

council: general assembly of the world's Catholic bishops with the Pope, which takes place at long intervals in the Church's history, and usually defines or clarifies church teaching.

curia: the Catholic Church's secretariat or civil service, located in the Vatican.

Council of Trent: a church council that took place in the 16th century, aimed at reforming the Church.

dicaster: see Congregation (above).

diocese: territorial division of the Catholic Church, presided over by a bishop.

Dominicans: a religious order founded in the 13th century by St Dominic, for the purpose of preaching correct doctrine.

ecclesiastical: whatever has to do with church.

ecumenism: the movement to achieve Christian unity, especially between Catholics and Protestants.

encyclical: an authoritative document issued by the Pope to the whole Church.

Eucharist: the central point of Catholic worship, also called the Mass. The Eucharist is both sacrifice and sacrament.

excommunication: an official Church sentence of expulsion from membership.

habit: a uniform worn by monks, friars and nuns.

hierarchy: the rulers of the Catholic Church: the Pope, cardinals and bishops.

Holy Communion: see 'Communion'.

host: the wafer of bread which is consecrated at the Eucharist, to become Christ's body, and is received in Communion.

Humanae Vitae: the 1968 encyclical, or papal document, in which the Pope reaffirmed the ban on artificial birth control.

Ignatian retreat: a retreat based on the writings of St Ignatius Loyola.

Jesuits: the Society of Jesus, a society of priests and brothers founded by St Ignatius Loyola in the 16th century.

Kiltegan Fathers: a society of missionary priests that began in Ireland in the present century.

laity: collective word for laypersons.

layperson: one who is not a cleric (which see).

liberation theology: Christian thinking that begins with the struggle of the poor and oppressed for freedom under God, and searches the scriptures for guidance in this struggle.

liturgy: the worship performed in Catholic churches, in particular the Mass.

Maryknoll: a society of missionary priests and brothers, founded in the United States.

Mass: another name for the Eucharist.

Mill Hill: a society of missionary priests, that takes its name from Mill Hill in London, where its head house is located.

ministry: service of others, for the motive of love of God and neighbour.

missions: locations for missionary activity (which see).

missionary activity: the spreading of Gospel teaching around the world, in response to Christ's command to 'teach all nations'. Often refers to such work in the Third World.

missionary: one who labours on the missions.

Modernism: a collective name for trends in Christian thinking, aimed at reconciling Church doctrine and modern scientific thought, which the Vatican condemned in the early 20th century.

monsignor: an honorary title given to certain Catholic priests who have been elevated to special rank.

nuncio: a representative of the Vatican abroad, with full ambassadorial status.

Oblates: the Oblates of Mary Immaculate – a society of priests and brothers, devoted to missionary work often in difficult or hazardous locations. Founded at Marseilles in 1816.

optional celibacy: an arrangement by which priests would be free to marry or remain celibate.

order: an international religious body of priests, brothers, or nuns, who take vows of poverty, chastity and obedience, and live according to a monastic-type rule. Examples: Franciscans, Dominicans, Carmelites. Some more recently founded bodies are called congregations or societies.

ordination: the conferring of priesthood on a person.

papal nuncio: see 'Nuncio'.

parish: a small territorial unit in the Catholic Church, usually with an appointed priest in charge.

pastor: the priest in charge of a parish. Also called 'parish priest'.

peritus: an expert in theology, called to assist the bishops in a Council.

priest: in the Catholic Church, one who has received the Sacrament of Orders, and is charged with presiding at the Eucharist, administering the sacraments, and being a go-between for God and his People.

priory: community house of certain religious orders.

provincial: regional head of a religious order.

Puebla: a famous meeting of Latin American bishops that took place in 1979 at Puebla, in Mexico, and was seen as encouraging Liberation Theology.

retreat: a period of one or more days set aside for prayer and reflection.

sacrament: one of seven principal channels of God's grace and help for Christians (for example, Baptism, Confirmation).

seminary: training school of candidates for the priesthood.

seminarian: one who is studying to become a priest.

sick call: request to minister spiritually to someone who is ill or dying.

superior: someone in authority in a religious order.

synod: an official gathering of bishops.

theologian: a specialist in the study of God and his dealings with people.

Tridentine Mass: Mass celebrated in Latin, according to a form of worship laid down by the Council of Trent, that was revised after the Second Vatican Council.

Vatican: the administrative centre of the Roman Catholic Church, located in Rome.

Vatican Council: usually means the Second Vatican Council, which was held during the 1960s to renew the Catholic Church in the modern world.

Vatican Two: the Second Vatican Council.

virginity: the condition of never having had genital sexual activity.

vocation: the calling by God to a particular state in life.

vow: a solemn promise made to God.

INDEX